HOUR OF GOLD, HOUR OF LEAD

Books by Anne Morrow Lindbergh

North to the Orient

Listen! The Wind

The Wave of the Future

The Steep Ascent

Gift from the Sea

The Unicorn

Dearly Beloved

Earth Shine

Bring Me a Unicorn

Hour of Gold, Hour of Lead

Locked Rooms and Open Doors

The Flower and the Nettle

War Within and Without

HOUR OF GOLD, HOUR OF LEAD

*Diaries
and Letters
of
Anne Morrow Lindbergh*

1929-1932

A Helen and Kurt Wolff Book
A Harvest/HBJ Book
Harcourt Brace Jovanovich, Publishers
San Diego   New York   London

Editorial Note

The diary and letter material in this book has been cut for repetition and readability, but has not been rewritten. Spelling has been corrected and punctuation standardized. Since this is a personal rather than a historical record, the footnotes were kept, in general, contemporary with the diary and purposely brief, confined to information essential to understanding the text.

The following abbreviations have been used throughout:

D. W. M.—Dwight Whitney Morrow

E. C. M.—Elizabeth Cutter Morrow

E. R. M.—Elisabeth Reeve Morrow

D. W. M., Jr.—Dwight Whitney Morrow, Jr.

C. C. M.—Constance Cutter Morrow

E. L. L. L.—Evangeline Lodge Land Lindbergh

A. M. L.—Anne Morrow Lindbergh

C. A. L.—Charles A. Lindbergh

ILLUSTRATIONS

Between pages 52 and 53

Charles Lindbergh's airplane nosed over on landing,
Mexico, 1929
Anne Morrow and Charles Lindbergh, Mexico, 1929
On wedding trip
Charles and Anne Lindbergh, July, 1929
Inauguration flights of the Transcontinental Air
passenger service
The Lindberghs in Army Falcon
Exploring New Mexico cliff dwellings
The Lindberghs with experimental Curtiss biplane
The Lindberghs with President Hoover
At the Cleveland Air Races, August, 1929

Between pages 132 and 133

The Lindberghs during an emergency flight, September, 1929
On Caribbean flight in Antigua, September 22, 1929
In Cristobal, Panama
Pan American Airways mail delivery in Port of Spain
Amelia Earhart and Anne Lindbergh, 1930
Anne Lindbergh in Bowlus glider
The Lindberghs during test flights, 1930
Testing their Lockheed Sirius
The Lindberghs in electrically heated flying suits

Illustrations

Dwight W. Morrow with Charles Lindbergh, May, 1930
Anne Lindbergh, summer, 1930
Next Day Hill, Englewood, N. J.
Anne Lindbergh with Charles, Jr., 1930
Charles Lindbergh, Jr., with his great-grandmother Cutter
The Lindberghs' temporary home near Princeton, N. J.

Between pages 196 and 197

Anne Lindbergh with Charles, Jr.
Mrs. E. L. L. Lindbergh with Charles, Jr.
Anne Lindbergh learning to fly
Anne Lindbergh with Charles, Jr., summer, 1931
Charles, Jr., summer, 1931
First birthday of Charles, Jr.
The Lindberghs and their Bird biplane
The Lindberghs starting on their trip to the Orient
Packing equipment in Ottawa, Ontario
After landing at Aklavik
Preparing for the flight from Aklavik to Point Barrow
Point Barrow, Alaska
Eskimos welcome the Lindberghs at Nome, Alaska
Charles, Jr., summer, 1931

Between pages 276 and 277

The Lindberghs in Nemuro, Japan
The Sirius before landing at Kasimigaura (Tokyo)
The Lindberghs as guests of the Prime Minister of Japan
In Tokyo

Illustrations

Outside the wall of Nanking, China
Anne Lindbergh speaking for China flood-relief program, 1932
The Yangtze in flood
The Lindberghs' house near Hopewell, N. J.
Reporters in front of the Hopewell house, March 2, 1932
Air view of the Hopewell house
Deacon Brown's Point, North Haven, Maine
Family group, 1932
Mrs. Morrow, Anne and Jon Lindbergh, 1932
Thor
Anne Lindbergh, 1932
Elisabeth Reeve Morrow, 1932

HOUR OF GOLD

Introduction

In biographies and autobiographies there is always a turning point in life when the young person emerges from the matrix of his background. How does the adolescent free himself from the protective shell of home and parents which shielded him during the vulnerable years but eventually became restrictive to his growth? By what means does he loosen the bonds? What doors does he open to discovery—self-discovery, actually? For it is self-discovery which enables him eventually to form his own structure and rules, always keeping some of the old, but adapting them to his own life and character. What are the accidents, the desires, the forces, one wants to know, that free him?

To be deeply in love is, of course, a great liberating force and the most common experience that frees—or seems to free—young people. The loved one is the liberator. Ideally, both members of a couple in love free each other to new and different worlds. I was no exception to the general rule. The sheer fact of finding myself loved was unbelievable and changed my world, my feelings about life and myself. I was given confidence, strength, and almost a new character. The man I was to marry believed in me and what I could do, and consequently I found I could do more than I realized, even in that mysterious outer world that fascinated me but seemed unattainable. He opened the door to "real life" and although it frightened me, it also beckoned. I had to go.

Romance was not the deciding factor. The shimmering haze of glamour that surrounded our courtship only blurred my feelings. I distrusted it. Romance was what the world saw and applauded in our engagement. Unlike most brides-to-be, it was *I* who was congratulated, not he. Hadn't I found and captured the hero of

3

the hour? As a gay member of the Embassy sang: "She was only an ambassador's daughter, but he was Prince of the air."

I did not see my husband-to-be as a Prince but though it was never put into words, the image was nearer to that of a knight in shining armor, with myself as his devoted page. The role of page came naturally to me. For years I had been an adoring understudy to my older sister. And I had early been cast in the role of page in a long succession of school plays, chosen no doubt for my small stature and limited acting ability. ("What ho, cup-bearer!" —"Yes, Sire, I come!")

Was this a good basis for marriage? Hardly. But perhaps it was a first step in a relationship. It was a role I could play until I grew up. I was an apprentice to someone more experienced in a world of which I knew little but which I was eager to explore. I followed; I applied myself; I learned. I leaned on another's strength until I discovered my own. It was not a bad beginning.

But there were other doors to liberation. Flying was a very tangible freedom. In those days it was beauty, adventure, discovery—the epitome of breaking into new worlds. From being earth-bound and provincial, I was given limitless horizons. From the cloistered atmosphere of books, writing, and introspection, I was freed to action. The practical work of learning to fly, of being a radio operator and navigator, of carrying my own parachute and my own "weight" as a crew member on the flights, gave me a feeling of enormous self-confidence. For the first time, I had a sense of value in the "real world" of life and action. Like the bird pushed out of the nest, I was astonished that—flapping hard—I could fly. All this was liberating.

But total freedom is never what one imagines and, in fact, hardly exists. It comes as a shock in life to learn that we usually only exchange one set of restrictions for another. The second set, however, is self-chosen, and therefore easier to accept.

The first restriction I faced was finding myself in the public eye. From the creative darkness of anonymity, a sheltered family porters and photographers in boats and planes. One man in an open boat circled around us in harbor for seven straight hours, his wake rocking us constantly, as he shouted demands that we come out on deck and pose for him. Finally we headed out to open ocean, trailing our anchor behind. I remember the night spent on a fishing bank, out of sight of land, with cans rolling around the hold and china smashing as our boat tossed in the waves.

I was quite unprepared for this cops-and-robbers pursuit, an aspect of publicity that has become a common practice with public figures. I felt like an escaped convict. This was not freedom.

When we returned to "ordinary life"—my husband's work surveying and organizing transcontinental and intercontinental airlines—it was more acceptable. We had no private life—only public life. The launching of passenger airlines, we recognized, was of legitimate interest to the public. We went everywhere together; we posed for photographs and my husband talked to newsmen.

We had no home; we lived in hotels, planes, or other people's homes. We traveled constantly, back and forth across the United States laying out the new Transcontinental Air Transport passenger route between New York and Los Angeles, or inaugurating new Pan American Airways routes to Central and South America. We stayed in Harvey Houses, private homes, embassies and legations. I was grateful to those friends or strangers who opened their homes to us, for I realized we brought burdens with us, of extra telephone calls, invitations, press pressure, and curious sightseers. My diaries and letters attest to the generosity of the Guggenheims in New York, the Bixbys, Knights, and Robertsons in Saint Louis, the Eastlands in San Francisco, the Madduxes in Los Angeles, and countless others on our trips around the Caribbean, in the Arctic and in the Orient, who took us in and gave us a sense of security and a precious taste of private life.

It was not many months before I realized that I, who passionately desired "real life," had only exchanged the insulation of conventional upbringing, a close family circle, and a cloistered life of books for the insulation of fame, publicity, and constant travel.

"Fame is a kind of death," years later a college friend remarked to me, contradicting the general assumption that fame is immortality. Fame is a kind of death because it arrests life around the person in the public eye. If one is recognized everywhere, one begins to feel like Medusa. People stop their normal life and actions and freeze into staring mannikins. "We can never catch people or life unawares," as I wrote to my mother, in an outburst of frustration. "It is always looking at us."

This is not to say I was unhappy. The letters reveal my happiness—our happiness. I was very much in love and there was (to quote a letter) "a kind of bright golden 'bloom' over everything; maybe it's just the way we feel—C. and I—when we get off together alone. All gold—" I obviously adored the flying. It was freedom and beauty and escape from crowds. It was privacy as well. There was too much noise in those early open planes to talk, but we could exchange notes. Flying also provided time alone, peace to sink down into oneself, to think, to learn poetry. (There was no one around to interrupt with magazines, snacks, or pillows in those early days.)

Thrown into a life of travel and action, I found it invigorating. Flying back and forth across the continent, stopping at small airports, meeting country crowds, gave me a new sense of the breadth and beauty of America and the warmth and vitality of people I had never met in my New England youth. To my surprise—for I had been a shy girl—I discovered I enjoyed meeting people: the pilots and their wives, the aviation personnel at the airports, who were often friends of my husband, even the strangers we took up on flights or met at trip functions. Talking to them was far easier, I found, than making conversation at the Embassy social functions. As a married woman, I had my husband at my side and developed a new confidence. "I always feel like standing up straight when he is behind me."

But I longed to gossip about these new experiences and people with my family. My reactions certainly come through the letters, but in the early years they are somewhat restrained and unnatural. I was afraid of being indiscreet. I longed to see and talk to my family as I had always done before.

My homesickness for my family now seems incredibly naïve for a young wife, and rather hard on a young husband. As the letters state, I found it difficult to believe I was married. I was happy in the new life but I missed my family terribly. How much of this is universal in the first year of marriage and how much of it was my particular problem of missing the freedom to gossip and exchange impressions with my sisters?

After a year of peripatetic living, constantly traveling, always on guard, avoiding all personal questions, speaking in discreet banalities, I longed for privacy, a home, an ordinary home. Everyone else, I thought with envy, has a home, family life, privacy, a baby.

The winter of 1929, waiting for the first baby, was not exactly a normal one. We continued our life in the air. We flew to the West Coast to supervise the construction of a plane with which my husband planned to carry on his air-route surveys. We made test flights. We flew up and down the coast. We experimented with gliding. I had already had some training in a Bird biplane. I received a gliding pilot's license after one day of instruction. We flew east across the country in our new plane, breaking the transcontinental speed record, two months before the baby was born.

Looking back with the hindsight of forty years, I feel those exploits on my part were of questionable wisdom. No doubt, since I had difficulty believing I was married, I could hardly imagine I was having a baby. All that flying around in open cockpits, being pulled off a mountaintop in a glider, and making a transcontinental record flight at what was then considered high altitude (without oxygen) was, I now think, tempting providence. But I felt young and strong and invulnerable.

The letters I wrote home about these adventures were not strictly accurate. The accounts were tempered to allay the anxiety of my mother or my mother-in-law, who, I realized, worried constantly and understandably over her son's exploits. Actually, I was frightened to death being pulled off the mountain alone in a glider, but I could not admit fear to my knight. Once in the air, however, it was an ecstatic experience I have never forgotten or regretted. The transcontinental flight east, on the other hand, was exhausting. I was seasick and in pain the last four hours of that fourteen-hour trip. (Since I had never been airsick, it must have been due to gasoline fumes and my "condition.") I could not interrupt and spoil the record flight and I did not want my fears or discomforts to get to the newspapers and make a story that would have a damaging effect on aviation, whose advance I had embraced as a cause, following my husband's example.

The first months of motherhood were totally normal, joyful, and satisfying and I would have been content to stay home and do nothing else but care for my baby. This was "real life" at its most basic level. But there were those survey flights that lured us to more adventures. I went on them proudly, taking my place as a crew member. The beauty and mystery of flying never palled, and I was deeply involved in my job of operating radio. Even more enriching to me was the experience of talking to the people we met in the outposts of the North, on our flight to the Orient across Canada, Alaska, Siberia. (Communication again!) I was enchanted by our visit to Japan, and awed by our brief view of China.

I wrote countless letters back to my family. Travel impressions they were on the whole, and somewhat played down. My inner censor was at work, keeping a strict watch on what I wrote. And my protective instinct about my family made me hold back on the more hazardous episodes. The intention of the letters was partly to reassure. I touched rather lightly on the dangers until we arrived safely home. A fuller account of the 1931 survey flight is in *North to the Orient,* the book I wrote a year or two later.

In explaining the unevenness of material in certain periods of my life I face a genuine drawback to an autobiography based on letters and diaries. When one is most active and involved in events—usually those of greatest interest and color—there is little time to write. Consequently gaps occur in the records of these early married years. There is no mention in the months before our survey flight of my learning to operate radio, which took weeks of study in radio theory and in the practice of Morse code. (At that time no practical long-distance voice radio was available.)

There is almost no mention of the hours of flying instruction given me by my husband in a Bird biplane. Even had I described it at the time, I would not have admitted how challenged, frightened, and infuriated I was trying to satisfy my exacting instructor. I remember going round and round the field alone in that plane, making one hideously bumpy landing after another. I myself was infinitely relieved, each time I hit the earth, no matter how hard, to get down alive, but he kept insisting that I go around again until I made a decent landing. And then, after all that hard work, there is no description of the absolute exultation of my first solo flight away from the airport, from the Long Island Aviation Country Club, over the towers of New York City to Teterboro Airport—my dream as a young girl at last come true.

Finally, I must admit that in rereading the letters of the last months of 1931 I am aware of hurrying through them (or was life itself hurrying?). They seem unreal. It is as if, in looking at my life, I were watching a swift-flowing stream, satin smooth on the surface, rushing headlong to the sheer drop of tragedy. Significantly, the letter that stands out most vividly at the end of that summer of letters, is the one after my father's death, news of which I received on board the British aircraft carrier *Hermes,* en route from Hankow to Shanghai. In replying, I let myself write from the depths of feeling. The hand of grief released me from the hand of the censor. There were other values, I was beginning to learn, more important than discretion or even privacy. As I discovered the following spring, in the abyss of tragedy, I needed to return to a deeper resource. I had to write honestly. So one can say perhaps that sorrow also played its part in setting me free. But that is another story. The first part of this book and this introduction cover the hour of gold.

1929

TO C. C. M.[1]　　　　　　　　　　　　　　　　*At Grandma's*[2]
　　　　　　　　　　　　　　　　[Cleveland, February 8th]
After one day of rushed preparation and two or three complete
reversals of plans, I find myself in Cleveland, starting for St.
Louis (and the announcement) at 4:30 A.M. tomorrow morning—
minus all my clothes and trunk! I have written all afternoon,
"Dear ——, I want to tell you before everyone knows that I am
going to marry—" It is all so unreal, but I feel happier—and yet if
someone should pounce on me and ask me what I was marrying
him for I should say, "Eyes—" Can't look in his eyes and do
anything else. I believe in his eyes, in what I think is behind
them, even though it doesn't always show in conversation. Well,
we're off!

Do hold your thumbs for me. Those terrible pits of fear and
doubt—"Let them not have dominion over me."

I *dread* the Embassy congratulations.

TO C. C. M.　　　　　*[En route to Mexico City, February 11th]*
Darling—
It is quite hot and very dusty and we have gotten so cramped—it
is as though one grew larger and could no longer fit into the
compartment but must break out of a window. Like *Alice*—remember? A dynamited train,[3] a burnt bridge have held us up.
The man in the compartment just outside is playing a raucous
gramophone, and because it doesn't make enough noise he bel-
lows along with it, "I'd rather be the girl in your arms than the
girl of your dreams!" He is very fat. The seat is getting too small
for him too.

[1] A. M. L.'s younger sister Constance Cutter Morrow.

[2] Mrs. Charles Long Cutter, mother of E. C. M.

[3] The train carrying the Mexican President, Emilio Portes Gil.

We have passed "Escape No. 67"[1] so I suppose we must go on with everything and that the announcement will be made tomorrow if I don't have another spasm. (I haven't had a real one since we left.)

Mother and I have exhausted our reading powers (I have finished *Elizabeth and Essex* and a *good light* novel, *Mamba's Daughters*), every known form of solitaire, and the train menu. Tonight all through supper, having ordered baked apple with cream (I hesitated between that and cornflakes), I regretted the cornflakes. And it occurred to me later that life might so easily be that eternal "If *only* I'd ordered cornflakes—"

TO C. C. M.   [*Mexico City, February 12th*]
Darling—
We're here—a night and half a day late!

Did Mother write you about the [code] telegram sent to Boyd[2]: "Urgent your telegram miscarried will announce plans on arrival Lincoln's Birthday unless interferes with your schedule as newspaper indicates. Major R. M. Kirk." Well, I never expected an answer, but Mother asked Daddy if there were a telegram for Kirk. *Here It is. I am wild with Joy.* To Daddy: "Have known Major Kirk for several years stop He has accurate technical knowledge and is reliable stop I endorse plan he suggests. Charles"—etc.! Isn't that *superb?* A masterpiece. It rejoices my heart somehow—the *play* of it. If he can do *that*—! And then it was *unnecessary* and he did it anyhow. Bless him.

And then to hear from him directly like that— It is reassuring and heart-warming. I have been hanging on to his hand in the darkness for such *ages,* it seems, and *now*— Oh, I am much happier.

[1] Notice alongside Mexican railroad indicating exit.
[2] Code name for C. A. L. A. M. L. had prearranged with C. A. L. a code wire indicating the day when the engagement would be announced from the U. S. Embassy, Mexico City.

Dear Charles—

I haven't very much hope in your getting this but perhaps you'll be in Washington a day or two and then go to New York. It makes me sick not to be there. I'm sorry it was all so delayed. Mother was a day late in starting, then we stopped in Cleveland, and then the accident along the line—to the train ahead of us—all combined to make the announcement delayed.[1]

All this has not been as bad as I expected. Everyone has been so extremely kind—overwhelmingly so. It's all horribly unreal, though. It's hard to hold on to reality (the reality of any happiness) when *so many* people are telling you how *extraordinarily* happy you must be! It is unreal. I feel nothing because I have been touched so many times in the same place. I wish you were here. I will try to be patient, though. I am such a coward by myself. There are a few very lovely things to tell you about and some awfully funny ones, and of course one moment of *pure joy*—a telegram about Major R. M., etc., that kept me going for days—*superb*. And it will last me quite a while still.

Oh, if I could only write and write—naturally, the way I do Con.[2] But then you would not have time to read them, or I to write them, for that matter—I am writing so many notes.

I won't expect to see you for ages. I will be patient—I know you have obligations and work. Please—I do understand. It doesn't matter. There are the mountains still, and riding, and singing, and the cherry blossoms are out, and there are always notes to write and dinners and the newspapers to tell where you have been.

I hope there is an unusually warm spell over all the North and West. It does not seem right that I should have the cherry blossoms.

Anne

[1] The engagement was announced to the press on February 12, 1929.

[2] A. M. L.'s younger sister Constance.

Hour of Gold, Hour of Lead

Dearest Con—

You wrote me such a dear letter but I thought you had had a lapse of memory, or something, because you didn't mention Charles or the announcement, and we were right in the middle of it! Now I realize what remarkable restraint you used and thank you, darling, for being so considerate. Before the announcement seems so long ago, and so immeasurably removed from me, that it is impossible to believe it was only a few weeks ago: the storms of congratulations, the unreal clippings, the showers of letters from every living person I have ever known and thousands from people I *don't* know. Life just completely changed and unreal, *very* funny at times.

Then suddenly one morning (after what seemed years) the papers' headlines that he was at Eagle Pass, and that evening he was *here*—in Cuernavaca! Now we have had a week, and again time seems to be playing tricks—I don't feel as if he were ever *not* here. I have not thought about time, about tomorrow or yesterday. It has been very wonderful—much nicer than ever before. I long to have you here. He has come into the family so, and we have so many jokes and he and Elisabeth tease each other. It is glorious. You *should* be here. Yesterday we were playing that game about people being like things to eat. You know: "What food is Mr. Ovey like?"² Answer: "A cheese stick." Well, he said very quickly, "Calvin Coolidge—grapenuts!" which I think is *superb*. (Don't, of course, repeat this.)

I suppose you want to know about the "Ace and Fiancée in Crash" episode. I wish I had written sooner, because the papers couldn't know very much about it and made it sound pretty bad.

---

¹ Mexican town, where Ambassador Morrow had a weekend house, Casa Mañana.

² Esmond Ovey, British Minister to Mexico, later Sir Esmond Ovey.

Besides, the whole thing was so interesting psychologically that I
would like to . . .[1]

I was flying at this time! He put me on the seat behind, with
the big flying suit and a pillow in front of me and another for me
to hold and put up before my head if we went over. He told me
to open the windows, so if we went over we could get out. I'm
glad I didn't know positively that we *would* go over because I
would have been so frightened. But when I said to him, "I don't
see how you can *help* being hurt," he said he didn't think it
would be such a bad landing. Then we flew over the field. I shall
never forget it—that casual group of people, curiously waiting,
watching for us, *suddenly* galvanized to petrified attention seeing
the stump and *no wheel*—all their hands pointing, everyone
running out, waving, shouting, (apparently) signaling us *not to
land*—those little ants down there below us, running around,
madly waving and absolutely powerless to help us.

It really was dramatic. We looked at each other and laughed
and circled the field again. We came down slowly (he cooled off

[1] Here a page is missing in original letter. What happened was this:
After takeoff from Valbueno field, Mexico City, C. A. L. and A. M. L.
landed in a prairie where they had a picnic lunch. On taking off again,
C. A. L. looked out and saw a wheel that had just come off its axle rolling
along the ground beside the plane. He realized that they would have a
difficult landing because the plane had a very wide wheel spread and the
axle would dig into the ground and probably cause the plane to nose over.
A further complication was that this borrowed plane had not been equipped
with safety belts, so that in the event of nosing over C. A. L. and A. M. L.
would be tossed to the top of the cabin. After discussion with A. M. L.,
C. A. L. decided first to fly around for several hours to reduce the load of
gasoline and minimize the danger of a burst tank and resulting fire on
impact. He also padded A. M. L. with seat cushions and told her to hang
on to the seat bottom. He himself planned to control the plane's landing
with one hand and with the other to hold on to a tube of the fuselage
structure. He landed on one wheel with the wheelless axle high, but as
the plane lost flying speed the wing dropped and the axle stub dug into
the ground, turning the plane upside down.

the engine), and I had one terrible moment of panic: "Now here is the test. Suppose you can't face it. You will just be ruined in his eyes. Suppose I can't. Suppose I *can't.*" Then we slanted down on one wheel, then a waver of the wing, a jolt—and I remember nothing until my back banged on the ceiling and I realized we had turned over and it wasn't a test at all, I'd never met anything. It wasn't so terrible, like finding yourself down at the bottom of a ski jump, not having jumped.

I was out the window and asking, "How are you?" He was out. "All right. How are you?" He was holding his hand. We looked at each other and smiled; he was breathing very hard; a truck came up. He talked quietly but with effort to a mad group of people, telling them he had dislocated his shoulder, would they guard the plane so no one would take souvenirs.

"Souvenirs!" a Mexican laughed and looked with amazement at a man walking out of a smashed plane with a dislocated shoulder and thinking about people collecting *souvenirs!* I can't write any more. I drove home through the traffic. It was terrible to see anyone suffering so, and I couldn't do anything. I wished I had been hurt a little. I had nothing—

TO C. C. M.   [*March 9th*]
Dearest Coz—
I am waiting for C. to have breakfast before he starts off to Brownsville.[1] It is not quite 6:30 A.M., and I feel so wifely and devoted, though all I had to do was to get up and take a hot bath.

Yesterday I took him riding with the Becks,[2] and they put him on Cream Puff.[3] Do you remember—a sort of bay-golden pony?

[1] To pilot the inaugural flight on the Pan American Airways route between Mexico City and Brownsville, Texas.

[2] Eman Beck, a long-time resident of Mexico City, and his family. His daughter Susanna was a friend of A. M. L.

[3] The Becks' horse C. A. L. rode in Mexico.

Sue said it matched his hair! Charles stuck to his saddle the way
Mr. McDonald used to tell us to and started off on a tear. Cream
Puff is the fastest horse and C. rode circles in the cross-fields with
her, while we were content merely to ride across! We went out
toward Los Remedios—you remember?—across fields of cactus
and barrancas.

C. loved it and the Becks loved him so I was very happy,
although it was one of those days when I felt like an egg poised
on a seesaw.

Charles is going so I must stop.

[*Mexico City, March 9th*]

Dear Mrs. Lindbergh,

I want to thank you for such a beautiful shawl. It was lovely of
you to bring it so far and give it to me. I feel as though I were
being given more than I deserve—not in gifts, I don't mean that,
but in happiness—and to have gifts too is an extra happiness. It is
hard to write this just because all words of thanks sound conventional and insincere, I think, especially when you have been
writing lots of letters. But it will be such a real pleasure to wear
your shawl—a favorite color of mine—and the sweet little coral
roses.

I wish that you were here. It does not seem quite right that you
should not be. I am sorry for this publicity that keeps things from
being as they should be. I am afraid, too, that it must have caused
you a great deal of trouble and discomfort in New York when
you landed. And perhaps even now you are being bothered by
letters and pleas and so forth—as I am. I think I understand a
little better what, in this particular, you have been through. I
remember your talking to us about the many letters and your
tolerance and humor about them.

Charles says with perfect faith that the newspaper accounts of
the one-wheel landing and of the revolution here[1] will not bother

[1] On March 3rd a rebellion against the government started in Veracruz
and Sonora. It was quickly crushed.

you—that you will know they are not serious enough to worry about. I doubt if I could show the same sense of proportion if I were in your position.

I am glad that you are back and only wish that you were here and hope you can be sometime again—at least that I can see you before very long.

Mexico City, March 12, 1929

Dear Con—

I have wanted you here terribly because C. has been so charming and delightful, and entered into the family—even more than at supper that night. He and Elisabeth and I have gone off on rides and we do nothing but tease each other in the most ridiculous fashion—about his being "a nice clean boy,"[1] about my skirts' being too short, about there being no men of our age as nice as those of Daddy's age—you just have to take a chance on a fairly nice person and hope he'll change (to C.). "That's what *I'm* doing!" C. saying that I made eyes at him in the plane the first time and he was shocked that the daughter of an ambassador should behave so indecently. C. imitating me making eyes—a scream! C. threatening to bring me a baby goat (I'm always gushing over them) if I will take all the responsibility, after he has caught it and brought it home! C. teasing me about calories, and collecting *all* the nut containers and setting them before me at meals. And lots of other silly things that grow up and mean so much. And if you were here there would be more. And then serious discussions about religion and people. He is really quite natural and unrestrained.

[1] So described by D. W. M. to a friend of his on the day the engagement was announced.

Dearest Con—

Charles left this morning. Tonight I am tired but it has been such a beautiful visit. I should love so to see you and talk about it. I am sure *sure sure* that it is right now, and the pangs are not *doubt* any more. Sometimes I am tired and mixed up and not still and happy and focused yet about it all. But it is not that heretical doubt. It keeps growing and smoothing out and I am happy.

Now this is a strict secret. Don't breathe or suggest it to anyone. People think we will be married *here* or in *Englewood* and we're just *letting them* think that—if they think it may be next fall, so much the better—and we will all go up to North Haven[1] and get married (I mean those of us who wish to!) on about three days' notice about the third week in June—perhaps. We are having a dreadful time deciding whom to ask. It is a terribly difficult problem, because it *must* be small and yet I love so many people and Daddy and Mother do, too.

I must go to sleep now. This is just a business letter—there is not one still pool of appreciation or thought in it. There has not been much time for that lately. I hope it will come back. I am tired of this dusty sunlight; I want one cool misty lonely walk in North Haven. I miss the vivid realization of things that comes from being alone and still. But you can't have everything—or everything in a hurry. I think we will have that—later. We seem to share more and more.

Please, darling, be careful of these letters—perhaps I have written too freely. It is so hard for me to learn to keep back the things I am feeling—especially from you.

Oh—I have forgotten to tell you about the best day of all. We went to Puebla, C. and I, and climbed up those dusty shelves of the tile place, and nobody bothered us or smirked or smiled or

---

[1] The Morrows' summer home, Deacon Brown's Point, on the island of North Haven, Maine.

even noticed us enough to try to sell us things! We had to dig in
the dust by ourselves. And we picked out bright bowls and dishes
with borders of blues and yellows and greens, searching through
stacks of dishes, clinking the dishes from one stack to another,
and the old Mexican woman sitting on a stepladder, wiping off
the dust from their rims with her apron, so we could see the
design.

A.: "Oh, *there*—there—look at *that* one!"

C. appraisingly, nodding but doubtful: "It doesn't match the
others you have here."

A.: "Oh, but it's so *pretty*—don't you think it's better to get a
pretty one than one that matches?"

C., large grin showing gradual conversion to my illogical view-
point: "Yes!" (So you can see what the collection must be like.)

When finally we had collected all together I discovered that
(quite typically) we had *three* sets of bowls—that is, three sets of
things to hold soup or cereals. That of course is because the meal
that comes most easily and fancifully to my mind is breakfast. It
is so delightful to imagine those sturdy little blue- and green-
rimmed bowls full of cornflakes and cream (the cornflakes all
gold and heaped up on one hillside and the cream in a bubbly
lake at the bottom, so that the flakes won't get soggy).

But one can't eat cornflakes three times a day, so we thought
we could use the littlest bowls for cups; they have no handles, of
course, so we shall have to cup them in our palms with both
hands, Japanese-fashion. And they have no saucers but we got
some small butter plates to put underneath them. Doesn't it
sound just like Mrs. Peterkin?[1] And you, the Lady from Phila-
delphia, will ask, "Why didn't you buy *cups?*" But they had *no*
cups in the whole shop; all was *"ventido,"* done up in baskets
under the shelves. Except for one lovely blue cup and saucer that
I got "just *anyway,* Charles, it's so . . . *pretty!"*

[1] *The Peterkin Papers* by Lucretia T. Hale.

Well, we probably won't use them for *years*. But perhaps when you are through school and college and taking a postgraduate course at Cambridge you can visit me *somewhere* and we'll get out the big bowl, the middle-sized bowl, and the little bowl and we'll all have cornflakes and cream.

Friday evening [Mexico City, March 15th]

Dear Charles—

Apparently you left yesterday morning—about two weeks ago. It is like getting back to school with lots of homework to do—all those piles of letters—and I am out of practice. I did *one* today and felt, "Oh, what a good girl am I!"

Cream Puff had a retrospective dreamy look in her eye this morning, a "gone-are-the-days" look, and Sandy[1] (back last night) remarked that he was "going to miss having the boy around," and I find that (in Lolita's phrase) "eet ees hate-*full.*" I think I shall be very happy, though, as soon as I digest some of the experiences of the last weeks and months. Of course one is happy *doing* things, but there is a different kind of happiness that comes from fully *realizing* afterwards the things done: the "recollection-in-tranquillity" feeling that comes when you are alone and quiet and see your experiences as a whole. But that takes quite a while.

Good night

Anne

Saturday

Today we were riding primly down the bridle paths and a man came galloping past and shouted, "Look out for the elephants!" Such a funny thing to say in a city park. There they were, two large wrinkly ones lumbering along. Their skin is so wrinkly, they look as if they had loose baggy trousers on, like Daddy's

---

[1] Colonel Alexander MacNab, U. S. Military Attaché in Mexico.

(not that Daddy looks like an elephant but his trousers do bag sometimes).

It reminded me of circuses: the smell of sawdust and animals and peanuts and garlic and heat and people; and ladies with very spangled dresses, and having a headache from sucking milk chocolate and from trying to watch the tall-silk-hatted man with a cracking whip *and* the glorious swings *and* the man falling off a tower of chairs *and* the Japs hanging by their teeth, *and* the clowns who paraded around underneath the audience doing stunts that inevitably ended in their house or car, or whatever they had, collapsing on top of them—all at the same time! You went to them of course. I loved them even though it always made me sick. I still like milk chocolate, too. I don't know that I would like them now, though—circuses.

(Did you know that "certainly God has played a great part in Col. Lindbergh's career"? In today's mail.)

The sun shone through the marmalade so nicely this morning (I know you're laughing—it *is* silly *"but* you don't *understand"*). I'm sure that's why breakfast is such a nice meal. You see, you haven't had sunshine for twelve hours and so you are extra glad to see it and to eat sunshiny things like golden toast and corn-flakes and marmalade—that is, *I* am because I like those things. (The cook has even stopped making those particularly large sugar-covered buns now, because no one eats them.)

Mr. Beck says the roads around Mexico City are *exceedingly* dangerous just now because there are no soldiers here to guard them. In fact, it is *very* foolhardy to venture outside of the city at all!

Sunday

Oh, I am tired of this eternal dusty sunshine. The sun doesn't seem half as precious here as it did those last March days in Northampton[1] when the melted snow tore down the banks and

---

[1] The reference is to Smith College, Northampton, Mass., where A. M. L. was studying the winter before.

you jumped in between puddles in the road, and when the sun glowed for a minute it was delicious, a *pale* gold sunshine (not red hot the way it is here), and you had to coax it to come in the window—with a jar of marmalade or narcissi.

No, what I want just now is North Haven. Wind to blow all the stuffiness out and a cool thick sea mist that pricks your face softly, deliciously, when you walk in it—and loneliness. I mean *sea* loneliness, not the *desert* loneliness that you might get here that is so dead. The loneliness you get by the sea is personal and alive. It doesn't subdue you and make you feel abject. It's a stimulating loneliness.

I have been reading *Othello* and it helps tremendously. There are such lovely passages that sweep you along, like a great wave or wind. I would like to quote them to you and I can't. Do you remember? Or perhaps you haven't read it—I did for the first time last year. She objects in one place:

> ". . . if I be left behind,
> A moth of peace, and he go to the war . . ."

(It is awful to be a moth, fluttering very uselessly, making a lot of fuss over nothing—the way I am now.) Oh, there is much more—can I read you some of it sometime?

> "If after every tempest come such calms,
> May the winds blow till they have wakened death!
>
> . . . .
>
> . . . If it were now to die,
> 'Twere now to be most happy, for I fear
> My soul hath her content so absolute
> That not another comfort like to this
> Succeeds in unknown fate."

Read it over again—no, not now, you are probably much too busy now—but read it over and over sometime. You *can't* say there isn't beauty in it:

"If it were now to die,
'Twere now to be most happy . . ."

This is all of my writing and absurdities that you can possibly read at a stretch. I'm sorry, but I love to write letters—that is, sincere ones.

Good night—
Anne

TO C. A. L.   [*Mexico City, March 19th*]
I looked up that quotation of Katherine Mansfield about what she calls "the act of surrender." You were right, it *is* the wrong word but she meant a *big* word for "giving," giving yourself. *Sacrifice* is pretty good but it has a kind of stoic idea about it which isn't right for her meaning. It is the act of giving yourself with abandon to work and art, in particular, that she means. Anyway, I like what she says of it: "It needs real humility and at the same time an absolute belief in one's own essential freedom. It is an act of faith. At the last moments like all great acts it is *pure risk.*" I think that is quite true and wonderful. Remember it.

Yesterday the 18th I got a letter from Ambassador Herrick[1]— very very nice—and the most beaming picture of you both, which showed, he said, what he thought about you. It was sent the 13th of February.

Did you see the awful picture taken the day we went up again, my skirts blown up terribly (Elisabeth: *"Which* dress is so short?")? I suppose that means another thousand letters telling me that I *am* a flapper after all and that the youth of America . . . etc.

I got the nicest letter from Vernon[2] today, congratulating us

[1] Myron T. Herrick, lawyer, banker, diplomat, U. S. Ambassador to France, who had welcomed Charles Lindbergh on his arrival at Le Bourget airport after his transatlantic flight, and had been his host in Paris.
[2] Vernon Munroe, friend and Englewood neighbor of the young Morrows.

mostly for going up in the plane the next day. That is like Vernon (he would have done it) and you, not particularly like me. I have no "fighting" instinct, I just wanted to follow you.

A little girl has just sent me "an original theme" about our engagement, the best line in it being "because they are both so reticent of speech that not even the associated press (!) will ever hear the truth of it."

Yesterday, three people tried to persuade me that you should have your portrait painted before the wear and tear of married life had taken the bloom off your youth and beauty! They were more tactful than that but that was the sad underlying truth—that you, poor boy, would *never* be the same again. Not that I object so to the portrait but just the implication that my nagging will bring on premature wrinkles! I have a feeling that I will be a fat middle-aged matron before you look a minute over nineteen!

We have just heard that Con can be here until the 3rd or 4th of April, which is too good to believe. I am so happy. It is such a treat to be with her. All trivial things we see and enjoy alike and together: a fruit stand, or two ducks in the road, or Daffin[1] begging with one paw crossed over the other, or the way Daddy eats an egg! She and Elisabeth and I are all the same age now. And the dear and intimate joy, after a party or dinner, of sitting on a bed with two wonderful sisters, talking and laughing about everything, knowing that every gesture, every quip, every smile is completely understood. Braiding up your hair and swinging your legs over the side of the bed and eating cookies and milk and laughing—oh, it is indescribable. I am sorry, just for that one experience, that you weren't a girl and never had sisters!

Wednesday night, late [*March 20th*]

I've just come in from a party. I was rather afraid to go. But it was gay and fun and stimulating conversation, and dancing afterwards, and more exciting conversation about reading and

[1] The Morrows' West Highland white terrier.

writing. And yet I am happy now to come back and realize, "No, that's not what I want. It *is* stimulating, it *is* interesting, but it's not what I want for any length of time—just once in a while."

Thursday [*March 21st*]

Tomorrow we get up at 5 A.M. to go out to a flower festival (an old Indian one and very beautiful) of Santa Anita. I wish you could be there too, Santo Carlos, because I shall be much too sleepy and grouchy the rest of the day to write about it to you.

It is the most amazing thing what *time* can do. I mean, it's remarkable how little time you can have been away before I think it's a year. And my watch has stopped, just to be symbolical.

"I told you butter wouldn't suit the works," sighed the Hatter.

"It was the *best* butter," the March Hare meekly replied.

TO C. A. L.   *March 25th*

Your letter was such a help—it came on Santa Anita day. I didn't expect one half so soon. You were good to write at the end of such a long day. But it was a joy. You see, that was rather a wasted day, except for half an hour of it. We were told it was a *very early* festival but well worth it. So—martyrs to the cause —we arose before five and chased out in a cold blowy dark morning to Mrs. Nuttall's,[1] where other martyrs were assembled, cold but eager. After that it was one long disillusionment—terribly funny but tiring. The whole thing was wretchedly organized. We didn't see anything worth seeing until eleven; we just waited for things to happen: waited for a Mexican breakfast, waited to find our float (it is a day when flower-decorated floats and canoes pole up the canal and crowds of Mexicans come for a whole day's holiday dressed in their old costumes and carrying and wearing flowers, to watch the floats), waited for the float to

---

[1] Casa Alvarado, the house of Zelia Nuttall, American archaeologist, friend of the Morrows.

be decorated, waited for the crowds, even, and didn't get home till one thirty.

I was going to write you a long and funny description of it all but I wrote it to Dwight and I'm too tired to write it over again. It's gone. Of course one half hour of watching that gay holiday crowd was gorgeous and worth it all. It gave you an idea of Mexico and the people more than anything I have seen, and I loved it and am truly grateful to Mrs. Nuttall.

We were low on the water and we looked up on either bank to bright crowds of people: women with wreaths of poppies on their heads, children with flowers round their necks, stamping their bare brown feet to a drum in the distance, and, against the sky, horses with gold-braided *charro*[1]-costumed men cantered by. Whole families squatted on the bank for the day. They twined poppy wreaths and sucked ice-cream sticks and bought tortillas and nursed their babies and washed their clothes and sang until they were tired out. *And there is a revolution going on in Mexico now!*

But of course there *would* be some hitch. We poled up the river through this gorgeousness until we came to the grandstand for the richer people and the judges of the floats. There I had a sudden chill to see forty or more cameras pointed at the floats. It was, of course, just for the floats but I felt very uncomfortable. I tried to sit inconspicuously for a while—and *then* that cannibalistic gleam in the photographer's eye when he sees meat. Well, it was nasty for a while and we got caught in a jam of canoes and floats.

I want to go home and I am sick of writing letters. I have about 110 *left* to write and I have been writing for two weeks steadily. And it makes me so stupid stupid stupid fat and dull. And I write you fat stupid letters.

Dear C. This is just an impatient exclamation, not a death cry!

---

[1] *Charro:* Mexican horsemen in fancy riding habits.

TO C. A. L.   [*Mexico City*], *March 27th*
I have just gotten your letter and I feel so cheerful. You see, when you get away I feel as though you were *never* coming back again, and it was so nice to hear such very real-sounding plans.

I'm glad your letter came because I had just begun to get very hard and angry about a front-page notice of the *Times* that you and I had given it out authoritatively (or officially or whatever the word is) that we were going to be married in June—place not given out yet. It made me *boiling,* first, that they should print an absolute *lie*—that we gave it out. And in the second place, that means more letters, advertisements, etc., and people writing and asking me when and where the wedding will be—and are they coming! And sort of waiting around and expecting things in June. It was an A.P. report. My, they make me angry.

Well, that's over. Oh, today—what do you think I did today! We went down to the big Easter street fair. You walk between lines and lines of booths flaunting *everything:* dusters, dolls, toys, baskets, pink lemonade (or worse), hats and children's wagons and minute little doll's tea sets, and pots and pans and lacquer boxes, and candy, etc., etc. I bought some *more bowls.* Why is it that all the pretty pottery is . . . *bowls?* In your old age you will have to live on cornflakes alone! But these were so lovely, with a blue and green border, and deep, sloping up gracefully like some kind of flower. They were *blue.* I'll do almost anything for *blue*— hills or bowls or eyes or neckties.

Friday the 29th
Today Constance and I went to the convent of Churubusco. You and Grandma and Aunt Annie[1] and Mother and I went once, but it was cold, and I remember feeling rather unhappy and not liking it. But it was still and sunny today. Con and I let the guide lead us through all the rooms in order to earn a peaceful let-alone talk in the garden after the guide was satisfied. He kept showing us

[1] Annie Spencer Cutter, E. C. M.'s sister, lived with her mother in Cleveland.

32

places where the monks washed their hands. He shouted "Lavabo" loudly, then in case we didn't get it he went through all the gestures with his hands. I was glad to see he really knew how to do it; his hands looked as though he'd never tried!

Then we sat on a log and took in the sun and the smell of honeysuckle. Do you remember? It brings up all of summer: July and dusty roads and crickets at night, and biting off the little green end to suck the honey out. Oh, but it would be nice to have rain again: a gentle, persistent, comforting rain on the roof. Do you remember how deliciously soothing it is to go to sleep to it, pattering softly and very comfortingly, and the gush of water running down the gutters, and the last sleepy thought before you slip off, like a refrain to that soft pattern, "How lovely and fresh everything will be in the morning!" Oh, you *do* remember? I am getting quite sleepy thinking about it.

Good night. Do I talk about silly little things? But I think most events are little and that it is only their connotations and their association with people and people's feelings that make them important at all. None of the "events" of my life here are at all interesting. It is only the beauty or association connected with them that makes them bearable.

Forgive me if they bore you. It is a help to write to you. Good night—

Easter night, postscript

Dear Charles,

That letter was so small and silly and futile i could not bear to have you get it alone, so I caught it and steamed it open again to add this. Oh, Charles, I am so sorry about Ambassador Herrick.[1] I wish you were here and I could tell you quietly instead of writing it coldly. I can't say anything because I didn't know him but I only know that you will feel badly.

Oh, Charles, I wanted so much to meet him. But I am terribly glad that he didn't die in Cleveland away from his work

[1] Ambassador Herrick died on March 31, 1929.

and the place he had filled so very well. Wasn't it wonderful that he got back there to France? It seemed *right* that he should be there. (What do you think—do you think it is a small thing I am saying?) But I am glad he died in office. Only that he did not see you again and you did not see him—that makes me sad. I am so sorry, and send you my love, good night, Anne

[*Mexico City, April 9th*]

Con, darling,

Last night C. and I had supper in the little office and C. read me the most thrilling article in the March Century called "The Magnificent Universe" by Edwin B. Frost. The heavens really do recede after you've read it; time and space and motion just mean unimaginable things and you feel like a millionth of a millionth of a millionth of a millionth of a millionth of a pinpoint! C. said that they now have a telescope so powerful that if the Capitol were placed on the moon we could see a dot there, and in ten years they will have a telescope made even more powerful which will be able to see *within* that dot! That is, we may be able to see if there is life on Mars!

The most stupendous leap into knowledge of these things has been made lately and yet we've really not scratched the surface (C. says). Leonardo—the most brilliant genius that ever lived—said at the end of his life, in which he was (besides artist) "hydraulician, hydrographer, geometrician, algebraist, mechanician, optician," etc., that "he had only been a child gathering shells and pebbles on the shore of the great ocean of truth."

Darling, C. is about to go. It won't be quite a month before we see you and spring—

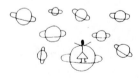

TO C. A. L.   [*Mexico City*], *Thursday, April 18th*
I am terribly sorry there *wasn't* a letter there. Yours has just
come—I think the nicest one you ever wrote me—and I hadn't
written you at all. I'm sorry. I didn't write because I felt so out of
tune with what you were doing—petty and rebellious and wicked
—so out of tune with what you were doing to help the Herricks.[1]
Parmely[2] sent me a telegram saying what a great help you were
to all of them. It is so seldom that one can be any help to people
who have lost someone they loved. And it is a rare and lovely
thing that you really could. I am glad, and it must be some
satisfaction to you. Then I think it was simply *miraculous*
thoughtfulness and kindness to send that telegram to me.

I wrote you one letter but it did not pass the censor[3] and I tore
it up. No, I'm glad I didn't send it—it would have shocked you
and I would have too if you could have seen my thoughts this
last . . . *week?* (Is it only a *week* and two days?) Thank God
we are leaving this place in exactly a week. I have let it do all
sorts of disturbing things to my mind and heart. Of course it is
not the place, just myself, you remember.

"O God! I could be bounded in a nutshell, and count myself a
king of infinite space, were it not that I have bad dreams." I
hope—I think it will be all right when I see you, but, Charles,
what *does* happen to me when you go off? Oh, these bad dreams.

So you see I did not write. Anyway these letters are futile
and baffling. I don't feel as if you ever got them or read them;
they drop into the sea. And I do not feel that I write what I like,
or you like what I write, and *that,* together with this interminable space and this interminable chilling reticence—well, it is
like beating against a stone wall.

---

[1] C. A. L. had flown to New York to meet the body of Ambassador Herrick, returned for burial in Cleveland, Ohio.

[2] Myron T. Herrick's son.

[3] See Introduction, pp. 5 f.

Oh, I know that it is necessary and I accept it, only . . . why *write* (*Ce n'est pas la peine*) a "halfway" letter? And oh, I love to write—a full whole letter. I don't mean sentimental—I don't want to write things like that. But I cannot write you what I want. Just the idea that "nothing written is safe" and that *someone else might see it* and that *I must be careful* muffles me, and then the fact that I have no conviction that this will get to you or, if it does, that you will let it in.

We had some musicians last night. They played outside on the porch and we sat where they could not see us in the parlor, and they played to the sofas and the granite pillars and the marble floors and . . . *silence!* Of course they *wilted*. Their songs simply sagged mournfully; their throats grew hoarse trying to reach us, touch us, warm us. Finally cowed, they faded out entirely and the men shuffled off discouraged.

That's the way I feel.

I have some things to read you. Some are too long and must be talked over; others—shall I put them down on the chance of their reaching you?

"J'ai besoin de vous voir, et de vous voir encore—et de vous voir toujours!"[1] (*Don't* get anyone to translate this.)

(Here Santayana is talking about the memory of great happiness or great experiences.) "All these count for nothing when they are once gone. The memory of them cannot cure a fit of the blues nor raise an irritable mortal above some petty act of malice or vengeance, or reconcile him to bad weather. An ode of Horace, on the other hand, a scientific monograph, or a well-written page of music is a better antidote to melancholy than thinking on all the happiness which one's own life or that of the universe may ever have contained. Why should overwhelming masses of suffering and joy affect the imagination so little while it responds sympathetically to aesthetic and intellectual irritants of very slight

---

[1] "I need to see you and to see you again—and to see you always."

intensity, objects that, it must be confessed, are of almost no importance to the welfare of mankind?" Read that again. Don't you think that is good and fair and true? It is an all-round statement of the experience, I think. Santayana writes like that— walking all around the subject. (I have saved some essays for us to read together.)

Oh, it is no use, all this that I have written. It is always, always *pushing* uphill. Do you feel it—this wall? Why can't I write you as I could write Con?

We leave here next Thursday, stop at Houston and Cleveland, and arrive home the morning of the 2nd *con muchissimo gusto*. I will write you anyway.

"ἄνευ δὲ σοῦ ὅσα μὴν διὰ σκότους ἡ ὁδός"
(Anabasis[1])

That's all right because it's Greek and no one can understand it and it means all I want to say.

Good-by ⚹

Oh, Charles, forgive this but it has been awful here. Let me see you soon—the first day. When I can talk to you it will be all right again.

Mr. and Mrs. Morgan[2] (here) are utterly different and terribly happy, married. Isn't that encouraging!

A ranch near Querétaro, Saturday, April 20th

Dear Charles,

I am writing you because I have wanted so to since day before yesterday. I wanted terribly to tell you that *for three days*—no, for two days, but it seems like a week—*I've felt almost the same!* Isn't that wonderful? I've felt almost as sure as when I'm with you—not quite, of course, that would be impossible. But I'm much much happier than I ever was before, and I feel much

[1] "Without you every road lies through shadows."

[2] Stokeley W. Morgan, Counselor, U. S. Embassy.

more courageous. You have been so patient and understanding that I wanted to thank you and say that I will try not to be wavering and worrying in the future.

Forgive that complaining letter from Mexico City. You know always what I am feeling underneath—deep, deep. You will understand and forgive that foam of irritation on top of the sea. I have been distressed about it since I left the city. It is strange, but the minute I got on the train and left I felt utterly different. I think one's feelings and thoughts, the real true deep ones, are better focused when you get away because they are detached from their stale associations: one's desk and room and bed and mirror. They become clear and just themselves, the way colors of a sunset or a birch grove seen upside down become clearer, because the colors are disassociated from their familiar forms. Do you see what I mean?

Oh, it is beautiful here. The air is not harsh and dusty but soft and there are fields and fields of smooth rich green shiny-leafed corn and of rain-colored wheat, coming up level around the trunks of occasional trees in the field, like water. And piles of big summery clouds in a blue sky. And clean air from the cornfields. I feel smoothed out and level like that—just as still and fresh and grateful as one of those cornfields. (I think there is great peace in *level* things, like the level line of wheat or the lines on a beach from waves or the horizontal lines of beech trees.) And I am happy, for we go home the day after the day after the day after the day after tomorrow! You do forgive me?

I know this is indiscreet—this letter—but I don't care, if it makes you forget the other.

[*En route from Mexico to Cleveland, late April*]
My sweet Con—
I haven't written for so long that I find myself desperately homesick for you, and realizing how hideous it will be when I leave with Charles. Though perhaps we are arranging it just right. You are going to be away now for four or five years[1] and perhaps by that time I shall be settled down.

We are in Texas now, on our way to Houston. I keep thinking of what you said last year: "It's so *green*, Anne, it's so *green!*" It is overcast and cool and damp, the trees heavy with damp green leaves. I feel as though I were inside a goldfish bowl. But it is rather nice for a change.

These little towns look so wholesome and sane and dear and yet quite foreign to me, with their "Coca-Cola" signs and "Lucky Strike Cigarettes." As though I were looking at a Kelly Springfield Tire advertisement in *Life*. Goodness knows they are shabby enough, these towns, but so clean and civilized compared to the Mexican ones. Clapboard houses, you know, painted white, and fences and clover and little children in bright blue, skipping, and shingled roofs and washing on a line (not on cactus or stones!).

This morning I woke up to a little boy's voice. He had traveled all night alone. He got off very proudly and his first words to his family were "Lindbergh's fiancée is on my train!" Such is fame!

New York City [*early May, 1929*]
Mother darling,
I have been sitting here thinking and thinking about you. And I can't say anything. I would like to tell you that you are wonderful. I sit most of the time apathetic, selfish, and unresponsive on the edge of your full marvelous life, and I seem to take you for granted. But one is rather stunned and is apt to forget or not to

---

[1] C. C. M. was a student at Milton Academy and later went to Smith College.

realize because you never seem to think you are wonderful! So I thought I would tell you once what everyone should tell you all the time—what everyone is saying but you don't hear it: that you are a simply marvelous person; a rare, beautiful, amazingly alive person, so all-touching, so all-sensitive, to everything.

It is the highest kind of culture. I have been noticing it more and more—all the time. Of course I realized it when we grew from one interest to another. It was amazing because every stage we went through and every new field we discovered—every new enthusiasm—there you were ahead of us, warmly sensitive to it as though you had just discovered it too. But you are that way with everyone, in a thousand fields. The trouble is that no one can really appreciate all of you, no one is big enough to get all the way round!

I thought this would be easy to say but it isn't. It is clumsy.

Darling, you *are* wonderful!

[Enclosure: Note to E. C. M.]
Darling—
I am going out with C. Plans indefinite, but I shall make him take me to Englewood sometime today. See you tonight. So happy!

[Written on the morning of the wedding day][1]
Englewood, New Jersey

Dear Mother,
You were wonderful last night, and you left me so happy and feeling very courageous and ahead-looking. Thank you, darling. I love you and I don't feel as though I were leaving. I have a permanent happy solid feeling of holding hands with both you and Charles.

Your Anne

[1] A. M. L. and C. A. L. were married on May 27, 1929, at Next Day Hill, Englewood, N. J., and went off afterwards on their honeymoon in a 38-foot cabin motorboat, the *Mouette*.

[*Written aboard the* Mouette, *May 27th*]

Mother darling—

This reminds of the letters I used to write on the train going back to Northampton! I feel a little the same way, too—superficially— a little choky about leaving but very happy and satisfied and warm about "what we got done." Oh, Mother— It was so lovely. I wouldn't change one thing: the walk around the old garden (and the new garden this morning with Con); lunch (although I was too excited to eat my favorite asparagus); every single person there—darling Vernon, Amey,[1] Aunt Maud and Dutch,[2] Grandma sweet and smiling, Aunt Annie [Cutter] and Edith [Yates][3]—all that lovely warm group. It was so lovely walking down the steps *with Daddy* into that group. I wouldn't change the dress, *the veil,* the flowers (that Elisabeth did so *beautifully*— columbine and larkspur), or any of it. Cutting the cake, kissing everyone! Wasn't Dr. Brown[4] *dear.* It was all perfect. But you want to know what C. thinks: *just the same thing!* Thought the ceremony beautiful, Dr. Brown fine, *loved* the dress *and* veil (didn't think he would but he did), was just as extravagant as you said Daddy was the other day.

But what he was most enthusiastic about was "the family, the whole family, and nothing but the family."

Tell Elisabeth that he looks at me fiddling with my fourth finger and says, "It will give the watch a rest!"

[1] Amey Aldrich. She and her brother Chester were close friends of the Morrow family.

[2] "Aunt" Maud and "Uncle" Dutch Hulst, old Englewood friends of E. C. M.

[3] E. C. M.'s younger sister, Mrs. Sheldon Yates; lived in Englewood.

[4] Dr. William Adams Brown of Union Theological Seminary, who performed the wedding ceremony.

May 31st

Mother darling—

We are in the harbor of Block Island. We have stopped to get water—a very dangerous proceeding as we don't want to be recognized. Charles has been preparing his disguise for three days (grown a beaver, in other words. Tell Con it's the "no-just-stubble" stage). He has a *very* dirty pair of pants on and a black-checked cap pulled over his eyes and dark glasses on. I am hiding in the cabin. Apparently they like him that way (as far as I can tell from behind the green-curtained windows): a crowd of a dozen men (Maine fisher type) are gaping at him and the boat and asking questions, mostly about the boat—cost, size, etc. But I have already wriggled with delight over the following repartee.

Gaping fisherman (doubtfully): "You own her?"

C.: "Oh no, just borrowed her for a while."

G. f.: "Alone?"

C.: "Alone just now."

G. f.: "Where ya bound for?"

C.: "Boston."

G. f.: "Where ya goin' to put in tonight?"

C.: "Don't know. Depends on when I get out of here."

G. f.: "If you come in again I'd like to have you stop up and see me."

C.: "Sure, that's fine—if I'm ever in here again. Doubt if I will be, though. My orders are to . . . Where do you live?"

In the meantime I wonder how much they can see through the green curtains and what they would say to see me with white sailor pants and a lavender shirt on.

Oh, there is so much to tell you, but I couldn't write from the beginning. It was very hot for three days and we spent most of the time sorting out cans and cans and *cans* of tinned soups, vegetables, milk, butter, cheese, fruit, fish, roast beef, ham, shrimp; *pâté de foie gras,* plum pudding, fruit salad, etc., etc., to say nothing of boxes and boxes of assorted breakfast foods.

I have never seen so much tinned stuff, boxes, and makes of

crackers outside of a grocery store. It took a whole day and most of the deck to sort them out. The baked bean tins towered on top of each other. C. had ordered small tins and they had sent the big kind. And of course there is no place for them. It took another day to hide them all. They peep at us now, like Easter eggs, from behind the extra beds, in the soiled-clothes drawer, in the medicine closet, on the towel shelves, etc., etc., everywhere! Tomatoes, beans, etc.

We have left the dock. Safe, with full tanks and icebox. One of the men, though, joking with a friend, said, "This guy told me he was Lindbergh—didn't you?" (to Charles). C.: *"Sure!"* Which of course was the only thing to say. Perhaps there has been a good deal of discussion in the newspapers about where we are. (Radio doesn't work.) Another funny thing. C. ordered two dozen bottles of ginger ale, which brought forth this comment: "Boy! There's going to be some tall drinking on that boat!"

Sunday—Point Judith Harbor

Today we spent the whole day cleaning, C. attacking the engine room etc. There is quite a lot of satisfaction, I think, in doing all the work for yourself (I mean in a small place and only for a while). But it takes most of the day, what with meals and dishes and pans and sink and icebox and stove and floors and decks and the bed to make and the bathroom to clean, etc. Perhaps I won't be so thorough in another week, but it is quite satisfying and hard exercise. I have been working so hard that I have not thought much about Sunday and home. I feel as though I had been away for years but not very far away or very permanently, for all day long I am thinking, "I must tell 'them' about this" and "How 'they' will laugh when I tell 'them' that."

It is funny, a week ago everything I did I would think with a shiver of almost dread and inevitability: "Next week I'll be *married* . . . when I wind this clock again, I'll be *married.*" It is so funny because it is all so natural and not a bit terrifying, not a terrific change or even strange, and—a great deal of fun. Only I jump a little to think that strangers seeing us would say, "A man and his wife." But perhaps they don't anyway. They are more apt to say, "A man and his little girl—or little boy!"

It is almost impossible to look back to when we first came on board, and of course you want to know. As for the wedding, I am glad I wrote even though it was just a little because I can't now. Just a few things: It seemed terribly short. I wish we'd stayed longer but the longer we waited the more difficult it made it, especially for you. Do you think it was awful of me not to kiss everyone good-by? It wasn't because it was a bother or anything, but I didn't feel that I could face it, somehow. A kiss of congratulation is very different from a good-by one. And that warm dear group—they all, everyone, meaning so much to me—I could not, I did not want to say good-by to them.

We did not get to the boat until ten. It was dark and smelled of salt and seaweed and we crunched over mussel shells going down to the water. The boat was lit up. It was really magical. We had neither of us seen it. It has two comfortable rooms separated by a roomy deck.

The first night we were too tired to unpack the china for supper but I brought out your knives and forks (which C. admires *very* much—more than anything else I brought). I had to use them. I am very clumsy about cooking, can opening, etc. I feel just like that impractical girl in "The Devil in the Cheese." C. with hands on hips looks at me gravely and says, "The soap powder, the sugar, and the brass polish don't belong together."

Love love love. More later. We are going out rowing.

· · · · · · · ·

June 7th—Georges Island, Maine (just outside Tenants Harbor)
I have not been able to write because we have been discovered—at Woods Hole—and ever since, we have been hunted with planes, amphibians, motorboats, etc. And we have spent the last three or four days just going as hard as we could, often at night

and spending the night anchored out in open water on fishing banks. Added to that, we have had the roughest weather so far. And though I haven't been seasick yet, it's not the most comfortable feeling in the world, hardly being able to stay in a bunk and hearing the dishes crash at every big wave.

We had to go into York Harbor day before yesterday for water, etc., followed by a flying boat and met at the dock by reporters. The York people were simply *great,* laughing at the reporters and giving C. every attention. The reporters got rather fussed—asked Charles whether he "and Mrs. Morrow" wouldn't pose for a picture. You certainly can always count on Maine people. They all called C. "Skipper"!

Today is one of those gorgeous blue Maine days: lots of little white clouds on the horizon, the pine trees sharp and black-green against sea and sky, and between islands, far away, the soft blue of other shores. This is our first rest since Woods Hole. We washed all the dishes, pumped out the boat, etc., etc.; got a whole night's sleep.

They found us again this morning—that terrifying drone of a plane hunting you, and boats. I don't feel angry about it any more—it is inevitable. But it was a terrible shock to wake up from that blissfully quiet existence of being nobodies, free to go anywhere, to stay quietly and watch and enjoy things without being followed, stared at, shouted at; to be waked by the harsh smirking voice of a reporter outside our window one morning: "Is this Colonel Lindbergh's boat?"

The Berkshire, New York, Tuesday [*June 18th*]

Mother darling—

You are not here. It was an awful feeling to have them say, "255 does not answer,"[1] and then that strange man's voice. But I had just about guessed it.

. . . .

[1] 255 was the Morrow telephone number in Englewood.

After the call—

Oh, I am so much happier. I could not speak to you, but I am so happy that you are coming. It seemed to me that I could not bear it not to see you. We might have stayed up in Maine a little longer if we knew you were to be there. We can't go up now, though, because C. feels he must get down to work. He has to inaugurate the TAT route,[1] starting early Tuesday morning, and he cannot tell for how long and he has business here before then. I think he feels that, the three weeks' vacation being over, he should not go away again even for a short trip to Maine. It would give the impression of not working even if it did not take time from the things he has to do here.

I feel, though, terribly that you should make the effort to come down when you have *just* gone up, and it is so hot here. That is why I was not more enthusiastic over the telephone, although I want you *awfully*. There is so much to talk about—past and future. I wrote Elisabeth about my great disappointment about the fall and North Haven, but I will surely see you in Mexico City later. But the September North Haven visit being off, I felt I could not *bear* not to see you now. And now I *will*. Oh, I am so glad, so glad!

Half an hour ago I was gulping (an awful let-down feeling) because up until the last day or two I took for granted that you would be here and I would see you all and have supper and pat Daffin and we would talk and talk. Somewhere on the trip we lost a day and two hours. (And I thought most sentimentally about you on the wrong day, for your wedding day.)

I felt quite reticent on the telephone because we had *just* arrived and the telephone operators, manager, bellboys, etc., are quite excited. I did not feel safe in speaking.

Tomorrow we rise at six, go out to Long Island for some aviation exhibition. It will mean the first time in public to-

[1] Transcontinental Air Transport route between New York and Los Angeles.

gether—crowds, reporters, pictures, etc.—and we won't get back till after lunch; then to a conference (and I have tea with the wife of the man C. is conferring with). It will all be quite an ordeal, but I don't mind—I'll see you Saturday!

Good night, darling. I am so glad I am going to see you. C. suggested calling Maine, bless him. Of course I wanted to but I am glad he suggested it. And I could hear you all so well. Elisabeth's laugh! Oh, it was lovely to hear it.

The Berkshire, New York, June 23rd

Dwight darling,

I thought so much of you on our trip. You know we went off in a thirty-eight-foot Elco motorboat. Went out the Sound, stopping at Port Jefferson and Block Island, and across to Connecticut, stopping at Point Judith Harbor, then up the coast to Woods Hole, Provincetown, then across to Cape Anne and up to the Isles of Shoals, then York Harbor and Cape Porpoise Harbor (Monhegan Island in here somewhere), then some islands off Tenants Harbor called "The Georges Isles," then up around Isle au Haut to islands south of Mount Desert Island, then home the same way.

I give you all the places because I thought so of you and wondered if you had stopped there on your cruises. "The Isles of Shoals" sounded familiar, also "Monhegan." It is perfectly thrilling to navigate—use a parallel rule and the compass rose and find magnetic, true, and compass course, and keep the needle on that number, *and actually get there!*

Of course with my usual carelessness, at the end of the trip I discovered that I had been counting the wrong lines in the compass rose. Charles made terrific fun of me and said I did it because those lines were "prettier." We went quite a lot through fog, especially coming home through Buzzards Bay and around the end of the Cape. Gosh, what a channel that is! We would see great hulks of ships suddenly rise out of the mist just off our bow, anchored until the fog lifted. That is an eerie feeling. And then stopping the boat to listen for bells and horns—to guide yourself by that alone.

Charles and I want to have you come along sometime if it won't be too tame for you after your sailing cruises. You and Charles can navigate, and I will clean up and cook.

Charles is an excellent cook and we had wonderful meals (not just pilot crackers and jam). But oh, in a rough sea when the condensed milk and the olives are rolling around in the bottom of the icebox and the jam has dribbled all over the ham and the asparagus stalks are hanging like icicles from one of the grated icebox trays!

I got back here just in time for my birthday, which I'd forgotten all about. What a darling you are to remember it and go to all the trouble of arranging to get a lovely present for me. I was *so* touched and happy about it. The bag is a very nice one and I haven't anything like it. I am going to take it on my first trip west tomorrow. It goes with all my dresses, which is a great consideration in flying because you have to economize in weight. Somehow you always did manage to get a "just-what-I-wanted present" no matter how busy you were or inconvenient it was for you.

Hotel Lincoln, Indianapolis, June 27th

Dearest Con,

This is our third day and I am rather tired. Yesterday, flying, I thought out long letters to you but now I cannot remember them.

The first day we did not leave Roosevelt Field until after three, and we went through a terrible lot of rain and mist over the valleys in western New Jersey and eastern Pennsylvania. It was quite lovely. That is *beautiful* up-and-downhill farm country. The fields were so green and even over a thousand feet up you could *smell* the wet earth. Some of the plowed fields—square—

looked like rectangular pieces of purple blotting paper, wet and drying out.

But over the Alleghenies it was *Bad*. Trying to go through very thick fog over mountains, not seeing ahead—it is terribly confusing and brings a cold terror to you. You see, the fog is so deceiving: it lets you get a glimpse of a hill and then while you are looking in the opposite direction it covers it up and you are utterly confused. We had to turn back once or twice and go around a mountain. I was terrified. Then we followed the cut of a river between and *under* the fog until we were past the mountains.

We got to Columbus[1] very late—that is, to the hotel, where as usual Charles is Charlemagne. It is amusing and always the same: that flourish as they wave open the door of the rooms. The bow and "Everything satisfactory? Anything you wish?" before you have even stepped inside. "Yes, please—a pitcher of ice water." Then the giggles of the operators when you first ask for something on the telephone.

But, of course, it is all royal and I shall be spoiled. Also I find it tremendous fun meeting the different people along the line. I never felt that I had any poise or dignity before. Now it is so necessary—a kind of defensive weapon surprisingly easy to put on and wield, and a solid comfort.

I was interrupted at breakfast at Columbus by two youngsters—overgrown, purposeful—asking for autographs. I gave my usual answer but they persisted, the girl speaking up smugly, "Usually when people ask for autographs they give their names, but *we're* not doing that—though we would if asked."

There were some very nice people at Columbus. Yesterday we

---

[1] At Columbus, westbound TAT passengers were transferred from train to plane for the flight over the Mississippi Valley to Waynoka, Oklahoma. Eastbound passengers were transferred from their plane to Pennsylvania Railroad coaches for the overnight, trans-Appalachian mountain journey to New York.

flew over completely flat farm country as far as we could see, all cut up into squares—a dark square of trees and a light square of grain—so that it looked just like Alice's checkerboard, and I looked for elephants flapping their ears for wings, galumphing over the horizon!

Really, this is much more fun than I imagined.

Hotel Chase, Saint Louis, June 28th

Mother darling—

I tried to write you from Indianapolis, but it has been very hurried. We haven't slept twice at one place, flying every day so far. But we are staying here today and tomorrow because something in the plane is being looked over.

That means we will probably leave Sunday morning, missing you and Con and Daffin by just twenty-four hours. It does not disappoint me as much as it might because I never had much hope of it, and this life is so strange that you really do not belong here. It just seems like something impossibly nice that didn't happen.

Yesterday was the most thrilling day. Flying from Indianapolis, about sunset we started to climb. There was a rainbow behind us, a glorious bow that was much bigger and brighter than those on the ground. We saw more than a half circle. It was so real and yet so vanishing—about to vanish—that it reminded me of the visions one reads about. Do you remember the poor monk who had a vision of an angel and then heard the monastery doorbell ring and was torn between his duty and the vision, finally went to the door, and came back to find it still there? It was so beautiful with great piled-up golden clouds behind, and I thought of your saying to me in Mexico that first morning, "Anne, you'll have the sky—the sky!" It was glorious of you.

Then we went up, up above the clouds, at dusk, fifteen thousand feet. At about eight thousand, looking down, there was a blue mist over the flat land so that a new horizon was made. It looked as though we were on a sea and the land, patchworked below the mist, looked sunk in many depths of blue water. Then up further through mist, it was very cold and suddenly out on a plateau of blue-gray clouds, as far as one could see, and the sky bright blue above us. It is an indescribable feeling—those cold blue motionless stretches of cotton wool. Like ice in their motionless stillness, but soft and piled up like feathers. I think it is more like a mammoth bed of gray feathers than anything else. Then we dove down out of this bright cold blue into sudden warmth and *dark*. The earth was dark and lights of towns peppered the ground. We came into Saint Louis at night but you could still see those two great rivers[1] and where they joined, broad, peaceful, and gleaming between the dark shores. It was thrilling.

Hotel Muehlebach, Kansas City, Mo. [*July 2nd*]

Elisabeth darling,

Did you know that Kansas City was in Missouri?! I always thought it was in Kansas, naturally. Well, here we are. How *do* hotels get these names? This one pronounced "mule-back."

. . . .

I started this letter about 10 A.M. It is now 12:30 but the bell rings every moment—everything from "Good morning, Mrs. Lindbergh, we're near neighbors of yours—Room 720. Coming into our rooms last night we were taken for you (snickers). Someone said, 'There's Anne and Lindy.' We thought that was real funny (snickers) and we'd sort of like to get a good look at you—thought we might drop in and really meet you." I answer without a quiver, "Thank you for calling. I'm very sorry but I'm afraid that will be impossible just now"—to an inventor who says he has a machine in which no one *can* be killed.

You know what this trip brings me, bango, first impression? A respect for the *average* college woman (her life, interest, general

[1] Mississippi and Missouri.

outlook, etc.) vs. the *average* noncollege woman. Of course that leaves out the unusuals on both sides of the question.

It has been great fun. I have met and talked with a good many people. Here is average conversation, questions and topics in their order.

1 Heat

2 "And how do you like Columbus?" (Indianapolis, Saint Louis, Kansas City, Wichita, Waynoka, or whatever it may happen to be.)

3 "You enjoy flying?" (followed quickly by) "Do you do any of the piloting yourself, Mrs. Lindbergh?"

4 What Mrs. X, her little Willie, young daughter Bovina, and oldest boy Albert and "baby" think of flying. (This works itself gradually down to school marks, summer camps, golf scores, calories, food, general health and illnesses, and eventually by this route back to)

5 Heat

and

6 "And how do you like Columbus?" (Indianapolis, Saint Louis, Kansas City, Wichita, or Waynoka)!

The average noncollege woman can talk for hours without a letup. The average man is *much* more interesting, on the whole. What an awful statement to make (I can see it in the newspapers): "Average man more interesting than average woman, Mrs. Lindy says after trip across!"

But in Saint Louis I met some unusuals (I have other places too, of course). We got into the field at night, over those huge broad peaceful rivers and the lights peppered over the banks (it was gloriously beautiful) and were whisked by Harry Knight, Jr.,[1] rather fat, amusing, and keen, to Mrs. Bixby's[2] very charm-

[1] Harry H. Knight, Jr., was a member of *The Spirit of St. Louis* organization, which financed C. A. L.'s flight to Paris in 1927.

[2] Wife of Harold M. Bixby, who was a member of *The Spirit of St. Louis* organization.

ing house in the country. A rather small low house, low ceilings and French windows (not formal, I just mean door-windows) opening out onto a dark cool garden. Inside, lovely prints on the wall, a piano covered with a Chinese brocade, bright zinnias in a vase. In a corner an old desk and, above, pictures of poets and writers (I remember only Goldsmith and Browning), and books; upstairs, an old four-poster bed and some fine rag rugs, and very dainty bathroom things like yours.

And the people (Mrs. Bixby, Mrs. Knight, Harry Knight, and Major Robertson,[1] friends of C.'s)—I felt immediately that delicious feeling, a combination of ease and stimulation, the immediate flash of familiarity and the challenge of unusualness.

Mrs. Bixby is quite striking-looking—young and assured and calm with the assurance of a woman who is happily married, has a lovely home, children, old enough (herself) to be settled and young enough to be very nice-looking, and who has enough time to take on the side university courses on Goethe etc.—and to pick zinnias! She is a kind of hostess to herself. I think "self-contained" in the fullest sense is the best all-around word. Enough fullness of life in her family, friends, books, collecting lovely things for her house, etc., *to be contained in them*. Do you see? A happy state.

Mrs. Knight was younger and utterly delightful. Lovely eyes, with that rather foreign detached look that always makes you look again—that kind of charm—interested in people, keen, sympathetic.

I went to her apartment one afternoon and we just sat and talked. It was simply glorious: I have had to be *so* on my guard, not saying anything at all personal or real. And talking to a woman is always different from talking to a man—a kind of quick flash about small things or fine distinctions (though C.

[1] Major William B. Robertson was a member of *The Spirit of St. Louis* organization.

really has this too). She is very keen and quick and frank, and it
was such a relief.

Clovis, New Mexico [*July 4th*]

Sweet Con—

I have been resting here after a night's trip from Waynoka, Oklahoma.[1] There are bugles outside—4th of July ones, perhaps—and
I lie with my eyes closed and think of the still palms and the
church dome at Cuernavaca. Do you remember the lovely time
we had there together once, in our togetherness and the peace of
the place? Not that Clovis bears any resemblance. A small Western town, flat and dry.

But Waynoka! I have *never* been in a place like it. It is smaller
than this—has four or five paved streets and a hotel (one of the
TAT men described it as "the kind you see in an old Western
movie") painted white with a large sign, "Baths," over the front
door. One big room downstairs for meeting, eating, registering,
buying and smoking cigars, spitting, and talking. At least I pre-
sume all this—I only looked at it through the open door. We got
a room at the Harvey House connected with the station and slept
well in spite of two or three trains going under our window. The
Santa Fe Railroad goes by there and stops. A small country
crowd tumbles out to the restaurant and gets a *terribly* good
meal.

It all felt very, very Western: the quiet, the lack of pressure
or touch with progress (not that Western towns aren't progressive, but a small, distant country town isn't). TAT has built a
magnificent field and hangar with attractive offices, the equipment being the most modern, efficient, progressive, down to the
last detail. All the town came out to see the dedication. Some

[1] At Waynoka, westbound TAT passengers were transferred from their
plane to Santa Fe Railroad coaches for the overnight journey to Clovis,
N. M. Eastbound passengers were transferred from train to plane for the
flight over the Mississippi Valley to Columbus, Ohio.

townsman said there hadn't been such a crowd since the dedication of the pavement!

I am simply amazed at the detail that has gone into this TAT line. They give so much care to comfort and luxuries. All the conveniences and comforts are beautifully planned out. Such things as soup in the middle of the morning "served aloft" and lunch, of course, and "lemonade or tea" in the afternoon. And an aero-car to take you from plane to train for your night rides. And showers in the stations where you change. And a map given to each passenger so he may study the country. I am going to send you the pamphlets.

Winslow, Arizona, July 6th

Mother darling—

Yes, you are saying that I should be writing thank-you letters, but in these little simmering red-sand Western towns I simply cannot. And as we are stopping at small Harvey Houses I hate to ask for extra favors like ink and blotting paper. Winslow is larger than Waynoka—has a daily newspaper. (Waynoka had a weekly one. C. and I had a long walk there in the cool dark.)

Last night we were in Albuquerque. The country is quite lovely—a broad flat valley between sharp and glorious mountains.

Over Grand Canyon today.

Yesterday we detoured and went over desolate country but very thrilling, over deserted canyons where the river was dried up and we saw the ruins of old Indian cities along the river bed. We went over several Indian reservations and saw funny little stone houses (like igloos) with a hole in the top for smoke, and round (enclosed with sticks) enclosures that served as barns. We took a great many pictures, and though it was very hot and dry and sandy it was thrilling. C. pilots the first passenger plane (going east) from Los Angeles back here to Winslow and takes back to Los Angeles the first passenger plane going *west*. On this second trip apparently Will Rogers,[1] Amelia Earhart,[2] and I sit as passengers in the back!

These places are incredibly dry. Your skin *crackles*.

Transcontinental Air Transport, Inc., July 8th

Con darling—

Isn't this exciting? This is the first passenger paying trip. I have so much to tell you. Last night we arrived in Los Angeles. This morning we are going back to Winslow, Arizona, in the big three-motor Ford passenger plane. It does not seem at all like the little open Falcon. It is beautifully comfortable and business-like; I feel as though I were on a private car. This morning (you will read it all in the paper, and *see* it too) there were *crowds* at the airport—the dedication of the ship. The Governor and his wife (*very charming*) and family, Mrs. Maddux,[3] very nice, sat with the TAT officials in a little circle below the bandstand. There were speeches and then "Miss Mary Pickford" stood upon a ladder and cracked a bottle over the nose of the ship. The ship was decorated like a float with flowers. Then many pictures taken. Mine with Mary Pickford. She is most gracious and lovely. But it all seems *so* strange and hysterically funny, somehow. A year ago, at North Haven, quietly, who could have seen that picture? I had the most enormous bunch of *gorgeous* yellow roses sent me. I could not even carry them.

The pressure (publicity pressure, of course, I mean) is quite *terrific* in Los Angeles. I know Daddy will gasp over that picture. Then we got into this huge ship. I am the only woman. The ship is beautifully decorated inside, painted a cool gray-green, with the most comfortable green leather-covered chairs, that are

[1] Known as the "cowboy philosopher," very successful in motion pictures, the radio, and with a newspaper column.

[2] The first woman to cross the Atlantic Ocean by plane, in 1928. She was lost piloting a plane on a transpacific flight in July, 1937.

[3] Helen Maddux, wife of Jack Maddux, President of Maddux Airlines.

adjustable. Little green curtains and blue-shaded lights. There is a white uniformed attendant shouting in my ear that he will get anything I want—reading or writing material. He gave me this when I started to scribble on an envelope (as is my custom).

We have each been given an envelope full of data on the TAT organization. I will send you some of it. Also I have been handed a large folding map (decorated à la old picture-map style) of our route. Postcards of places along the route. The "courier" has just offered me a little aluminum table to write on; there is plenty of room for knees and a table. There is a radio operator on board who looks as though he were playing a kazoo; he has a round metal box fastened to his mouth and he is *talking* into it.

This is desolate country. We have crossed the mountains— nothing but sand, gray sand and grayish-red sandy mountains and old craters, a black spreading mass running out from the cones. I cannot see Charles; he is in front.

The courier tells me that we are passing over "the Devil's Playground"—the farther end of Death Valley. The sand stretches look baked and blackened, but we are cool—much more so than in the Falcon, where there is sun on your head and a hot wind in your face.

I am *crazy* to have you take this trip. You simply must. Even Mother would enjoy it. It has not been rough at all. There is room under each seat for a small bag like Mother's. Tell her she need not be separated from it even here. I *always* think of Mother with that bag—we are always moving or traveling, I guess. I can see her going to Heaven and saying at the gate, "No, please, I think I'll take this right along with me"—that constant remark to porters, officials, friends, family.

Oh, you darlings—how I relished your letters. It was like coming home to find them. Two from you, one from Mother and from Elisabeth, and the telegram. I had to wait all day for them—a long day. A three-and-a-half-hour flight over the desert; the ceremony in the Governor's offices; Charles pressing a button

57

to start the first train from New York with the TAT service; then to "lunner" or "dinch" or some meal (we had had only an early breakfast) at five thirty and back to the hotel, where at last I read them over and over.

I'm so glad you had a good time at the dance. I laughed at your suggestion that those who came back over and over *did* really like you. Remember my letters to you last fall: "He asked me to go up again, so maybe he isn't *just* doing it for Daddy." Beware! Pat yourself on the back with both hands and say, "Constance, my dear, you certainly were the belle of the ball!" It's a nice feeling—try it.

I agree about *All Quiet.*[1] Terrific—very compact and wonderful. It took me by the teeth and shook me as a dog a rabbit, and I could not get over it. C. read part and was absorbed.

We are just passing over Needles. Isn't that a wonderful name for the hottest place in the world! A fifteen-minute stop at Kingman. We walked out of the plane into a long awning (like a wedding); the awning is on rollers and is rolled up to the door of the plane; you walk through it to the "station."

At Kingman we took on two square tin cupboards and one large thermos. The little table was set up by me, covered with a lavender linen tablecloth (tied on), and on metal plates I had passed me a delicious meal: cold chicken or tongue, etc., salad with sliced pineapple (and no dressing but cream cheese on the side), white and brown bread—brown, the kind Mother would like, rather rough and grainy with a slightly bitter taste, sliced grapefruit, cake, and coffee (hot).

Transcontinental Air Transport, Inc., July 9th

Sweet Con—

We are on our way back today. Tonight we get to Los Angeles again; tomorrow, early, we go to San Francisco! I hope we stay there for a while, because I am a little tired of moving around

---

[1] Erich Maria Remarque's war novel, *All Quiet on the Western Front.*

and because the strain of feeling "in the public eye," of having to watch every step and word, especially in the high-pressure places like Los Angeles, is rather terrific. I have to keep *so* reserved and taut and on edge for pitfalls.

I have made many breaks that one would not naturally think of, such as answering a question asked me by a reporter who did not say he was one and who I thought was a TAT official; speaking to C. in a hotel when the transom was open; answering near-personal questions asked me by some friends I was introduced to, when a reporter was behind them.

I think that is the worst problem: how to keep up a polite conversation and yet say *nothing* personal, bearing in mind every second that everything you say (even if she is not at all connected with the press) may be repeated and made into a "story." And yet one mustn't be rude, and "personal" covers all the natural questions that are asked me. "Do you pilot a plane?" "Were you ever afraid?" "How far up do you come on him?" "Do you ever get sick?" "What were your feelings when you first went up with him?"

It is a terrific strain to avoid the question quickly and politely or answer it in a general way, like an oral examination or fencing. I feel taut. Of course there are the old stand-bys of C.'s I am learning: "That is a rather difficult question, Mrs. X," and "This has been a very pleasant trip," and "Well, I wouldn't exactly say that," and "Thank you" and "Really?" and then always at the last extreme one can use as answer to an indiscreet question merely the "Bright-Insane Smile." That always baffles them.

Also, I want to stay in San Francisco because we are staying with some friends[1] of C.'s—the man whom I like extremely. The most interesting thing, almost, on this trip (as in Mexico) are the many and varied people I have met; many, utterly new types to me but very nice. I keep wanting to describe them all minutely

---

[1] The Thomas Eastlands of Burlingame, California. Banker and broker interested in development of aviation.

and intricately but I am afraid of indiscretion. He is the keen man-of-the-world, discreet, kindly, and cultured—the kind we know in the Firm.[1] You know, the same timbre as Mr. Lamont,[2] Mr. Grenfell,[3] M. Monnet.[4] I recognized it immediately. I have not seen anyone like him on this trip, and I felt at home. You know, I might have met him at one of those Partners' dinners in London, in between caviar and after-dinner coffee and cigarettes and men's voices discussing the debt question.

TO E. C. M.   *Burlingame, California, July 13th*
                                       Outside San Francisco
Darlings—
I feel so very far away from you. We have been visiting the Eastlands for three days here. It is great fun to be in a family again, but I want my own family. C. is away all day or locked up in a room talking airlines and engines and "efficiency." And I have met people and seen gardens and houses etc.

It seems so strange to be in this kind of social life with none of you here. I do not feel at *all* married. This is the first chance I've had to write. I think C. finds the social end rather tiring. It does not seem so much of an effort to me. It is rather a game, this meeting many kinds of people and trying to keep things going.

For instance, I feel as though I've scored a point when I am not baffled by a young and shy German gentleman, when I am able to (instead of sitting in red and painful silence—red because he is blushing) bring out my three and only points of contact: 1, the Parker Gilberts;[5] 2, the Harz Mountains; 3, *All Quiet on the*

[1] The firm of J. P. Morgan & Co., of which D. W. M. had been a partner.

[2] Thomas W. Lamont, partner of J. P. Morgan & Co.

[3] Edward Charles Grenfell, head of Morgan, Grenfell & Co., London.

[4] Jean Monnet, French political economist. Worked with D. W. M. on Allied Shipping Council, later responsible for European Common Market.

[5] Seymour Parker Gilbert, lawyer and financier; agent-general for German reparation payments (1924–30); later, partner in J. P. Morgan & Co. His wife was nicknamed "Mrs. Gib."

Western Front! As a matter of fact, I think I get two points for that, because both point 1 and point 3 brought that bright and grateful flash of recognition. The Harz Mountains did not score at all, but perhaps I didn't pronounce them correctly! It reminds me somehow of surf riding. The *Harz Mountains* was only a gentle ripple that took me nowhere, but I was swept along quite nicely on *All Quiet,* and I rolled ahead for miles on *Mrs. "Gib"!*

C. thinks it's better not to make any effort (unless they interest him). Perhaps it is less tiring on the whole, his way—you give none of yourself and take none of them. But it is so *deadly* dull. Still, it is a nervous game and we are both rather tired after the high pressure of the last two weeks. C. has to work all day and then talk too at night, sometimes.

. . . .

We have just had a heavenly weekend in a log-cabin camp in a valley of tall redwood trees and a little mountain stream. We were there all alone, walking, canoeing, etc. There was no noise except for cones falling on the roof at night. It was heavenly.

Today C. took up two planeloads of managers of railroads and families. Most of them had never been up before and were very nervous. I sat trying to look as calm and casual as possible, hoping it would have some effect. I tried to convince them that there really were three motors and that there is no such thing as an "air pocket." However, the noise is just bad enough to prevent any point from getting across.

Mrs. Railroad (leaning across to me): "Don't you sometimes hit air pockets and fall for miles?"

A. M. L. (loud and clear): "There is no such thing as an 'air pocket'—there are just *currents* of air going up or down."

Mrs. R. (vaguely horrified): *"Really,* really—you *really have* been in an air pocket! Helen, she says she *has* been dropped in an air pocket."

A. M. L.: *"There IS NO . . ."*

Mrs. R.: *"What?* . . . Oh, *Willie,* sit *down* in your seat. Don't move around like that in a plane."

I am about to explain that it won't upset things even if he does move around, but I know that's hopeless.

Did you meet Dr. Merriam[1] when he was in Mexico? Very amazing and interesting scientist (geologist and archaeologist). We are trying to get some photographs for him.

To my *great* disappointment, and C.'s too, Will Rogers was not on the first TAT trip. I will tell you about Amelia Earhart sometime. Now, just that she is *very* likable and very intelligent and nice and amusing.

This is a divine country—there is a kind of bright golden "bloom" over everything, like autumn, and you smell eucalyptus leaves burning in the ditches, a rich spicy smell and warm and golden. All the hills are covered with stacks of golden wheat, and the sea glints at you from all directions, and yellow gorse runs along the roads and falls over the cliffs, and I kicked up golden dust when I opened the gates for C. as we drove through fields and farms today. Maybe it's just the way we feel, C. and I, when we get off together, alone—all gold, that extra golden bloom over everything!

Falaise,[2] *Sunday, August 4th*

Con darling,

We have been so rushed lately, since we left Los Angeles about the 20th, that I have not written any letters. And I have wanted to about so many things. A wonderful rush-of-joy feeling to find that two letters were at Los Angeles from you and one from Mother. Then the "Picture Gallery" (C. tantalized me by open-

---

[1] John Campbell Merriam, palaeontologist, President (1920–38) of Carnegie Institution in Washington.

[2] The Long Island home of the Harry F. Guggenheims, close friends of C. A. L.

ing it *very* slowly and looking at it first). It delighted me—its neatness and compactness (C. thought so too). And the pictures were very real and dear. (You know what a joy it is to see a *new* picture of people you love—you have not gotten accustomed to it and it means not a photograph but *the Person himself*.) Yours is good but not as nice as you look. You usually look prettier. Elisabeth is good, though a little lifeless. Mother is good except *for the mouth*, which Miss Selby has retouched and made very *hard*. It hurt me to see it and I wanted to look at Mother so I put a strip of paper over the mouth. Now I can look at it with comfort. Daddy very good. Dwight not the way he is now but sweet.

· · · · · · · ·

Washington, August 6th

I am always longing to write you about people. So many that are amazingly different and yet whom I like tremendously. The thrilling part is the people utterly different from the type I have met.

Mr. and Mrs. Maddux (airlines etc.)—I just love them, both of them, and I have never met either before. Mr. Maddux is quite tremendous, I think. He has been a rugged stubborn pioneer all his life in different fields, but there is nothing of the *reckless* pioneer in him. Just a tremendous slow fearless force pushing ahead. It is a strange combination. He has had the most amazing experiences: faced death in different ways and yet you know he did not get into those situations from recklessness. He would be slow to move and then with the vision in his eye he would shoulder ahead with a sure indifference to any obstacles.

He has had these experiences: trapped in a submarine for hours under water, has come down in the desert in a plane, walked for miles until he found a Mexican hovel miles from the railroad, etc., etc., and yet seems very simple and sometimes childlike: a great Saint Bernard dog's simplicity. Mr. Eastland told me that he "wanted to adopt Mr. Maddux"! That's *just* it. Mr. Eastland was a great joy to talk to about people. We almost always agreed. Mr. Maddux has vision, I think; started bus lines all over the Southwest, the Lincoln car business, and now these Maddux airlines. I think he is a great man.

Mrs. Maddux is very keen and bright and quick—birdlike. Takes half the business on her shoulders, is amusing and quick to notice details and understand people through them. She is hearty and sanguine and real.

Their house was a strange combination of the newest and best in radio, plumbing, appliances, etc.—and lights inside a red and green glass parrot; heavy dark plush curtains and sofas; and wall lights in the semblance of candles dripping over the edge. Do you understand? Things that used to be such a criterion for me.

Well, I have spent much too much time on them, but they are wonderful.

Then we stopped at Dr. Kidder's[1] archaeology camp in the Pecos Valley near Santa Fe. Pecos is a heavenly high cool green valley between mountains and the cliffs of a mesa. On the curve of the thin stream are the red squares of walls of the excavated city, and on the red bank opposite, between green pines, is the Kidder camp. He is hearty, cordial, interesting, with a marked Boston accent and mind.

What struck me most was that onto this red soil of New Mexico he has transported, whole, the atmosphere and machinery of a boys' school near Boston. The Headmaster attitude: the young acolytes in their respective tents learning to be as He, the Headmaster's wife who tirelessly looks after all the acolytes, the eating house with its long table (like the Cabots') and the Headmaster at the head, the bells for meals and rising (rise at six, breakfast at six thirty, a "getting ready" bell and a "forward march" bell before each meal).

---

[1] Dr. Alfred V. Kidder, archaeologist, specialized in Indian civilization; member of the Carnegie Institution, Washington.

I do not mean this in a denigrating way. We enjoyed it *tremendously* and liked them. They (Mr. and Mrs. Kidder) are the kind of people that you feel are made out of a very fine high-grade material—wonderful old oak or finely tempered metal. *Quality*. You feel this immediately, before seeing, or regardless of, what they do. It is an inherent *quality*. They have a large family, and the whole camp eats, sleeps, and lives Archaeology, and we did too. The little boy, age four or five, plays with an ax and one stumbles over squares of rocks and sand he has built—his "ruins"—when you step out of your tent. (C. made a great hit with him because he can wiggle his ears, and I because I can move my forehead up and down so fast!)

It has been amazing to step from one circle concentrated on some specialized work—seeing nothing else, and seeing the world from that angle—to another concentrated on another specialized work.

At the Madduxes' it was all airlines and planes and engines; at Pecos, ruins, etc.; at the Edisons', [in New Jersey], scientific inventions, etc. I wonder sometimes if they are all different worlds or the same one seen from a different angle, the way you can look through a window with different-colored panes and see a green world, then a yellow world, then a red world.

The Edison world was thrilling. I itched to write you about that family, especially how the sons each took different qualities of the old man and how they were going in opposite ways. The tone and quality of that old late Victorian house.

The interesting committee[1]—listening and watching each very different man: Dr. Stratton of MIT (Daddy knows him), Ford, Dr. Perry of Exeter, Eastman (Kodak Co.), Edison's son Charles.

They all spoke of Daddy too. It has been strange and thrilling to me to go all over the country and have men speak to me (out of these specialized cells) of him, admiring him, knowing him. It

[1] Committee, of which C. A. L. was a member, charged with selecting the winner of an intellectual contest for boys sponsored by the Edison Company.

has also been amazing to me how Charles can concentrate first in a green world, then a red one, and command the respect of the best men in the field, even though it is only in showing interest or asking intelligent questions, and comments. It reminds me of Daddy.

All this talk of Charles reminds me of a saying they have in the Edison family if one starts boasting about one's own family. At a certain point the boaster is interrupted by the casual question, "Some relative of yours?"

I have just gotten an invitation for us to spend the weekend with President and Mrs. Hoover. C. says we must accept. Of course we want to and I think it is lovely and considerate of them to take us to their camp; also very unselfish. You'd think they'd want to get *away* from guests and entertaining at their camp. Still, it annoys me to *have* to accept anything; it seems illogical, especially as C. and I have to go back to New York for a conference of his and then *back* here again for the weekend.

It worries me to be so dependent. Life seems so unsettled. Suppose we had had that invitation for the weekend we were going to spend with you in North Haven. I tremble—Charles' plans are so unpredictable. I shall not be sure of seeing you for that precious time until I can kiss you.

I don't dare think about North Haven. When I get your letters, I am simply absorbed. Really, when I finish them I *wake up* from them, the way you do from a very vivid dream of people. And I continue to carry with me all day not only the related facts of your letters, but a vague sense—like a mist around me and between the people I am meeting—of actually having been with you, of actual presence. I suppose that is because Mother and Elisabeth and you write such vivid letters and we know *just* how to make each of us comprehend what we mean to express.

We have been rushing a good deal lately, crossing from Santa Fe in two days. The last day—6 A.M. Kansas City, 12:30 A.M. Newark airport—was a hard day and we spent that night (what there was left of it) *in a hotel in Newark.* I thought so of Mother. I knew she would appreciate how funny that seemed to me—a hotel in *Newark*—just like camping in "Idlewild" camp (is that its name?) on Palisade Avenue. Then some wearing days at the Edisons', then one lovely one with the Guggenheims, then this trip to Washington, tomorrow to New York. The next day back to the Hoovers' camp, then straight to Detroit to see Mrs. Lindbergh, then back (I hope) to New York and you.

I wish I could talk to Mother. Mrs. Hoover's secretary's note says, "Life at camp is simple and one needs only informal clothes—something like a jersey dress, a silk sports dress, and an informal afternoon dress and informal dinner dress." I know just how *"informal"* that sounds! I feel like cabling Mother, "Will flowered chiffon be formal enough for 'informal dinner dress'?" Still, I don't feel exactly afraid or even shy. C. is responsible for that. I always feel like standing up straight when he is behind me. It is quite marvelous what it does to you. "Ramparts," you know.

These are just the things that have "happened." There is so much else I have digested and thought about on those long flights when there is nothing else to do. Charles and I scribble absurdly silly notes to each other, with lots of pictures and quips. It is delicious fun. If only he had written letters like that!

P.S. They have torn down the old house.[1] I knew that was coming but I didn't realize so soon, and was casually looking for that familiar rock of security and time: the house. It was a terrible shock to me to see just the stone foundation. It was almost as though it had been cut down in one slash before my eyes, because I had been so sure of it that a picture of it was in my mind as we came down over the hill—I had almost seen it—and then it was razed. I had never imagined that plot of ground without the house.

[1] The Morrow house on Palisade Avenue, Englewood, where the family had lived from 1909 to 1928.

And everything the house meant had come up behind me and taken me by surprise. It was a definite physical shock, as though I had fallen on the ground and lost my breath. And what have they done with it all? How can it just "vanish"? What has happened to the heavy green door with the brass knocker?

[*Washington, August 13th*]

Elisabeth darling—

I write from the White House. I keep thinking of how thrilled we were when Mother or Daddy used to send us a letter on White House paper.

I long to talk to you. We have had really a lovely weekend— "slow" riding (suited to my taste), walks down the stream, and around a fire at night. For opinions I must wait. President and Mrs. Hoover have been very kind. She is the most tireless, energetic hostess, every moment given to thinking of and planning for her large brood of guests. He has a nice dry wit. I love the Herbert Hoover, Jr.'s. Very charming and nice.

It was quite a big party and poor Mrs. Hoover had to arrange us for every meal. After two days she was saying distractedly to me, "Mrs. Lingrin, you sit next to me, and Colonel Lingrin, you go *there* . . . no . . . then you're too near Mrs. Lingrin. Well . . . oh dear . . ." etc., etc.

The most interesting thing, though, was riding past a mountaineer's house miles from a town or road. Now, there is a rough cart road built up the mountainside for the Hoovers, and he is moving away—to "quieter lands." He cannot read but has had handed down to him parts of the Bible which he has by heart, and some old songs and hymns which were handed down. He goes about the mountains preaching. There are eight children; none of them ever been to school. The wife can read a little and taught the first child but gave it up with eight children!

We met the boy of twelve—shaggy-headed and bright-eyed. He had been given a pair of shoes, some new clothes, and a jack-knife. He was about to return his respects by giving the President a possum he had caught. Two little barefoot girls (ten and six) sat on a big rock and watched us gravely with no sense of shyness. They were very pretty, with small faces, cunning turned-up noses, and grave eyes.

The ten-year-old had her fair hair done up in a "Zorn" knot behind. We asked her if she had ever been to school. She looked at us, turned away, and gave a long spit and then answered politely in a clear, assured voice, "No, Miss, 'ndeed I've never been to school at all." We asked her what she would like for a present and she said quickly, "A doll."—"What kind of doll?"—"It don't matter, Ma'am, any kind of doll, jes' so long as it's a doll—that's all."

They really moved me quite a little—at least that sensation of *stopping* in your mind, a kind of still island in the stream of thoughts and emotions. You have to stop and pay attention to it and you're not quite sure what it means to you but you go on thinking about it.

I have found a delightful and slightly nightmarish book about children; the book grows and fascinates like a child's dream after playing "pirates" in a four-poster bed with the sheets as sails. *The Innocent Voyage,* by Richard Hughes.

We are on our way to Detroit. "Off again, on again, begin again, Finnegan."

Detroit

Elisabeth darling—

We dropped down in Cleveland for a night, surprising Grandma and Aunt Annie. We called up, and C. said quietly but explosively (if you see what I mean), like very *very* softly putting a bomb on a doorstep: "This is Charles," but she did not get it. Finally, *"Charles and Anne"* brought recognition.

Williams and Aunt Annie motored *miles* to the airport, while I paced the floor wondering if it were all a dream—such a strange way to come to Cleveland. And yet coming over the city I got that unmistakable coal gas smell that we used to get as we climbed out of the sleeper into the dark station, and I thought of all the *first* memories of Cleveland: a second breakfast (after we had stuffed on the train on cornflakes, muffins, etc. It was always such fun to eat on the train), with cream in that little-pitcher-with-red-cherries and *honey*. Then we went into the sitting room that had an artificial log burning. Then that funny game with glass marbles, and the *St. Nicholases;* and outside, very grimy snow and roller-skating and Ruth Thompson with pale braids.

Aunt Annie came at last, and we squeezed hands excitedly. It was *such* fun to see her. It was a wonderful warm feeling and we talked and talked. It was like coming home. Grandma met us at the door—so excited, the angel, that she tried to kiss C., who was very embarrassed.

Then we had milk and scrambled eggs and I was so happy to have C. there and they were so happy and Aunt Annie snooped around trying to find "vita wheat" and ketchup for us.

Grandma and I walked in the garden (where behind the hedge a camera man hunched and when accosted shouted, "Miss Morrow, won't you let us take your picture?"). Grandma worships Charles, says, "That boy lives in a higher plane" (no pun intended)!

We left about noon for Detroit and flew through thunderstorms. Now, after a three-day visit, we are en route to New York. Charles, and his mother, and I. Darling, I had such a lovely visit with her and C.'s uncle.[1] I cannot tell you how happy I am about it all. I love them both. I feel that I know her much better and she is really wonderful—so unselfish and spunky —and I love her quick, sharp Irish wit. It is exactly the impression I got from that first letter, only more interesting, for that

[1] Charles H. Land, Jr., mining and mechanical engineer, who lived in Detroit with his sister.

wit and tartness that puzzled us, now seems one of her chief charms. I think Daddy was quite right in his first impression of her. Do you remember how enthusiastic he was?

Charles is dear with them, so gay and naughty and very small-boyish. We all spoil him and adore doing it.

The uncle is quick and shy at the same time, and it is a very charming combination. We all had such a gay informal lovely picnic time together. It is a rare relationship, those three, and I do not want to hurt it in any way.

And I think—I *think* she likes me! Oh, I *do* hope so.

C. feels he must go to the air races in Cleveland for at least two days, and they start on the 24th or 25th. So we plan to go for the first two days, then straight to North Haven—everything permitting. I'm afraid we can't be there long, but I thought it best to go first to the races in case C. gets beguiled by North Haven and can stay a little over the promised "two or three days." The trip south is scheduled to start September 20th (all of this is private, you understand).

I must stop. This has gone on for weeks on such varied paper. There is one funny joke that I have meant to tell you. In Los Angeles Mary Pickford invited us to "Pickfair." C. and I have been considering our names carefully in case of a future "eagles' nest." "Lindmor" and "Charlanne" have been discarded for C.'s brilliant suggestion, "Spengustus"![1]

Chagrin Falls, Ohio, Tuesday [August 26th]
Beau Manoir Farm [the Herrick home]

Mother darling—

I have just had a delicious hot breakfast from the most enchanting yellow breakfast set, upstairs in a sweet little French room with French flower prints on the walls. And now I'm sitting on the terrace alone (except for two little French statue boys, each

---

[1] Combination of A. M. L.'s and C. A. L.'s middle names, Spencer and Augustus.

holding a bird and a pannier of flowers, behind me and surrounded by hedge). It is quiet except for someone raking leaves in the paths and the sound of roosters. There is the smell of burning leaves. And the little dogwood next to me has about four bright red leaves. "Max," an aristocratic gray schnautzer, sits at my feet and looks across the lawn with me. It is a very Galsworthian–*Forsyte Saga* atmosphere.

Mr. and Mrs. Parmely [Herrick] are just as kind and cordial and nice as they can be. They have taken me right in, and they worship Charles and seem to understand the kind of life he and I like and go to all sorts of trouble to give it to us. This is a long, low, small-roomed, low-ceilinged house and perfectly charming; the most enchanting old French prints and French furniture (little dressing tables etc.) and sometimes the paneling of an entire French room.

Some lovely Chinese porcelain and modern French bronzes.

Thursday

I have just sent you a telegram—I wanted to put in it my *extreme* impatience to see you. The Herricks are lovely to us and I have met so many dear friends of Charles', but I am simply pacing the bricks of this house in my wild impatience to get to you. From C.'s first saying that we wouldn't come at all, then just for a day, now we are staying over a week—over Labor Day. We came in a little Moth with very small baggage capacity. I took my small brown bag (like yours) and the old *minute* dark blue E. R. M.-going-to-Cleveland-tra-la-la bag. Into which I managed to put 3 pairs of shoes (evening, street, and sport), 5 pairs of stockings, silk wrapper, 1 slip, 2 pairs drawers, 1 combination drawers and slip, 2 bras, my 3-piece wool suit, 1 riding blouse, 3 hats (1 straw one), 1 bright blue silk suit, 1 pink flowered street dress, 1 linen tennis dress, 1 linen coat, 1 light blue silk afternoon dress, and 1 evening dress—to say nothing of a Mennen's powder tin, comb, cold cream, toothbrush, and perfume. Whee—

You can imagine how squashed everything is. Unfortunately, I prepared for boiling weather and it gets damper and chillier every day. Each morning I come down hopefully in a sleeveless linen dress and shiver back into my one warm suit.

We are, as you can imagine, somewhat lacking in those things which an exquisite French maid is supposed to take out and lay on the dressing table or bedside chair: brush, bedroom slippers, clean nighties, and handkerchiefs (I forgot to list those—I took about six), etc. Each night I find, like "the little Princess," Sara Crewe, new luxuries laid out for me, like a Paris nightie *all* lace with a few silk patches, velvet slippers, a velvet bed coat (which I adore).

The races after the fourth day are pretty deadly. The same things are done every day; some of them are very thrilling, but after you've once seen them . . . The most interesting things are the *autogiro*—a plane with a windmill effect on top which does *not* draw it vertically upward, is *not* connected with the motor in any way, but acts as wing space and allows the autogiro to float down leaf-fashion and *settle* awkwardly like an old hen. It settles down about vertically and could land on the North Haven terrace.

Then the gliders are interesting. They start them like a kite, towing them behind a car until they rise about five hundred feet, then "glide" down.

. . . .

Oh, I long, *long* to be with you. I dream about North Haven every night. I feel, though, that if I stay here as long as C. wants perhaps he will stay longer in North Haven. At any rate this will not shorten our visit.

The Berkshire, New York, September 5, '29

Mother darling—

I am writing you in the desperate feeling that we will never get to North Haven. I have felt superstitious about it from the beginning because I have counted on it overmuch all summer long: the quiet, the apartness and all of you, and the feeling of being completely alone and natural and oneself instead of the usual constraint with everyone else.

But there has been delay after delay, and I'm sure Charles is as wild to go as I am. First the air races—for a day. Then the stunting kept him there; he felt he couldn't stop, having started.[1] It was quite a strain, that week: the noise, the dust, the speed, the people and excitement, publicity, press at the field, and waiting for C. to do formation stunting every afternoon. Then there is a certain strain just in being a guest. Charles was quite tired at the end, and I too. Then here in New York, C. said he must have one day for business; but we made all plans for today.

But the last and really serious delay and justifiable one is this lost ship.[2] I have thought of that until it is an obsession. It seems so terrible and close to me. I can picture it all: the plane, the trip, the pilot, the families saying good-by to all those passengers. Did you notice they were all single passengers and from all over the country? And this terrible false report and this *hideous* waiting, waiting, and searching.

It seems to me the most terrible accident in all the history of aviation, because the best in every way that can be done is being done on that line. It is just one of those ununderstandable, hideous accidents. There is still some hope but it is *desolate* country and they had no food with them and only a little water. Of course in a good part of that country are Indians (and so water), and it might take them days to get back to civilization.

[1] C. A. L. was flying as a member of the Navy "High Hat" aerobatic team.

[2] A TAT trimotor transport disappeared en route from Albuquerque to Los Angeles on September 4th. It was later found crashed on Mount Williams, with no survivors.

Charles can do nothing here. The search is organized—all that can be done is being done out there—but he feels that it would look rather brutal, especially to those friends and relatives waiting, if it came out in the paper that he started off on a "vacation" to Maine when this terrible thing is still hanging fire.

We have been telephoning and pacing the floor all day (C., that is), and I am going to get dressed and try to take him out to Englewood and out of all this for supper.

Oh, darlings, I long to see you. Each morning I wake and think, "Will I be in North Haven tonight?" And I am still in the Berkshire Hotel. If we can't get up there, at least I will see you here again. That will be something—in Englewood in lovely Indian summer weather.

[*En route to Saint Louis, September 6th*]

Dearest Mother—

I am glad I did not have to speak to you this morning—it was hard enough to hear Daddy's simple echoing "You can't get up here at all?" I don't remember *ever* in my life being so disappointed. I think because I have wanted it so terribly and so patiently (that is, believing we would in spite of each new obstacle) and so long.

But I do not really grudge the time spent on *this* trip. Charles could not refuse to go. It is an emergency and I do not feel impatient about it. But I do grudge *bitterly* the week at the air races. I know Charles feels badly about that too. But we could not tell; we just didn't "gather our rosebud" while we might. I think perhaps Charles feels worse than I do because he feels he is to blame, but he isn't. He spoke of how *wonderful* you were about it over the telephone.

Well, I shall just think of seeing you in Englewood before we go south on the first announced trip on the 18th.[1] That trip, as I

[1] Flights over the Antilles, South America, and Central America, including the inauguration of the Pan American Airways route to Paramaribo, various route surveys, and archaeological exploration flights over Yucatán.

wrote you, will take from ten days to two weeks (counting the return trip to New York), which brings us back to New York in the early part of October. Then we may spend a month getting ready for the big trip.[1] C. has arranged for another special ship,[2] and we may go out to the West Coast to get it (all this is confidential).

We are on our way to Albuquerque in a Lockheed Vega—a very fast ship. The weather is bad so I don't think we will fly at night but stop at Columbus.

I am stuck in a small front cabin which is mostly wires and gas tanks and baggage. To get this pencil (my fountain pen giving out) I have just moved from my right elbow (not *on* it but *near* it) to my knees: two leather coats, three emergency bundles (slickers, bedding, food, Red Cross kit, etc.), and two suitcases. The pencil was in my diary in the *bottom* of the bottom suitcase. But it was worth it! I think that episode epitomizes "Morrow life," don't you?

We are now crossing the Alleghenies—the worst part of our trip to Columbus. It is foggy, as usual, but not impassable.

Tell Con she had better marry an aviator. I am "sylphing" beautifully with this life.

. . . .

We arrived Saint Louis at 9:45 our time (7:45 theirs) and left New York at 3:00. We made it in 6 hours and 45 minutes—record time. Up again at 4 A.M. and on for a nonstop to Albuquerque. But I feel rested and ready for the trip.

[1] The Lindberghs were planning a trip around the world, starting with a survey flight over the great-circle route between New York and Tokyo.

[2] A single-engine, tandem-cockpit, low-wing monoplane with which the Lindberghs later surveyed Pacific and Atlantic air routes; the first of a number of planes produced by the Lockheed Aircraft Corporation under the name of "Sirius."

1929

[*En route to Albuquerque, September 7th*]

Mother darling—

We left Saint Louis at about 5:30 and are now on our way to Albuquerque—a long day, but I feel ready for it. It is very bad weather—low fog. Sometimes we fly high trying to get over it, sometimes just above the treetops or skimming the Missouri River.

Last night I was terribly tired when we got in. I shall always love Saint Louis. It has taken us in twice when we were tired and at night. It means welcome and peace and a rest. Last night I was unspeakably grateful—first, to see the broad sweep of lights of the city flickering through darkness and patches of fog, then the reflection of lights in water (that meant a river and Saint Louis), then the square lighted field. The fog was bad and we lost sight of it from time to time.

At last down and the friendly hands and faces of Major and Mrs. Robertson and sister. They drove us to their home; gave us scrambled eggs and milk and toast and salad and ice cream (that Mrs. Robertson ran out to get us). And then a delicious sleep. C. says there were mosquitoes around our heads all night, but I was too sleepy to wake up—I dreamt they were planes. This morning the Robertsons woke us and *got up themselves* at four; made breakfast and put up a lunch and drove us to the field. I can *never never* thank them for what they've done for us in these last twelve hours. I feel so rested and well.

Every once in a while through a hole in the fog I look down and see a train chugging along like a child's toy. It looks so safe and slow. Fog is very terrible. It comes about you before you realize and you are suddenly blind and numb and cold. It really does seem like death, though I am not so frightened today: it is flat country and we have parachutes.

Now we are riding on top of a sea of cotton, the sun shining brilliantly. For a while we were on top of this sea of mist and beneath a *new* sky of clouds. The sun broke through holes in the new sky and threw spotlights on this floor of mist. Now it has broken completely through the high clouds and the sky is blue above us. There must still be some mist between us and the sun, for on our right side C. has pointed out a strange rainbow phenomenon. There is a small *complete* circle of a rainbow riding along beside us and in the center of it is the shadow of our plane. I feel as though I must be somewhere on top of the world, in the great polar wastes of ice. . . .

We have passed through Kansas and are now in Oklahoma. It is 9:55 Central standard time. Through Kansas it was overcast but we flew below the mist. Now we are flying through it again—very bad. We have passed the fertile plains, the checkerboard Middle West, and this country begins to look really Western—barren rocky hills. In Saint Louis we had many rumors of the ship but none plausible or verified. I cannot help remembering the Frances Smith search[1]—I feel just as hopeless about it.

. . . .

Kansas, Oklahoma, Texas, and New Mexico were rather nerve-racking, with no time to write, and we arrived in Winslow about five Saint Louis time; nearly ten hours in the air. You know by the papers what the news was here about the ship. It is terrible but a relief to have it found. I can tell you more when I see you. Everyone here is shot to pieces, and I have never seen Charles so tired. He said it was about the worst flying weather one could have—our trip.

Tomorrow we start back. C. will inspect the wreck from the air, spend the night in Albuquerque, and start the next day for home. We won't do any emergency-speed flying, though.

WE WILL NOT GO TO NORTH HAVEN FROM . . . SAY THE 11TH TO THE 15TH IF WE CAN FIND ANYTHING ELSE TO DO INSTEAD.

(This is a code message—see if you can guess it!)

---

[1] Frances Smith, a freshman at Smith College, disappeared in January, 1928. Her body was discovered months later in the Connecticut River.

En route to Havana in trimotored Fokker¹ [September 20th]
Mother darling—
It is only saying good-by that is so hard—one feels further away
that moment than any other. Strange, isn't it, that I should feel
quite near you now, and that I should (probably shall) feel
nearer you in Caracas than when I was kissing you good-by?
Funny, isn't it—distance is mental and not physical? Or is
imagined distance greater than real? Or is it just another way of
saying that what matters is being away from a person—not how
far away? Besides, I have talked more to C. about the trips, and
everything is sufficiently vague and promising so that I can hope
perhaps to see you before we thought; but I don't dare state a
supposed plan for fear it may change.

We have just left Florida and are flying along the Keys. The
water below is a pale blue satin with scallops of rose near the
marshy islands. It is smooth and shaded like the inside of a shell.
There are big clouds piled up, castley ones, around the horizon.
Ahead, this sheet of pale blue satin melts into the sky. There is a
boat below us which has cut a white slit through the blue.

Now we are leaving the circle of the Keys and cutting straight
across the water to Cuba, about a hundred-mile water hop.

There are two reporters and a photographer on the ship as far
as San Juan—tomorrow night. I have been introduced to them
and they are very considerate and nice, and all arrangements have
been made so that I am "not to treat them as reporters at all"
except that, as they are writing up the trip, they want to send
back "comments" on the scenery (by radio) every ten minutes. I
feel like "the little small red hen," safe on her perch but slightly
dizzy and ready to fall any moment!

It was such fun to see Betty Trippe² this morning and compare

¹ After visit to North Haven. Beginning of Pan American Airways flights
over the Antilles, South America, and Central America.

² Elizabeth Stettinius Trippe, wife of Juan T. Trippe, airplane pioneer,
organizer and President of Pan American Airways, later Chairman of the
Board of Pan American World Airways.

notes on cramped baggage space, short-notice trips, and photographers. I am *so* glad they are along. She is now writing reams on a small pad to her mother.

I read Forster's *Aspects of the Novel* on the way down. Some reporter got the name and it caused a lot of comment. "Are you doing any *writing*, Mrs. Lindbergh? I noticed you were reading," etc., and I replied, "No, but my distinguished mother, Mrs. Dwight Morrow, is composing a very modern novel called *The Painted Pig*"![1] What will they say when they find *The Egoist* in my bag? Or *Crime and Punishment* or *No Love* by David Garnett?

The horizon is towered now with pillar-of-cloud-by-days. The white columns are reflected in the water below us.

The courier shows me a large map from time to time, has passed us cotton, chewing gum, and crackers at different intervals for ears, jaw, and mouth respectively. "No, thank you. I never chew." The courier says that the blue line on the horizon I have been watching is Cuba. It is now 10:45 and we left at 9:51. Miraculous. . . .

12:45—after leaving Havana

We stopped at Havana for about forty-five minutes. Oh, it looked beautiful flying over it; the country so rich and green, and the water that divine turquoise, and a red freighter pushing out of the harbor leaving a foamy line behind. I saw Morro Castle and the plaza on the other side of the narrow entrance (to the harbor) and the bandstand square, that stood in front of the Miramar [Hotel] (that was) and the statue to the *Maine*. The harbor has four arms to it and little ships everywhere.

We landed and stepped out into a crowd of Cuban officials, bouquets, officers, and cameras, to say nothing of a waving craning crowd of Americans behind a fence.

But the shock was the foreignness of it: the bowing high

---

[1] The title of a children's story by E. C. M.

Cuban officials, dark, good-looking, and polite, and Spanish being spoken around us—such a change from Miami, suddenly in Latin America from being in the most blatantly American city. One very high official (Cuban) presented (or *had* presented) to me a beautiful bouquet of sweetheart roses. I was introduced while the flowers were in my arms, and I had been photographed with them, and I was bowing as graciously as I could. Evidently that was not enough. He stepped most graciously up to me and said (naïvely), "I am the ———— of the Republic de Cuba and it was I who gave you the flowers."

Then we were rushed into the station and met a hundred or more people.

Then something happened that may have consequences. I have been refusing to speak to reporters and continued to say here, "I have nothing to say," despite their pleading, "Just one word about Havana or Cuba . . ."

Then Charles pulled me aside and said that it would do no harm to say something about enjoying the trip or Cuba and probably would be rude and ungracious to refuse to, so I said simply, "I cannot give you an interview but of course I enjoyed the trip and I am happy to be in Cuba."

They were all delighted and took it down so avidly that I fear the results: "Mrs. Lindbergh gives first interview. Speaks at last to Cubans, after refusing Americans, etc."

. . . .

We are sailing over the Keys and shoals off the coast of Cuba. These "Keys" or islands are like lily pads floating on this silken sea, which is mottled and colored in bright greens and pink. In a curved white beach harbor there are little fishing boats, very still. The sea and sky, too, are iridescent and silky. It is an unreal iridescent world, like some of Conrad's descriptions of the South Seas. It is still and beautiful but iridescent and as if about to tremble and break, like a soap bubble.

At last I have seen some flamingos, flying in flocks below us, and so far below that they looked like bits of pink sand blown across the water, or across the surface of a mirror. These reefs are too beautiful. Some are really pink around the shore the way one imagines "coral reefs," and some hold pools and coves, blue and green like the inside of an oyster shell.

4:15—just out of Camagüey, Cuba

Camagüey is a small inland town surrounded by cane fields. A huge crowd of Cubans were held back by guards. A pretty little Cuban—daughter of the Mayor—came up to me with a bouquet of tuberoses and pink roses as large as herself. I tried to accept them gracefully with one hand and shake her hand with the other. All this was put on record forever by cameras. Then we pushed through a crowd of warm hands and staring eyes while all around me I heard these so-foreign-to-me people say immediately, *"La Señora! La Señora! La Señora Lindbergh."*

It was weird—these people I didn't know at all, who couldn't even speak my language. But they were friendly and charming about it. They were frankly curious and pleased. But they were not at all fawning or begging for favors. The Mayor's daughter bantered with me gaily for not speaking Spanish when I had lived in Mexico, and other girls offered me fans—it was so hot— and someone asked me if Betty Trippe and I were *"hermanas"* [sisters]! It was all rather casual and fun.

Then a reporter asked C. for a few words, at which C. in his masterly way said, "We are very glad to stop in Camagüey, even if for only a few minutes. We wish it were longer." Then we hurried back into the plane as fast as we could.

· · · · · · · ·

Without any doubt I have just seen the most beautiful shore-line in the world!

We rose above the harbor to the left (turquoise reef-water formation), climbed up over some mountains on that jut of land (green rugged wrinkled mountains like some of the foothills to Popo and Ixta[1] from Cuernavaca), climbed and climbed, and suddenly abruptly over the edge and down at the feet of them curled the sea, a misty violet blue. It was breath-taking: the rugged green tropical mountains dropping into that deep blue violet; added to this there were big heaped-up golden clouds piled over the mountains, superbly beautiful and wild—untouched. I feel as though we had come over those peaks *first* of any men, and seen the sea.

September 21st, en route to Haiti

Last night was so weird and dreamlike. We arrived at Santiago in the evening. The town, backed by rugged mountains, faces the sea. A narrow entrance to the harbor (like Havana), guarded by a castle, widens to a small bay scattered with islands. It is much more beautiful than Havana.

We stepped out and had, in their usual order, (1) the national anthem, (2) the huge bunches of flowers, (3) the introductions, (4) the triumphal home-from-the-wars ride through the streets. I have seen so often the newsreels of C. doing this—sitting on the American and Cuban flags in the back seat of an open car. It was quite thrilling riding through those dark streets lined with dark faces, horses prancing beside us, faces lit up in the lighted doors and lighted windows, little boys running beside the car, all grins and teeth gleaming, almost under the feet of the horses. Then the cry *"Muchacho! Muchacho!"* And all the time running beside us like fire went the constant cry, "Ah . . . Leeendbaug! Leeendbaug! Viva Leendbaug"—and hands pointing and eyes fixed on us.

The town has *great* charm and is untouched by tourists: narrow streets, pink and blue and green stone houses like Nassau; balconies, bird cages, and tropical vines. We drove up to the main square, quite beautiful, with two bell towers on the old

---

[1] Popocatepetl and Ixtacihuatl, volcanoes.

church, and stopped in front of the state building or palace and walked up many steps between white uniformed officials, up more carpeted steps to reception committees, an *enormous* bouquet of flowers (the national anthem), introductions, etc.

I am a little vague about all of this and only remember that in taking a picture one man held a huge Roman candle that shot sparks all over everyone and started a small fire in some Cuban's straw hat; that we were passed fruit punch cocktails and very buttery cookies—I didn't have time to finish mine and held it crushed in my glove for an hour; that just as the spokesman started his lyrical and complimentary speech the band struck up.

Oh, that speech! Many *"elegantes"* and *"gloriosos."* It was all so comic and dreamlike, but everyone else was amused, too, and gay and spontaneous, and I left the hall feeling very lighthearted and pleased—as though we had been playing "king and queen."

> *En route from Puerto Rico to South America, September 22nd*
> *Government House, San Juan, Puerto Rico*

Con darling—

Someday you must take a cruise, by boat or plane, through these islands, stopping two or three, *at least,* days in each place. I want to do it. It's strange, I didn't want to go terribly—that is, I wanted this trip someday but I wasn't crazy about going *now.* And it has been indescribably beautiful—beautiful with that kind of extra unreal glamour, with which one thinks of the Caribbean in the winter, in Northampton (or Milton). I write pages about "the most beautiful harbor I have ever seen" and another most beautiful rises out of the sea.

Haiti: the harbor of Port-au-Prince was, I thought, the most beautiful in the world—until I saw Saint Thomas. You come in between two long arms of land and an island. The sea is turquoise and lavender in places, and the crinkly mountains come straight down to it. (They look crinkly as your fingers do when they have been under hot water.) And they are that rich tropical green. Port-au-Prince is at the foot of mountains and dazzling in torrid sunlight. (Their public buildings are made out of some glistening white stone.) A look at the crowds made you exclaim suddenly, *"All Negroes!"* I have never seen so many black people.

A somebody Drummond (?) came up. He was the United States Chargé d'Affaires, I think, and had been in Mexico under Sheffield.[1] We bowed to a large bouquet and shook hands with some Haitian officers and were whisked in an open car (the leather of which burned our behinds!—sun had been on it) to the stupendous glistening white palace. The streets were narrow and bordered with a mixture of new stone houses and old painted wooden ones that looked oddly French or Swiss: funny carving and knickknacks on them (Haiti was once French, you know). The old French wooden market place was charming. Up marble steps, between black officials in spotless white uniforms who spoke in exquisite French and bowed gracefully, to an elaborately French-furnished anteroom.

We "awaited" (yes, the word fits) the President of Haiti.[2] He is half French and half Haitian and a very cultured man, well read, and writes poetry. He was quite beautiful, distinguished carved features and the most polished manners, and spoke exquisite French and English. Also all the Haitian cabinet, in spotless white uniforms, with long curling black mustaches. They bowed, toasted us, and asked polite French questions. Also Mme Président and five or six sons and daughters.

I tried to say that I *"trouvais le paysage très belle."* I wanted to say *harbor,* but I had forgotten the word and could only say futilely, over and over, *"L'approche . . . l'approche est très très belle!"* Also, while I was having a picture taken on the balcony with Mme Président, C. rushed out to say we had to leave (we have only about forty-five minutes in each place) and I had to

[1] James R. Sheffield, preceded D. W. M. as U. S. Ambassador to Mexico.

[2] Louis Borno.

explain that he wasn't objecting to the picture but *"Il faut que nous partons . . . je regrette . . . nous retournerons . . . j'espère."* None of which sounded quite right to me—suspiciously unsubjunctivated!

So we bowed again to the mustachioed Ministers (who were most gracious and poised). Really, I can't describe their *surprising* ease and carriage. These were polished men of the world. Even the educated Negroes in America cannot have that ease and *condescending* grace. That's it—condescension. They have never been in a position to be condescending—always the other way round. They may be more educated or charming or interesting than some Haitians, but they can never get that natural (imperceptibly) arrogant ease. They have had too many humiliating knocks.

I read a Haitian paper all in French, quite a good one: a plea for independence (we have had an advisory committee working with their cabinet, and Marines stationed there since 1915), an article on disarmament, foreign affairs, and a whole page on modern literature with a poem or two.

You know their flag is merely a red and a blue stripe. The story is that a leader of the revolution vs. the white (French) rulers— saying that the French tricolors represented the white man, the Negro, and the mulatto—tore the white out of the tricolors, symbolically making a new Haitian flag. I think that's quite gorgeous.

Then on to Santo Domingo, where Columbus first landed (we didn't see the town at all). The story is told about Haiti (and its wrinkled mountains) that Columbus, wanting to describe it to Queen Isabella, crushed a piece of paper in his hand and said, "It looks like that!"

On to San Juan, Puerto Rico. I would like to spend a month there—a town surrounded by that green-blue water and backed by tiers of rugged hills that change shades of lavender in the evening. The trade winds blow there all year and it rains, not in seasons, but as in the North, so it is cool and fresh and green all year. It was here that the Spaniards hid the gold from Mexico, waiting for ships to take it to Spain, and here Sir Francis Drake fought for it, and Hawkins died and was lowered into the sea at night.

I don't know whether I can give you any idea of the amazing and unreal beauty of it. It is mostly the tropic water, of course, clear, still, and gemlike, and these volcanic peaks—greener than the fields of England—pushing up through it. Then when you set a town down at the feet of these and make a harbor out of a semicircle of peaks, and the houses perched in tiers up the hills—white and green and pink houses with red roofs and green shutters and palms pushing above the roofs—and the water is still and gemlike and the peaks are still and wild—then you have Saint Thomas.

(I have just passed C., in the pilot's cockpit ahead, a bottle labeled "Gordon's Special Old Tom," the liquid a milky green . . . which turns out to be lemonade!)

5:30

The mountains of Trinidad are blue ahead of us. I love flying in a sea boat, in and out of the sea and coming into harbors at night. Trinidad is *almost* South America.

Adios

C. says sometime these islands will be a day's trip from the U. S. and you and I will go on one of your Smith College vacations.

En route to Paramaribo, Dutch Guiana, S. A., September 23rd
Government House, Trinidad

Elisabeth darling—

I have written Con a Cook's tour of the Lesser Antilles. Do you remember this is the route we saw "Colonel Lindbergh" trace with his finger in Mexico? It is the most utterly beautiful coast-line—that is, island line—I have ever seen: steep green volcanic mountains plunging into blue water. Magical and unreal. I believe in Drake and Hawkins and pirates and Spanish galleons now. This was their hunting ground. Port-au-Prince, San Juan, Puerto Rico, Saint Kitts, Guadeloupe, Martinique, Trinidad.

We have been in an amphibian since Puerto Rico—all the curve of the Lesser Antilles—watching the color change from bright turquoise in the morning to a deep violet at night, coming into harbors with fishing ships below us, anchoring in a harbor at night, the volcanic mountains towering above us and the fishing sails.

We stop three or four times a day in these harbors, circle over the pink and white and green houses and red roofs, and palms, and sail down onto the water. Then a thousand little boats filled with blacks row up or they swim out to us, black sleek arms and bobbing black heads like seals. Then the British Governor rows out—he spotless white—and we shake hands and bow to large bouquets. (We can't carry any extra weight in the plane: we are in *two* crowded ships already. I am the only passenger in this; the Trippes are in the other. C. and copilot in front, radioman and I in back.)

We have started very early every morning, getting up at five and flying till dark. I have lost all track of the days. It was amusing yesterday at Saint Thomas (the most beautiful harbor of all). We arrived at eight and were preparing to fly on to one of the thousand little islands in the Antilles chain (Saint Kitts) when the Governor called to us that, it being Sunday, the chaplain at Saint Kitts had telegraphed him to persuade Colonel Lindbergh please not to arrive at Saint Kitts before ten because they were having a church service and he felt we would distract the worshipers. I can't tell you how amusing and sweet that seemed to me. Poor man! Of course he was right: that minute little island where no plane had ever landed (and C. was the first to fly over it two years ago), two amphibians droning over their neat little whitewashed houses and still palms.

As a matter of fact, we had to circle the town five times before we landed. I could not hear singing from the erect brown stone (incongruously) Gothic church, but I looked in its open door and windows wondering if the congregation was trying to sing "From Greenland's icy mountains, from India's coral strand." There was not a person to be seen in the dusty streets—white in the sun. All were seething on the beach; some black legs (with pants and dresses rolled up) were running in the water. The pier was jammed, too, with the British officials, the Governor "of the Leeward Islands," and a large *Welcome* flapping from the Customs House.

"Please not to come before ten"! It is hard to express how quaint that sounds. I hadn't even remembered it was Sunday. Somehow in these terrific spaces and distances, when time changes with each stop, when all that matters is the original time clock, from sunrise to sunset, daylight is just *daylight,* advancing or receding.

When one is on schedule merely to get in before it is dark on this route for establishing swift communication, when one brings word from one small island to another in several hours which used to take four days, time seems very arbitrary—ordinary clock time—ten o'clock, Sunday, on the little island of Saint Kitts in the Lesser Antilles. "Service from eight to ten, Sunday": a minute toy world with round wooden trees and Noah's ark people on round stands and a tiny church one could pick up by its steeple!

I am rather worried about these islands. I like them because they are as untouched as Nassau used to be, and this line is bringing to them the fate of Nassau: tourists, drugstores, hotels, but also prosperity, education, sanitation.

Why do progress and beauty have to be so opposed? I guess they're not; that progress and *charm* are, for charm means (perhaps) "people lived here a long time"—association with people, traditional customs, old ways of living and building and walking and eating and painting and whitewashing and sailing and fishing. And of course newer and better ways of living change all that. I suppose it *is* better. I feel that it's quite a terrible responsibility to sweep away all that without weighing carefully whether it is *"better"* as well as *"newer."* But people never seem to doubt it for a moment; they swagger right in with reckless assurance that "Progress is the thing." *Real* progress I suppose *is*—not exploitation.

We were also reminded of Sunday in the harbor of Trinidad. Lots of canoelike boats came up, rocking and weighed down with islanders; one very precarious, old and tippy and crowded with gleaming-toothed, smiling Negroes, was named "Faith in God." I don't know if it was his Sunday boat or not—but appropriately named for any day in *that* boat!

Our dinner at Government House was an exact replica of the one in Nassau. "His Excellency" talked to me about Nigeria, Africa, his last post. We drank "Gentlemen, the King," and had a little "gramophone dance" after supper.

Foreign diplomatic service never seems to change English people at all. No matter how full of "atmosphere" the place, it never seems to get under their skins. They are all true to form— they take with them all over the world their uniforms, formal dinners, taffeta evening dresses (or changeable silk), and "gramophone dances." I suppose it's very nice for British subjects—sort of like the Catholic Church, the same service everywhere! They were certainly very kind and cordial: let us go to bed early and even got up terribly early to see us off.

For three hours we have flown over the flat thick jungle of South America; now going up a muddy river bordered with palms and thatch-roofed huts.

Paramaribo is pronounced Pára Mári Bo. I think it sounds just like a nursery rhyme:

> On a palfrey I will go
> Straight to Paramaribo!

or

Tell me, strangers, do you know
The road to Paramaribo?

En route from Port of Spain, Trinidad,
to Caracas, Venezuela, September 26th

Con darling—

We have been down in South America (the top), are now going west along the coast, bound for Caracas, Panama, Belize, etc.

I would like to tell you about Paramaribo—much the most "interesting" place so far. Paramaribo is in Dutch Guiana (on the Atlantic coast). It meant to me what it probably does to you: another Latin-American colony. I expected something on the order of Nassau; all these Antilles islands have been like that— stone houses washed with pink and green, palms, hibiscus, shuttered porches, etc.

We flew over flat swampy jungle for one day, going south over Venezuela, British Guiana, to Dutch Guiana, arriving at dusk. As we circled the town it was a great shock to find a small European wooden-built town, only like no town I have ever seen: square neat little houses with gables and shuttered windows—not just one gabled window but *six* sometimes on one house. In the center rose two Flemish spires of a wooden church. Carved and quaint but wooden and distinctly Flemish. Along the river (it is on a river and the sea) ran a stone waterfront; lots of small fishing boats and a large crowd on the pier.

When we were rowed up we could see a green square flanked by these stiff quaint Dutch houses, towering palms, and shady big-leafed almond trees. On the dock there were women dancing and nodding and jumping up and down in the twilight—great big Negro women dressed in the most *delicious* costumes: enormous cretonne skirts with bustles behind and in front, and medieval-looking stiff cretonne caps made of a square kerchief.

We stepped on shore and a black band struck up the martial tune (as though it were a national anthem) of, what I found out later, was "Lucky Lindy."

Then we marched along the waterfront between them all shouting and smiling and throwing at our feet cloths of cretonne or batik. These, I found out later, were their headkerchiefs. They were paving the way for us with them—Sir Walter Raleigh fashion—and it was a special mark of honor to spread down their headkerchiefs! Evidently there were not enough to make a way from the dock to M. de Munnick's house, where we stayed, for I saw them picking up some we had already stepped on and rushing to put them ahead of us again. Like a child's game: *"Don't step on the cracks!"*—nodding and bobbing and singing, their big skirts swaying in that half-light under the grotesque almond trees.

We had dinner at the Governor's house: all Dutch people. There is only one American couple in Paramaribo. My card, "Mevrouw Lindbergh," put me next to the Governor. I thought at first they had misspelled Morrow and then realized it was "Madame." But doesn't "Mevrouw" sound *matronly?*

He was the most cultured, charming man; speaks perfect English. He had a delicate twist of scholarly humor that reminded me of President Neilson. He seemed like a scholar in being the kind of man who sees things with the detachment of one slightly out of the action.

After supper we went through the weirdest nightmare of a procession. Apparently they had planned to parade C. through the streets in an open car hung with red, white, and blue lanterns and a kind of open canopy decorated with ribbons and lights, and boy scouts with torchlights going just behind and running alongside and a band following us!

"Come on! They are ready!" The chief manager (a large blond Dutchman, out of breath) started to push C. into the canopied car. C. drew his lips together and said in his "I-do-not-quite-hear-

you" voice, "What is that . . . you wish?" It was explained
impatiently. In the iciest of polite tones C. said, "Oh, I'm afraid I
couldn't do *that,* sir." They were amazed. Finally it was decided
that C. and I and the Trippes were to ride in an undecorated car
and some of the dinner guests in the decorated one; Juan Trippe
by accident got into it too.

Then we started. The band struck up "Lucky Lindy." The
lanterns bobbed and a singing crowd of blacks ran and shouted
alongside. C. gritted his teeth and didn't look to left or right—
that look of contained bitterness. I felt terribly for him but, I not
being the cause of the procession, it did not irk me as much and I
could look at it detachedly—a wild mad dream, through these
narrow streets between old peaked wooden houses lit up weirdly
with the flashes of torches and swinging lanterns. Peering, glossy
faces, hands pointing over the carved balconies and out of the
windows.

Here and there a man on a balcony was burning some green
powder that made a poisonous and blinding green blaze like
lightning. And all the time the band pounding behind us. Sometimes when a very familiar tune (the *most* familiar—there were
only *two*) was started a sigh or a shout would run through the
ecstatic crowd around us, and they all started bobbing and
jumping and dancing—a wild mob.

I was fascinated by the different types of faces: Negroes, many
of them still in that costume; slim, delicate Javanese (like the
British Indian) with silk turbans and batik skirts (I love their
finely chiseled features and deep-set, sad eyes). Then a balcony of
Chinese faces, then a Dutch face, leaning out of a shutter-framed
window. The houses were simply enchanting and so foreign and
medieval to me.

After this we went to a grand open-air circus where in their
different rings we saw "Javanese," "Bush Negroes" (with tom-
toms), "Red Indians" and "British Indians," and Paramaribo
Negroes dance.

Everyone wants to give us things, do things for us. It is lovely of them but so embarrassing; they would have us at receptions and parties all night and day and load us with flowers and presents which we can't carry in the plane. We are always saying, "I am so sorry but we can't . . ." They do not consider that you need sleep or rest. The minute you arrive you are rushed to dinner, taken to meet officials, drink toasts, hear speeches, say over and over again to hot faces and wet hands: "Yes, I enjoy flying."—"Yes, it was a very beautiful trip."—"Well, *we* are very glad to *be* here."

They say regretfully, "Oh, do you really have to get up at four tomorrow? What a shame!" But they never think of altering *their* dinner-party time. They don't mind delaying us dangerously (it is dangerous to arrive after dark) as long as they get an hour to toast, shake hands, present flowers, make speeches. Of course some people—generally hostesses—have been lovely, but they cannot control a whole visit. Still, we are unspeakably grateful to them.

> *En route from Barranquilla, Colombia, to Cristobal, Panama,*
> *September 29th*

Mother darling—

It is rather hard to get air-mail stamps in all these countries, and envelopes, when we get in so late and leave so early. I keep writing to you and Con and Elisabeth but never sending letters. I wrote Con about Paramaribo—an old wooden Dutch town on the South American coast.

Trinidad did not seem to me to hold the old character, did not quite live up to expectations, perhaps because we did not see it except in a rush. Also, in Trinidad the most maddening incident on the whole trip occurred. I enclose the article. I tremble to think of the U. S. A. edition of it.

At a private dinner at Government House a "lady" guest (along with others) asked Mrs. Trippe and me the usual questions about the trip. She said nothing about being a reporter but went home and *wrote the whole thing up*. The other guests—the Chargé d'Affaires, etc.—knew she was the wife of a reporter and often did such things (reported people unawares). And yet no one told us or warned us beforehand and took it as a great joke afterwards. They certainly look at these things differently.

Not only did this woman write up "ten minutes with Mrs. Lindbergh" but on the points where I had been careful to evade her questions—I always evade them with anyone: on women's flying, being seasick, and what does one do in the plane (I always answer vaguely, "I enjoy flying very much")—she made up a whole lot of rot—*sheer rot*. The whole thing made me utterly sick. I dream at night now of meeting accusing (hitherto kind and nice) newspapermen of the U. S. A. saying, "You *never* give interviews!" and desperately trying all night to explain. The British were very kind to us in Trinidad and *very* nice, but that one incident colored the whole visit.

It doesn't seem to me that I have ever heard about the natural beauty of Venezuela. The mountains and harbors and sea are gorgeous—towering wild green peaks. Caracas is one of the most beautifully situated cities in the world, I think—high, with green mountains all around, cool, and, from the air, red-tiled all over—neatly at the foot of green mountains. The people and houses remind me of Mexico.

We met such charming Americans, British, French, and Germans in the diplomatic circle (besides, of course, charming Venezuelans). Had a cool night and tropical fruits for breakfast, overlooking date palms and red tiles of the city. One painter of the "Washington-crossing-the-Delaware" type, but better—Tito Salas—has done huge murals of the life of Bolívar. I asked him, through an interpreter, what he thought of Rivera. "Interesting but barbarian." That's what most Venezuelans think, I am told, though most would leave out the "interesting." They are afraid of his "Bolshevik" ideas.

The old General Gómez[1] is the most wiry, magnetic, slight little man—quick, nervous hands and a keen, quick, changing expression. He twirls about and suddenly faces the man behind him or to his side in an electric manner. He adores C. Took both his hands in his. He says of C. in Spanish, "What a straight stick of a man!"

I am having the most terrible time with my Spanish—that is, not knowing any. They all expect me to. "No," I say sadly. *"Lo siento mucho"* (my one phrase), and then they let out a stream of incoherent Spanish. I find that I remember words, many of them, a few phrases even; but it is impossible to make a complete sentence. Of course the words do help. You can let them drop out helpfully when someone else is fumbling with a sentence!

Panama—September 30th, Mrs. South's house—The Consulate Coming to Panama is really like coming home, because of association[2] and also because everyone speaks English and, oh, it is so *clean,* so *clean* and neat after the narrow, hot, poor streets of many of these South American towns—not picturesque, but clean and prosperous and no mosquitoes or flies. I never appreciated it before. There is an "epidemic" of smallpox here, though no one in the Canal Zone has any. We were, however, all revaccinated last night on arriving.

I think probably we will *not* stay here a week but proceed in a leisurely fashion home, not stopping anywhere long except a day or two in British Honduras to take pictures for the Carnegie people.[3] I am glad. I am tired and anxious to get back, though the flying *never* gets tiring, just these teas, receptions, dinners, etc. Listen to today's schedule. Up at seven (in Cristobal); called on

[1] Juan Vicente Gómez, President of Venezuela 1922–29.

[2] A. M. L.'s uncle, Brigadier General Jay J. Morrow, was Governor of the Panama Canal Zone 1919–24. She had visited there as a young girl.

[3] C. A. L. was to pilot Carnegie Institution archaeologists over unexplored jungle areas in an attempt to locate the ruins of lost Mayan cities.

three officers on France Field after breakfast; pictures, etc. Flew across the Canal (which was wonderful—Uncle Jay should do it, if he hasn't) to Balboa Heights and Panama. Called on the President of Panama; pictures, etc. Back to the Legation, where we are staying; twenty minutes to change and get to a huge formal lunch at the Union Club, where I shot my isolated words of Spanish at a Panamanian grandee who spoke no English or French; back to the Legation; ten minutes and off to make social calls on various officers here. Tonight we have a huge dinner at the Union Club. Tomorrow morning we go back to Cristobal.

This is what we have been having, only worse, because here are no huge hot crowds surrounding us, and no foreign language (on the whole) to cope with, no parades through the streets, no very solemn official welcomings in hot crowded rooms with champagne, roses, and long speeches—and we are not rising at five to fly all day.

C. says we will never do "all this" again. I pray not, though the actual flying has been the loveliest I have ever had and not really exhausting in itself, not half as tiring as train or car in spite of the long hours. The Trippes have been such fun, and wear so well. I think they are remarkable. The more I see of them, the more I think it. They both have a wonderful sense of humor and are such a reassuring comfort in hot moments.

I am relieved to have had my first "forced landing," as it was perfectly harmless. We arrived over the Barranquilla field with one hour's more fuel supply, but C. was afraid to land with so many people on both sides of the runway, so we dropped notes asking them to clear it and circled around for about an hour. C. did not know how much gas there was left, only that we were low (there are no gauges on that plane). As we left the field after many circlings and climbed steeply up and were turning to land in the river, suddenly "sput"—both engines stopped dead.

Everyone in the plane was up straight. We could not make the river. We turned, and there below us and ahead was the sweetest little lake I have ever seen. C. nosed for it, and in that moment before we had had a chance to be frightened (I shall always bless him for it) he turned around with a reassuring grin and said, "I think we'll make it, but hang on tight!" It looked like marsh with stumps in it and might have turned us over. But we came down easily and spanked over the water with no obstacles and came to a stop in the middle of this wild lake. Then we all stuck our heads out and laughed. The radioman lit a cigarette. C. reached for a tin of nuts. Betty and I giggled helplessly. "Thank you *very* much!" She bowed to C.

But how to get out? After a while two or three *cayucos* came up with natives speaking no English. Then we started. *"Donde está el camino?"*—*"No hay buques más grande?"* (the last was mine and was greeted by puzzled and derisive laughter by the natives). Also much hand pointing and "A Barranquilla?" and very fluent impatient speeches from the natives in the boats. Finally the owner of the land (with a straw hat on) persuaded us to board a *cayuco* (all in Spanish) and motioned, *"Ah, otomobile a Barranquilla—sí, sí!* etc." C. and Juan teased Betty and me, saying the men were bandits and would kill us for money, and the man with straw hat evidently understood a little and acted up with throat-slitting gestures.

On land we got into a little *ahoto* and bumped off on a dark road with native cowboys galloping behind us shouting and weirdly calling. I really didn't think we were heading toward Barranquilla. Then started a long fight to get to the right official. At every group of houses we stopped for information, and no one spoke English. We wanted to get to the American Consul. It was a nightmare. We changed cars, accumulated officials, and all the time hopelessly trying to explain, *"Vamos a Legación American."* Mr. Trippe suggested "Aeroplano field?" And C. came out proudly with his one phrase, *"El campo de aviación"!* Finally, after approaching the city, one unnoticed youth in the front seat turned around and said in slow but unmistakable English,

"Whair ees eet you want to go?" We shrieked! He had known English the whole time.

And in Barranquilla, all anyone said when we arrived was a casual "Oh, you landed in the *laguna,* did you? We thought so," and reproachfully, "You missed the tea that we planned for you."

One of the funniest things happened last evening at the Union Club dinner, and C. and I have laughed about it and compared it to Daddy. Some rather kindly sentimental old lady was talking to me and holding my hand for a long time. Suddenly and quite casually, as though the most natural thing in the world, Charles took her hand and gently pushed it away. I looked at C. He was not angry or smiling—not aware, evidently, that he had done it. The lady looked not offended. It was not done rudely or even, apparently, intentionally. It was an action as queer and as natural as a dream action. She looked a little dazed, and as if a friend had suddenly shown a slight tendency towards insanity.

C. said afterward that he was rather sleepy and he saw this hand and didn't like it there so long, and, utterly without thinking, he gently pushed it away! He said it reminded him of the gentle way Daddy absent-mindedly pushes someone out of the way.

En route from Panama to Managua, October 5th

Dear Sue,[1]

I have completely given up hope of ever again sitting quietly at a desk and writing you the long pen-and-ink letter I have had in my mind for so long. I have been traveling literally ever since we were married and it is impossible to write in an open plane. Though strangely enough I have often felt in an open plane not as though I were writing a letter, but as though I were actually spending an afternoon with someone—one is so completely

[1] Sue Beck (see note p. 20), who had written to A. M. L. about her engagement to the archaeologist George C. Vaillant, later author of *The Aztecs of Mexico.*

alone and apart and secure from interruptions. And I have told you exactly what I feel about your news. I hope it clicked in successful mutual telepathy!

Your letter reached me on one of the "off again–on again" stops in New York. It made me very very happy—first that you had told me about it, second because I think it perfect and inevitable and *right*. Sue, I just *glowed* for a whole week afterward with that news.

You said I would be shocked. I was surprised but with a surprise of recognition, if you see what I mean. You see, when we rode together you talked so much more of George than of anyone else. I remember thinking once or twice, "If I didn't know better I'd think she was in love with that man—that's the way I talk and think of C." Perhaps you don't realize how often you quoted George, or brought him into the conversation. And I loved it because I had met him and thought him one of the biggest, most vital and interesting men I had ever met. Naturally, he seemed a realer person than that rather dreamy, charming, introspective figure I had never met [a former attachment]. But I didn't say anything—I didn't want to stir up any indecision in your mind.

I hope you have that marvelous "swept out to sea" feeling that has complete faith and security underneath, because it does seem so right and wonderful to me. And unbelievable. The people I care most about and think are "rare" *never* seem to marry other "rare" people. But you two are matched in "rareness" and "keenness" and "aliveness." (Do I sound like a maiden aunt congratulating you?)

Perhaps I know a little that conflict between the person who means sweetness and dearness and old association bound up with charm of place and time—a world very dear and lovely and . . . *safer*. And then the other: tremendous, overwhelming, and inevitable. But I am sure, sure, *sure* that the second is the soundest.

It seems to me I have heard nothing but praise of George everywhere this summer. Dr. Kidder at Pecos, who spoke of his brilliant work. He also told me this delicious story which C. and I would like to adopt. Dr. Kidder said they were often awfully bored and bothered by silly onlookers while excavating and George hit on the best method to shock and disperse them. He would put a pipe or cigarette nonchalantly in his mouth and then very casually strike a match on a recently dug-up skull. It never failed to have effect.

I have quite changed my mind about "archaeologists" and their work. C. and I have had a lot of fun this summer with Dr. Kidder, Morris[1] (at his camp only, in the de Chelly, del Muerto region; we didn't meet him), Morley,[2] etc. We fly over mesas and spot ruins and photograph them. C. enjoys it and likes the men—they talk to him on a natural basis and *not* about aviation. And he doesn't have much of that. I was—we were—slightly chagrined at the beginning to have some kind archaeologist naïvely tell us that the biggest help we were being was having the name "Lindbergh" associated with archaeology, as it would bring public interest, and their work, in the end, depended on that!

As for that "Maya City" that the *Times* had a nightmare about, C. loves to say coldly (to pseudo-archaeological fans who say, "I am so interested, Colonel Lindbergh, in that Maya city— the 'two pools like eyes'—*do* tell me"): "As a matter of fact I located a ruined wall almost covered by tropical vegetation."

(This letter seems to me very sentimental and I really mean it all. Isn't it awful when your feelings, frozen into words, turn out to be sugar roses!)

[1] Earl Halstead Morris, archaeologist, specializing in Southwestern areas of the United States.

[2] Sylvanus G. Morley, archaeologist.

Hour of Gold, Hour of Lead

En route from Mérida to Belize [*October 11th*]

My darling Con—

Your letter was such a miracle. It arrived day before yesterday in Belize—a very wet, muggy, desolate day and Belize is the most isolated spot on earth. It rains there all but three months of the year. It is below sea level and at high tide the place is a marsh; no flowers grow because of the salt water always *six inches* below the surface soil.

The houses are all built on stilts and old and rickety; the place is rather dilapidated and lost-looking. It is the wettest place I have ever seen—the spongy ground, the wet streets, the decayed houses. It was here [they say] that they once had a pestilence and didn't dare bury the dead because of the water carrying the disease (they have to put stones in the coffins to sink them below the water, as it is). Anyway, they *concreted* two hundred or so bodies into a closed tomb.

It was too wet to fly so we stayed in Government House (*very* nice and dry) and felt homesick. I am wild, wild, wild to get home. We start in a day or two.

We have just come back from Yucatán. Mérida is the most charming place. First of all, the ground leveled off out of jungled hills into flat fertile cleanly marked-out fields—neat little adobe cities with Spanish churches in the squares. We were welcomed by smiling Mexicans, who would not take *no* for an answer when we said we were too badly dressed (I was in riding pants and had *not another* thing with me) to come to their house to dine with the Governor. The streets are beautifully paved and clean, with little green squares, many old Spanish churches; lots of old square cabs trot through the streets.

It was Sunday and all the Indian women wore spotless long white smocks gaily embroidered around the neck and hem, a bright rebozo around their shoulders, and their sleek hair brushed back into a low pug tied with a bright red or green or purple ribbon—like a carnation stuck there, or a cluster of bougainvillaea. In one of the busy squares that evening I saw groups of them strolling sedately under lit-up trees with young men.

I must tell you about Flores, an old little town on an island in a lake in the remotest part of Guatemala. The lake is tropical blue and the houses run around the island in a circle, also the palm trees. There is a lovely story about Flores. (It is inaccessible even now; the road to Belize is passable only by foot or mule.)

It is said that Cortez rode in there one night and his horse had hurt his ankle. Cortez asked the townspeople (amazed, no doubt, at such a traveler—they could not have crowded around him, though, with more interest than around us, all jammed into *cayucos*) if they would keep his horse, and to take the very best care of it. He would come back someday for it. So he went on and they—delighted—fed this precious animal on nothing but *flowers!* And he died and they grieved and set up a statue to it which walks the streets at night one day in the year (of course!).

. . . .

We had one exciting day of finding mounds of ruins in the Quintana Roo country south of Yucatán.[1] The thick jungle growth trails over mounds and masonry, like a blanket of snow; one can see nothing but an outline, usually. But it gives one a weird feeling to see a bit of wall—white masonry sticking nobly out of the tangling jungle, still fighting for breath. Unspeakably alone and majestic and desolate—the mark of a great civilization gone. Do you remember Milton on "the extinction of the Venetian Republic"? It gives you that feeling of bowing to an old and vanished power.

I would like to spend a week at Chichén Itzá—white and beautiful in that green fertile land. It is quiet and cool at night, a

[1] The Lindberghs' flights were made in collaboration with archaeologist Alfred V. Kidder. They were flying a Pan American Airways "S-38" twin-engine amphibian.

charming Yucatanian told me, and you can walk along the white stones and smell mimosa.

At one of the Maya ruins—a spot on the coast—Tulum, we landed, climbed up the cliffs, and walked into white stone temples. In one we found a modern Indian shrine of the Santa Cruz Indians. (All they have left of the Spanish religion is the cross, which they worship in their own old distinctive "idolatrous" fashion.) There was a little wooden cross covered with a doll's dress, and guttered candles around it. And four sea urchins (white and pearly—you know) laid at its feet and two or three red beans and seed pods. It was so sweet and like a child ("My little Son, who looked from thoughtful eyes . . ."[1])

. . . .

We are almost to Miami. Hallelujah! ⅄

Washington, Sunday, October 13th

Mother darling—

Oh, it is so heavenly here in Washington. It is dry, and a tang of cold, and the air is fresh and golden, and the trees are golden too, and the gutters where the leaves have scattered down . . . It is not a soft tropical gold but hard and firm and healthy, as though you could dig your teeth into it, like a stinging, fresh, cool apple.

My heart and blood rise up in it and I feel alive and I want to just walk and sing. I have not felt that way for so long. In those damp hot countries one moves only to sit down again, and life seems hopeless.

Oh, it is glorious, glorious here. Last night I dreamt of Northampton: the pile of leaves in front of the library and the birds on the steeple of the church as you walk downtown with your head in the air, and the gold-underneath-russet look the stubbly fields have, even long into November.

[1] Coventry Patmore, "The Toys."

"Because I see
New Englandly."

We have been looking in vain for places along the coast and have limited ourselves finally to (1) hills in Virginia (inland), (2) inland Connecticut. And perhaps hills *east* of the Alleghenies, in New Jersey or Pennsylvania.[1] And C. wants a farm and cows, and to really make it go. And I think that would be fine, as long as I don't have to plan cow barns and keep cow accounts. But C. knows enough about it to make it go (he did before, you know, as a boy). And I think it would be marvelous recreation for him—so utterly apart from flying.

Of course, we are certainly going to have trouble with publicity. It will all have to be done under someone else's name and the publicity run on a *false* place—the *second* break won't be as great. Then if necessary we can keep a policeman there. There is no doubt about it: if there is a road (and there'll have to be to run a farm) people *will* come from everywhere and do their best to gape and giggle and spy on us. If the policeman doesn't work, at least we will have done our best to live in the United States and will have to try somewhere else.

I have gotten utterly bitter about it. I have no patience, no understanding, no sympathy with the people who stare and follow and giggle at us; who ask questions, crowd, want to know about our private life. I don't think at all any more when I see that *leer* of recognition on someone's face and the elbow nudging someone else to look. I just feel a bitter *"you brutes"* and I turn and stare at them with as cold and as amazed and as insulting a stare as I can. But it doesn't often scratch the surface at all. Most people *like* to be stared at.

Oh, Mother— It is so wearing. I wonder if it will ever slacken. Think of the people—any person, any two people who can be alone on four square feet of beach in Miami, or on a park bench

[1] The Lindberghs were looking for a place to build a home.

anywhere, alone and independent, and we can't get it where there is *anyone* around.

Today, I don't dare go out and walk in the streets and watch little girls roll hoops or stroll through the Freer Art Gallery because of people leering and nudging and craning their necks and following. Oh, it is brutal. We never can catch people or life unawares. It is always looking at us.

It is like being born with no nose, or deformed—everyone on the street looks at you once and then *again;* always looks *back*— that second look, the *leer.* No one else gets that. President Hoover doesn't get it; Daddy doesn't get it; they get a dignified curiosity. But that look, as though we were a public amusement, monkeys in a cage. There are so few people in the world who treat us *naturally.* Either they have an amused curiosity, or they flatter and fawn, or they burst with pride and patronage and carry us along on their arm in a "see-what-I-have-here" fashion. On this trip I have met several rare exceptions. But, strangely enough, they are mostly foreigners: a Yucatán girl (married to an American in diplomatic service—Mrs. Muse), a Russian girl, the Dutch Governor of Dutch Guiana. There are others. But these were *absolutely* natural.

And then it works both ways: if *they* aren't natural *I* can't be.

Of course, if we were with people longer I suppose they would be more natural. I am just talking about first meetings. On the trip the radioman and copilot, the archaeologists, and the Trippes were all natural. But they were unusual people.

Well, I have just burst; but it does get very nerve-racking.

[*Englewood, October 30th*]

Mother darling—

I am very hungry for you. I have not written because I have felt so wretchedly and because I can't think of *anything* else. Tell Elisabeth not to start making bibs with rabbits until we are sure!

We are looking at apartments, but after one batch I was so tired that I could not face another. And this nausea seems to increase. If that would vanish and you were here I would be perfectly happy. I shall hope for Cuernavaca. . . .

. . . .

A week later

Darling Mother—
Everything continues the same or worse! I saw Dr. Foster[1] this morning and asked him if he thought there was any doubt, and he said no. Of course I suppose there is still a very small chance, but I can't wait any longer to write you.

This weekend I decided to go up to Milton. Dr. Foster said I'd feel just the same wherever I was, so I decided to go, staying with the Brandts.[2] No one knew a thing about it. C. wore a cap and goggles; we ate hot dogs and had a beautiful trip through oak-brown New England. I noticed all the little birches; they are very dear to me—I think they are young girls, sisters, for they always flock together. It used to seem to me that they were the pure delicate *spirit* of New England. They rise, feathery smoke, from the stony hills of New England and seem pure breath—spirit.

But then I think elms are really more spiritual—not as delicate but *mature,* spiritual wisdom and rest. Elms have dignity and birches have none: they just have grace, a young sisterly grace, all leaning together. They play with you, run along beside stone walls and hide behind other trees in a forest, glinting sidewise their white skin here and there between the black bark of other trees. One couldn't imagine an apple tree *running.* Don't you think they are like little sisters?

All of which is ridiculous, but it was all I had time to think of. We got in late. Con was waiting at the Brandts', very happy. We

[1] Nellis Foster, Morrow family doctor.

[2] The family of Laura Brandt, a Smith College friend of A. M. L.

sat in bed together the next morning and wiggled our toes and talked. A little shopping followed in which I disguised myself: all hair under my hat, my hat on the very back of my head and a pair of goggles on and quite a lot of lipstick. It was perfect. C. in an awful cap, also goggles. I said to Con, "They're *still* looking at us, Con."

Con, in her ironical tone, *"Yes,* dear, they certainly *are,* but for an entirely different reason. They wonder why that *nice* little girl is riding with those two hicks!" We laughed until we ached.

Never since the flight across has C. accomplished such a thing as that weekend. Also we saw much of Connecticut, Rhode Island, and Massachusetts, and C. was quite enchanted by it. (I tried not to say, "I always said New England was the place. . . .")

By the way, the last morning I said to Con that "they" thought all this sickness might mean a child.

"Yes," said Con, without quivering an eyelash.

A.: "Why, Con, aren't you surprised? It was much more of a shock to me."

Con: "Well, it couldn't be very much of a shock—I've been thinking about it for three days" (in her most emphatic matter-of-fact tone).

A.: *"Three days!"*

Con (in a slightly "aren't-you-tiresome" tone): "Why, yes. It's such a funny way to be sick, and you were so mysterious about it."

Isn't that *just like Con?*

I talked to Dr. Foster this morning. He advises my having the child in a New York hospital. I told him I'd rather have it in the house in Englewood—sentimentally. I wish you were here to argue for me. C. will, though. He agrees with you about *no hospital* but home and thinks Englewood would be fine.

C. is anxious to get hold of his new ship out west, but I dread the trip west now. We won't go until I feel better. When we get the ship, then I shall plead for a trip to Mexico.

Of course you understand that I don't want it mentioned, hinted at, etc., or *anything*—especially till we know.

The Berkshire, New York, Wednesday [November 6th]
Mother darling—
Yesterday I spent the afternoon with Amey. It was such fun. She called up about one and asked if I didn't want to go to a movie on "bees and ants and things." Then Amey and I had tea and a talk. I have been refusing dinners with her so I thought I would try to explain, meaning to tell her but not expecting her to guess. So I said I had been seasick for a week or two, casually. But Amey is too quick. She said gently and sweetly, "I hope it's a *nice* kind of seasickness," and she got it immediately.

It was next to having you. She said gaily, "Well, Anne darling, I am so *delighted* that you are feeling seasick!" and we laughed and Chester came in and played one of my favorite smooth melting Brahms Intermezzos, and we had tea and I curled up on the sofa and looked across at her Rockwell Kents and the Persian print.

Apparently I can't surprise anyone with this baby. Everyone accepts it as a matter of course—almost as an "I told you so." Even Amey. I suppose most people think of it as following marriage and I . . . just don't feel married. We have no "little room" to do over in sky blue or anything. I'm not sewing on "tiny garments," and it all seems quite marvelous, inconceivable, and ridiculous. That afternoon was the happiest I have had for ages and ages, and they had to *push* me out.

Now, having found *just* what we want in apartments, we have decided that we hate New York and that C. doesn't have to get to New York every morning at 8:30, so why not look for a small plot near New York on which to build, as substitute for an apartment? (Not to take the place of the farm.) C. won't get away in an apartment: too many calls, etc. He hates sleeping in the city. He can't *even* get out and walk in the streets there. He thinks, of course, Long Island would be best because of the flying

fields; it is quicker to New York; also we are more apt to be able
to get land near a big estate: get the protection we wouldn't have
from a community. I hate Long Island but it would be more
convenient. As long as it wouldn't be our real farm home, I don't
care so much—just so we can be independent. I am wild to settle
down *anywhere*.

TO E. R. M.   *Englewood, Thursday* [*November*]
Darling, I have meant to answer your many wonderful letters. I
have loved them. But I have felt so miserable, and there was no
news, except the walls of the Berkshire and meal after meal going
the same way. Bless your Dr. Foster—I love him, and *except for
the nausea* I have been perfectly well.

C. and I are enthusiastic about your school.[1] We felt like
wiring, "Please accept our application now!" But felt that would
be a little indiscreet—especially considering the uncertainty.

But why couldn't you get a small *modern* house on the East
River somewhere? An apartment seems cold and New Yorkish
and fashionable. I agree about the sunlight *and* the *modernness,*
but I *hate* apartments and they will be expensive. You could
modernize a house quite successfully. Besides, I think stairs are
good for children and I'm *sure* they enjoy them, like taking a
train. It is a novelty and excitement, and banisters are *thrilling.*

(Also—small voice No. 999—what happens when "Unknown
Soldier" steps into this picture? Will he be janitor or what?)

Friday morning
I am sitting in bed. Dr. Foster recommends breakfast in bed, so
here I am, fallen to it at last. Emily brought it up. I love Emily. I
have lately had a fit for finding the really old-house things among
all the Elsie Cobb Wilson.[2] There are so few of the *old old* ones,

---

[1] Elisabeth Morrow was planning a nursery school which eventually was
started by her and Constance Chilton in Englewood, N. J., as The Little
School.

[2] Interior decorator.

like Mother's blue-clovered soap dish and those Venetian glass green swans (filled on Thanksgiving with nuts and peppermints!). I think I shall have to explore the attic.

I am reading Chekhov's letters. They are not as *intimately* satisfying as Katherine Mansfield's but bigger—he was bigger and more interesting. He was marvelous and took hold of life. He has newer things to give one. He was a doctor all his life, you know—scientist and writer.

Friday

I have spent the whole day redoing my room—rushing up and downstairs loaded with *all* my Mexican china, Mr. Ovey's tray, college books, Lowestoft bowls and dishes. Robbed the guest room of a comfortable chair until my sofa comes, and desk chair. Emily and I have had the stepladder out and we have held up tapestries and pictures at different angles all day and pushed in tacks.

The results are not a drastic change but somehow much more livable, as I have around me *all* the things I like that will, without stretching it too far, *fit*. Elsie Cobb Wilson would go into contortions of horror, but never mind. Why keep all that Mexican china in the attic? Now I have it up on the highest two shelves of the bookcase, with Mr. Ovey's tray and the Count's[1] pink-lady-picking-a-rose dish in the big top arches. Then on the little chest of drawers I have put a Lowestoft bowl, two of Mrs. Bliss's[2] vegetable dishes, two plates, two salt cellars; above is hung a piece of tapestry and that suave lady; she is eighteenth-century and goes with the Lowestoft. On the wall flush with the windows I have Chester's two Mexico pictures.

Over the bed is another tapestry. (That's not quite right, I'll

---

[1] René d'Harnoncourt, friend of the Morrows in Mexico; later Director of the Museum of Modern Art, New York.

[2] Mrs. Cornelius Bliss. The Blisses were New York friends of the Morrows.

admit. I need your eye there. Perhaps a long picture or series of pictures.)

I've found some more "old" things around, that green bronze lizard paperweight, Con's [baby] shoes bronzed, and the Peter Rabbit tea rest. I leap to them.

Saturday

What did I break in all this upheaval? Yes, I *did* break the *best* thing in all my travels up and down stairs: one of Mrs. Bliss's platters. I felt sick and cured of moving things. It can be mended, as it is broken clean in half, but never used—*hélas*.

I wish you were here. What am I doing this for if not for you to come in and sit in my extra chair and have tea with me and say, "Well, I don't know about *that*." And then we would laugh foolishly and I would admit, "Well, there *is* something funny about it."

When am I going to see you? When I feel better? But Charles has a lot of ideas for "when I feel better": first, the trip west to get the "ship" and tests on it taking two or three weeks; second, a record trip back across the continent (all this is very private and visionary); third, a record trip from Miami to Panama, straight, and then to Mexico from there. It sounds a little exhausting. Anyhow, I am not much better, though I keep down more meals. And this begins the third week.

Chekhov pursues the argument that "peoples and historians have a right to call their elect as they like, without being afraid of insulting God's greatness or of raising a man to God. . . .

"In exalting people even to God we do not sin against love, but, on the contrary, we express it. One must not humiliate people— that is the chief thing. Better say to a man 'My angel' than hurl 'Fool' at his head—though men are more like fools than they are like angels."

He says, too, that it is obligatory for the artist *not* to solve a problem, but to state it correctly. "In *Anna Karenina* not a single problem is solved, but it satisfies you completely because all the problems are correctly stated. . . . It is the business of the judge to put the right questions, but the answers must be given by the jury according to their own lights."

It is rather stimulating to think of *Hamlet* and *Tess* through that statement.

What a long letter! Keep it to nibble at like plum cake, though it won't improve at all with age and hasn't many raisins in it to start with.

Englewood [*November 16th*]

Darling Mother,

Amey has just called up, so I am going to try to go in and meet the Neilsons[1] with her. I feel much better. Also, tonight we have tickets for La Argentina[2] and we are going to try to go in, a little late, sit in the back row—*very* much disguised: C.'s hair oiled and parted in the middle, eyebrows blackened, and a dark mustache (if possible) and eyeglasses; I, my hair much disguised, and lipstick and glasses. We are going in separately and will act like strangers—unless we pick each other up! Of course if it works it will be grand. If it *doesn't* . . . La Argentina won't have a chance, for we will bring down the house. I am quite squeamish about it but I think it will be fun. Added to which, if I am sick *once* all day, C. won't let me go.

Englewood [*November, 1929*]

Mother darling—

La Argentina was not particularly successful because my disguise didn't change me *at all* and no one noticed it. Oh dear, I shall have to break it to you and I hate to—and now you know, you've

---

[1] Mr. and Mrs. William Allan Neilson. He was President of Smith College at the time A. M. L. studied there.

[2] Spanish dancer.

guessed: I've had my hair bobbed! Please don't say "My darling, you will never be the same again, I just can't feel the same way about you," because I couldn't bear to have you cast me off. Please don't. I have always been saying I wanted to try it sometime and I did it in a rash moment as Charles has been teasing me for months to do it and I've been saying, "I don't *want* to, I *won't* like it. What have you got against my hair as it is?" etc. So the last time he said, *"When* are you going to bob your hair?" I said, "I'll make an appointment this afternoon and it'll be a splendid disguise for La Argentina," and went ahead thinking, "If it *is* ugly, as it probably will be, it will be a good time to have it done. I won't be being social and I can let it grow again in these months."

Oddly enough, I like it *very* much and Charles *adores* it and says he'll never let it grow again. But it looks about the same from the front—a little fluffier and more apt to curl—so that no one knew the difference at La Argentina, and we were stared at and the word was passed around and C. left in the middle. (As a matter of fact, people were much nicer than I imagined and though the word was passed around that we were there, they had difficulty in finding us because Charles looked so *awful*. He did *not* wear a mustache, though.) But it was pretty nerve-racking and C. didn't enjoy her at all, and I, less than before.

1930

Written at Wichita, January 2nd
(Only about three more flying days to the coast!)[1]
Mother darling,
We are now heading south, and we're halfway and more over, and it is warmer. I have not caught cold, but one isn't exactly cozy in an open ship in winter in spite of Tweedledum's clothes.

In Detroit I saw Anna Fay,[2] who was a *darling*—and "Fay" is enchanting and unbelievable and Anna Fay is dear with her. They all seemed to know I was having a baby. But Anna Fay was lovely about it and the publicity. They have a lovely house, warm and bright. Anna Fay took me up to her bedroom (while Dan entertained callers below) and it was quite delicious. She was nicer and nearer than ever before and very understanding and perceptive.

She was talking about the general problem of our being able to have a home and live quietly and—on top of a statement, "I don't see *how* you stand it"—she added very simply, "Of course, you have each other, and that is everything." It surprised me very much and I loved her saying it. That isn't a new thing to say, but in the direct simple way she said it, it wasn't a platitude. And she talked about Fay's being a miracle—"just a miracle." Well, you know, people are almost afraid to talk about miracles now, seriously. I loved that, too.

The chamois suit came so quickly. I am wearing it, instead of riding trousers, waist, and sweater. It takes up less room and is lighter and warmer. My nose was described in a Columbus paper as sticking out of the back cockpit "like a red grape." I ask you!

[1] The Lindberghs were on their way to California to supervise the final construction and take delivery of their new monoplane.

[2] Anna Fay Prosser (Mrs. Dan Caulkins), childhood friend and neighbor from Englewood, now Mrs. Leighton Stevens.

I wish you could see C. and me heaving through a hotel lobby. You know, it really isn't bad, that is, we don't attract any more attention that way than in ordinary clothes. C. says we might just as well walk through the lobby with *nothing* on at all. We *couldn't* attract any *more* attention. And some of the people might even look the other way.

In Saint Louis yesterday I took a walk in the light rain. I walked down quiet streets ("Kingsbury Place" etc.; both ends are shut off except to the residents) of nice quiet brownstone respectable homes with fair-sized lawns and brown forsythia bushes and sand piles around them. No one walks in those "Places" except children and baby carriages, and it was very restful. I looked at all the wreaths in the windows, and in one window saw some lovely red cyclamen and thought of you and walked home and tried to telegraph you one. I tell you about it because I doubt its ever getting to you—and, if it did, late, of course. But I wanted you to know how I thought of you. New Year's Day does not mean anything in *particular* to me, except sermons in the Sunday School chapel and—long, long ago—resolutions. But I knew you would all be together, and that meant a lot.

I learn a poem or two every afternoon resting after the day's flight. Then they help to amuse me flying, when it's too cold and dreary to look out. And I group them in my mind, the sad ones and the happy ones, under various unsatisfactory headings. It seems to me that there are a lot of melancholy poems and a lot of pleasant ones but almost no lines of pure distilled joy or sorrow. You hardly ever get a poem that gets you around the throat.

For sheer happiness, I should say Rossetti's "Birthday"—brimming and overflowing. And for sorrow, I can't find anything that moves me as much (except some lines of *Lear*) as the one Sir John Beaumont wrote on his son's death. I think the first four lines are perfect and compact and heart-rending. It's in the Oxford book, so you must know it.

OF HIS DEAR SON, GERVASE

"Dear Lord, receive my son, whose winning love
To me was like a friendship, far above
The course of nature or his tender age;
Whose looks could all my bitter griefs assuage:
Let his pure soul, ordain'd seven years to be
In that frail body which was part of me,
Remain my pledge in Heaven, as sent to show
How to this port at every step I go."

It's a silly classification because the most beautiful poetry probably won't come into it. I have so much time when there is nothing I can do with anything but my mind (or memory, rather).

Perhaps you will have time like that on the boat if it isn't rough. Oh, I hate to think of your last hectic days. Is there *anything* as horrible as *starting* on a trip? Once you're off, that's all right, but the last moments are earthquake and convulsion, and the feeling that you are a snail being pulled off your rock. I hate it and it is ten times worse for you.

You did so much for me during Christmas: I felt so relieved about things.

I wonder about Con's parties and if Elisabeth is getting rested. Give them my love.

Darling!

Los Angeles, Monday, January 5th, I think
We are staying with the Madduxes. I feel well and I have gained weight, but I am terribly glad to be quiet here for a while. The Madduxes are lovely to us. But we are a burden anywhere and mustn't bother them too long.

It isn't warm enough here to *sit* in the sun, but there *is* sun, and green grass, and a yellow rose over the next wall. And this morning I woke up and heard *birds*. It sounded like June. I wish it were. You and I both quietly at home in Englewood.

This afternoon we are going to fly in the new Lockheed. C. can't wait. He says there are some changes he wants made. He says it *must* be made less drafty than the Falcon, and he thinks he may make the cockpits closed, which would make the trip back *much* easier. He and I (probably) are going to make a trial trip to San Francisco. On the trip east, I reserve my judgment. I will not overtax myself. Don't worry. I wish I could see you, though it would only mean saying good-by again.

[*Los Angeles, January 13th–14th*]

Sweet Con—

California is cold—very, very cold—and the houses seem under the illusion that the sun provides enough heat—or the reputation of southern California. But it *is* fun to be here.

The trip out was not as bad as I was afraid, although one can't really be *warm* in an open Falcon. But C. is putting closed-in cockpits on the Lockheed, and it *is* the most thrilling ship. Really, I didn't expect to get such a kick from the first flight. It was one of those few moments in life when you are absorbed and over-come by the utter perfection of a thing, like seeing a perfect rider swing a perfect polo pony, or watching the Panama Canal locks open, or hearing Harold Samuel play Bach. The power, perfect control, flexibility—a machine smooth as syrup and sensitively obedient. Well, I felt the thrill(lllll!) of flying for the first time.

Charles is, of course, actively happy and alive.

Then, the people. Of course there is Mrs. Maddux. I've talked about her to you. She is just as splendid as ever, and Mr. Maddux (who is head of the western end of TAT), who got a wire from the East saying he was making a big mistake on the economy policy he was taking and he wired back (it is *just* like him and I *love* it), "The man who never made a mistake never done any-thing!"

The biggest surprise, though, was Amelia Earhart, who was here the first four days. She is the most amazing person—just as tremendous as C., I think. It startles me how much alike they are in breadth. C. doesn't realize it, but he hasn't talked to her as much. She has the clarity of mind, impersonal eye, coolness of temperament, balance of a scientist. Aside from that, I like her.

I am sitting with my back to the radiator and the table in front of me, just as I always did in college. They don't expect cold out here and the rain is the dismalest, coldest, penetratingest rain—worse than Northampton Sunday rains.

I want an open fire and a room full of flowers—spring flowers—against the gray windows, long window boxes of narcissus and daffodils and a big flip jar full of fresh white freesias on the table in the middle of the room. And red tulips where the firelight will reflect in them. And bookcases up to the ceiling and two large roomy desks and you at one of them, and Daffin in front of the fire. And for lunch (on a yellow tablecloth with mimosa in the center)—and we would make it ourselves—clear (canned) soup and a poached egg apiece, and FRESH asparagus on toast, and you would read me your latest story.

I love you and miss you. . . .

Saturday [January 18th]
[Written in the air]

Mother darling,

We are on our way to San Diego. C. is taking Mrs. Maddux, her son Junior, and me in a closed Lockheed. Mrs. Maddux, Junior, and I expect to go for sunny drives while C. plays around with a giant glider he's interested in.

Last night we had dinner with Mary Pickford and Douglas Fairbanks at "Pickfair." I was rather afraid to go—and had a *delightful* time. She is very sweet, with a kind of fine good sense. I felt she was solid and dependable and sincere. I suppose all that doesn't fit the picture and doesn't sound complimentary but I mean it to be. As for him, I think he's *perfectly* charming, and the most delightful fun, and a very entertaining, interesting talker. He gave you that refreshing feeling that he enjoyed life richly and keenly. I liked him immensely and they both made me feel at home and gay—and I thought I would feel stiff and stupid. Charles had a lovely time exchanging tricks with him but was beaten all to pieces.

. . . . . Going to land . . . . .

Monday, back in Los Angeles

Another hideous crash. I can't write any more now. A very good friend of the Madduxes and his wife were on board. And there are fifteen other families—sixteen people. . . .

Los Angeles [January 24th]

Dear Mrs. Lindbergh—

I know you have been thinking about that last TAT-Maddux crash.[1] I don't know how much publicity it was given in the East. Of course it was overwhelming here and overemphasized in our minds because of the nearness. Mrs. Maddux has been taking care of the baby of Mr. and Mrs. Brown, friends who were killed on the plane.

I know that by the time you get this it will be out of most people's minds, but some of the papers here have carried such spectacular and horrible stories, and incorrect, that I thought perhaps you might wonder what the people who have investigated and thought about it (Charles etc.) consider accurate. Charles *did* give a statement out to the papers but they are usually twisted before they get correctly to the people who read them.

The weather reports were *not* bad when the two TAT-

---

[1] A TAT-Maddux trimotor transport crashed at Oceanside, Cal., en route from Agua Caliente to Los Angeles on January 19, 1930. There were no survivors.

Maddux ships left Agua Caliente in the late afternoon (a Western Air ship also left about the same time). But the ceiling became lower and lower. The pilot of one of the planes considered it too unfavorable even to *try* to get through and turned back. The Western Air ship tried to get through and turned back. All three engines *were* going perfectly on the plane that crashed. And there was *no* fire until the plane hit the ground. All the passengers were killed instantly from the impact before the tanks burst and caught fire. The pilot (from the position of the wreck and condition of it) was not trying to land but turning, and had lost sight of the ground and the horizon.

This is, of course, all from Charles' statement. You are probably sick of reading about it and I won't say any more. I think everyone who thinks about it feels that, though it was "due to weather," the pilot should not have *been* in such weather. Two other ships turned back. It is brutal to say that, perhaps, and I do to you only because things like this always make me feel (for a few awful, weak, superstitious moments) that bombs are bursting all around us and the next one will hit us.

I wouldn't admit that to Charles. It *isn't* sensible or sane or logical, but perhaps you sometimes feel it too even though you are a more courageous person than I am. And when I think that sneaking bomb-bursting thought, I sit down and make myself try to understand, brutally if necessary, why such an accident happened. And I come out with two definite conclusions about Charles (that you know but I am going to say anyway).

1. That he does know when to turn back. He does not rely on weather reports but uses his own judgment about what weather he can go through. He looks at it and knows. No one can be perfect, but he is very, very good and doesn't take that kind of chance if he isn't sure.

2. He is one of those rare people who do their best in an emergency, instead of their worst, the way most people do.

I suppose this is an indiscreet letter, Charles would say, and perhaps it ought to go down the incinerator.

San Diego, California [*January 30th–31st*]

Dear Mother,

I read every day about you—at least about the delegation[1] in the paper. Yesterday Will Rogers said he's been somewhere with you and Daddy and *Elisabeth* over the weekend. The *Elisabeth* staring at me from the *Los Angeles Times* sounded so nice. I felt as though I'd had someone telephone me from London: "I saw *Elisabeth* yesterday." In fact, I always take the Will Rogers Morrow comments as personal telephone calls to me. I can just see Daddy when Will Rogers talks about him. I can see Daddy smiling, with his trousers a little baggy. There's something in the tone of Will Rogers; he doesn't *say* "in baggy trousers" and he isn't rude or anything, but . . . I see Daddy in baggy trousers just the same!

I read about the conference—columns of it—every morning diligently, and it's just like squeezing oranges for orange juice: so little juice to all that squeezing and straining. In fact, I get practically no information except that committees are forming to form committees to form other committees to decide on procedure.

Then I read Will Rogers, and feel comforted.

We are back in Los Angeles after the most exciting day. Gliders! Elisabeth will appreciate that. Do you remember, Con and I begged her to bring back a glider from Germany? C. has a friend in San Diego, Hawley Bowlus,[2] who has built what he calls a "sail plane." It has a tremendous wing span and a small body (no engine, of course) and looks just like a great gull—perfectly *beautiful*. It has no wheels but just skids onto the ground, landing on its shiplike keel. Is that what you call the ridge on the

[1] D. W. M. was a member of the U. S. delegation to the London Conference on Naval Disarmament (January 21 to April 22, 1930). Accompanied by Mrs. Morrow and his daughter Elisabeth, he had sailed for London on January 9th.

[2] Hawley Bowlus had been factory manager for Ryan Airlines, Inc., the company that built C. A. L.'s *Spirit of St. Louis* in San Diego, in 1927.

bottom of a boat? Hawley Bowlus has painted the body (fuse-lage) a deep sea blue and the great tapering wings are silver.

The pilot sits in the front; there is only room for one, of course. Hawley is very interested in the project from the point of view of teaching young boys and girls to fly, as it is inexpensive to build, needs no gas, etc., to keep it up. Also, it is so much safer than power flying—slower, of course, and you land slowly and lightly in a few feet almost anywhere. And it is wonderful training for the prospective power pilot: knowledge of air currents, landings when his motor has failed. And it is *such* fun.

C. went up in one a week ago and I wanted to try it. So yesterday I was towed behind a car across a field in a training glider. The car goes faster and faster, pulling the glider behind it, and you point the nose up a little, and up you go. Then they cut the rope loose and you glide down.

I didn't make very good landings with this and bounced lightly like a balloon. It was terribly funny.

The day before, C. had picked out the highest hill around there called Soledad Mountain—next to the sea—for me to be cata-pulted off in the sail plane. No one had gone off there before but you could tell it would be a perfect place. A steep slope down to unobstructed fields. And quite a range of hills that would give ascending currents to soar on. C. was sure I could do it and not be hurt. (It's almost impossible to get hurt in them.)

When we got up to the top of the hill, the sail plane perched on the edge, the nice little green fields below—it felt terrific. All the men were ready to pull at the elastic cord and shoot me off. Camera men all set and ready for a show (taking it as a matter of course). Hawley pacing around nervously, giving me futile last instructions. (I knew that no matter what he told me I would not remember his words and when I got in the air would act instinc-tively, and that was what C. was counting on and what gave me confidence. As soon as I got into the air it felt natural and the controls were obedient and it was familiar ground after the *Fledgling*.[1])

Just the same, when I got into the cockpit and all the people stood around and C. said "All set?" and Hawley said "All set?" to the men on the ropes, I felt like a lamb about to be sacrificed (right on the top of a mountain, too!). (Even C. admitted that at that moment he was "getting quite a kick out of it," seeing me all alone and about to be pushed off.) Then I thought, "Well, it's just one of my flying dreams. The mountain is just the same, steep, way down, and you just flap and glide off." Then the men started running, pulling the rope. I heard the keel scrape and I was off! In a second.

Oh, the relief of getting off! It was quiet and the ship rose steadily. I was not frightened now; there was plenty of time to think; the ship responded easily to the controls. And it was so delicious, so still. I picked out my route (more or less as C. had instructed): along one hill, across to another, and down into a green field—a very conservative route. I did very little soaring because I felt rather timid about getting too near the sides of hills. I didn't want to experiment this first time. But I felt the ship go up to currents in each crevasse in the hillside.

When I was quite near the field I heard a bird singing. Then I turned around the field to face it the long way and skimmed along the ground and it stopped, without any jolt, like a sled plowing into snow with a slight crust. Then I jumped out, lifted up the tail to see if the scraping had hurt anything (it's very light), and looked at the road. Cars were stopping and people (a few) came up. "We've been watching you. We wondered what you were doing so close to this field. We thought you were a plane." They stood around grinning. "Where did you come from?" I, in my white overalls, pointed up to the mountain that *looked* in the clouds.

[1] A training plane in which A. M. L. had some flying instruction.

One excited lady called over and over, "She's all right! She's all right! This little girl came all the way down from that mountain, and she's all right!"

"How are you going to get up again?"

"Oh, I'm not going up again," I said with a pleasantly insane equanimity. "This is where I meant to come," standing with my feet squashing the newly planted beans in the field. They looked puzzled but I was perfectly serene and happy. Hadn't Charles pointed out this field from the top? Here I was, it was all right, I was right next to the road and he would come soon. It took quite a while. I wished I had stayed up longer, of course, and tried more to soar. I didn't take advantage of the wind on the many hills. It had been absurdly short—only about six minutes—and yet the ship glided so slowly and easily that my hair was hardly blown. I just wore a band around it. Now I am wild to have Con and Dwight and Elisabeth try it.[1]

C. agrees that it is more sheer sport than a power plane. A big hawk circled C. when he was up, curious and unafraid, and Hawley says he has sometimes used them as guides to ascending air currents.

I think it especially appealed to me now because we have been so enveloped and weighed down with this last summer's and this winter's accidents. That is, I have been so in an atmosphere that talks and thinks the problems and responsibilities of a commercial line.

Well, I have written and written about it. Please don't worry about its being too tiring. I feel tired today a little but only from the excitement and getting up early, and have felt no other ill effects.

We have been bothered again by newspapers with reports of all kinds: that C. had ordered a room in a maternity hospital for April; that the baby is coming any moment and that's why we

[1] A. M. L. was the first woman in the United States to obtain a glider pilot's license.

are waiting around Los Angeles, etc., etc. I hope the glider publicity knocks that story on the head.

You see, I will have to be quiet so soon. We will be going back to New York in a week or two, and then I will do nothing for four months. C. has a trip to Panama to take.

Our plans now are: tomorrow San Diego, Saturday someplace in the hills for a week for Hawley and C. to experiment on gliders, then a short trip to San Francisco, then home.

March 4th, Pebble Beach
(C. is looking for gliding spots and winds)

Dear Mother—

I cabled you because I don't want to miss you and of course you expected me to be in Englewood by now. You see, they are putting a folding landing gear on the ship, which means building an entirely new wing. C. didn't expect to be able to build this into this first ship. But it is a device that he thinks a great deal of and hoped to put on a ship someday. It means more speed in the air and altogether makes it a newer, neater, more efficient ship. As it's only about three weeks more, C. wants to wait. The ship and anything he does with it will mean more with this new improvement, and he doesn't know when he can get out here to the factory again. If it is going to take longer than that we will go back on the ship as it is. C. has to get back for business and we think I ought to be seeing a doctor again (though I feel *splendid*).

I rode in it on my first trip cross-country, up here to San Francisco. They have put on an arrangement so that you can pull an isinglass cover over your head and make a closed cockpit. Not a breath of wind gets in and it is really *warm*. I have never really been warm in the Falcon except over deserts in the middle of the summer in the middle of the day. Also, I have a great deal more room in the cockpit and don't have to sit in one position all the time. It is a great luxury to me—really as comfortable as a closed plane. Then there is no partition between C.'s seat and mine, though our heads stick out of different cockpits, so I can poke his back and shout at him whenever I want to.

For cold weather we have had *wired* flying suits made (like an electric pad). C. has put a small generator in the ship. The wired suits have been tried before and will not burn, fizz out, or give shocks. Noise and vibration are less in this ship. Lunch boxes, thermos bottles, coats, pillows, will stay on the floor as there isn't any draft through the cockpits and a great deal more room.

Altogether the trip back does not frighten me. It will probably mean only a long day and no staying up all night. I will be comfortable and warm all the time, be able to take good food along, and sleep. And it won't be nerve-racking because we will fly only in good weather.

It is getting in and out of a ship that is tiring, and fighting cold or fear in bad weather, and, of course, a cramped position. So much for the Lockheed and plans.

I have wanted most to write you about people—your friends and Daddy's—I have seen.

The Coolidges.[1] We called on them just to pay our respects, for about ten minutes. She came up to me so very graciously and sweetly and said she really thought of me as nothing but "Anne." And she asked about all of you, and Dwight and Constance. He was so nice too and not at all hard to talk to or clamlike as the cartoons have made him. In fact Coolidge was very amusing in that inimitable dry fashion all the time we were there. He said to C., "You look just as well as your pictures said you were," then, with a look at me, "You look better than your pictures said." Talking of flying, with C., he said, "We had a Republican senator from our section for years. He went flying in Washington. Now we have a Democrat."

---

[1] Calvin Coolidge (President of the United States 1923–1929) was in D. W. M.'s class at Amherst College.

Another night we met Will Rogers. He sat and talked to an admiring circle until after twelve. He certainly adores Daddy and spoke so warmly of him. I loved him for it. He has a way of not exactly describing people but letting a few phrases in about them so that you just see them. He described Daddy walking up and down the room after the "I do not choose to run" statement[1] came out, and arguing with Will about it. He described him in Mexico too, very jovial and beaming at a Mexican banquet with music and gay songs and many-sized glasses on the table. And Daddy looking up with a glowing smile at Will and saying, "Imagine going to war with a people like this!" He did it beautifully—I could *see* Daddy's eyes.

I think Will Rogers is a wonderful person, keen and clear, with a touchstone for the reality in people and situations. And he is so *very* kind and gentle; most clever people aren't. But then he is much more than clever. Don't you think he is very generous and hearty in his admiration and interest in many kinds of people?

I have thought about both of you here. It is the loveliest place I have seen on the West Coast. Great hills coming right down to the sea, cliffs and rocky juts of land with single twisted cypress trees clinging to them, a white line of surf and here and there the rocks are broken by beaches of white sand. It is very green now and yellow flowering acacias bend over the roads. At Carmel, five or ten minutes from here, there is a group of charming little cottages and gardens full of flowers. It is some kind of artists' colony. I have seen about five enchanting little houses for Elisabeth and me. We were always picking out little houses in which to spend our dotage. So many wild flowers, too: yellow gorse and something blue, a wild lilac, I think, and blue flags along the cliffs, and little yellow johnny-jump-ups over the hills. In Carmel I read on a tin mailbox R. JEFFERS![2] I know he lives here. It makes it not so "arty," I think.

[1] Coolidge's statement prior to the Presidential nominations of 1929.

[2] Robinson Jeffers, poet.

Darling Mother,

We are now in our last week (weather permitting) and are packing up. We're shipping everything back. Jack Maddux has to go on to New York to TAT meetings, and Helen is going with him tomorrow night. They are letting us stay on for our last week here—the angels—and then *home!*

I am crazy to get home—to be settled and having nothing ahead except June.

Everyone on earth knows I am going to have a baby—not that I look so enormous, and I dress carefully, but I suppose everyone has read the story (it's come out over and over again) and my coats and scarves tell the rest. Such solicitous care I have never had. Chairs pulled out for me, things picked up for me, milk offered me, an arm offered for big steps, etc., etc., questions as to my health, information about obstetricians, etc. At first it bothered me; now I think it rather a relief—sometimes very funny and sometimes very nice.

Except I do *hate* and *dread* the curious eyes of an airport crowd, trudging the gauntlet of those eyes and cameras to climb clumsily into a plane. But I don't think I'll have to do that again. We've made our last trip and we'll leave very early in the morning; there won't be any crowd, and if we don't stop till New York that means only one *last* getting out in New York to go home—no hotels to tramp through, no snickering in the lobby, no waiting around while C. talks to officials.

Really, I think this all-the-way-across trip will be much more pleasant than if we took it slowly. There won't be any all-night traveling that I worried about. We'll leave at daylight and ought not to arrive in New York later than 8:30 P.M. (Los Angeles time) that evening. We'll be sure of good weather before we start.

Los Angeles, April 10th

Dear Con—

We are working hard on navigation. In another five minutes I must stop and go back to it. A good navigator and instructor[1] comes every morning at 10 and every evening at 7:30. I work all morning and all evening and some of the afternoon, and C. works when he is here. It is absorbing and not very hard.

I had forgotten what fun it is to do nothing else but work on one definite subject, thinking about it and in terms of it all the time, especially when someone else is doing it with you, so you are thinking in the same terms. You use a sextant to measure the angle the sun makes with your position and a watch set on Greenwich time and some tables and charts that do the spherical geometry for you and get your line of position. If you have the moon and the sun or two stars you get *two* lines of position that intersect and show *exactly* where you are. It is thrilling.

We hope to use it on the way back to show us if we're on or off course. But it takes quite a lot of concentration and your mind is quite blind when you look up around you. For instance, C. asked me the date.

C.: "The tenth, isn't it?"

A.: "Yes, the tenth."

Then we laugh and remember that we are thinking in *Greenwich* time. It is the 10th in Greenwich, the 9th in Los Angeles. Also (this sounds madhouse but perhaps you'll see it) I have been working so much with graphs and charts that I see everything in intersecting lines like that. Last night I laid my clothes on the chair this way 　　 and C. put his this way 　　 , the result being 　　 . I looked at it, felt a little dizzy, and said, "You're Arcturus and I'm the Polestar!" So you see we are turning into maniacs.

[1] Harold Gatty, navigator for Wiley Post on his flight around the world.

Dear Mother—

Yesterday you got home—no, it was the day before. How I would love to be there! I imagined that first morning with the trunks and bags all over your back hall and Isabel quietly and swiftly going deeper and deeper into them, and perhaps Aunt Edith there saying, *"Bee,* you *must* tell me *all* about it—just start from the *very* beginning!" And perhaps Elisabeth will rush back [from her teaching] for a meal and perch on a chair and add spicy bits to your stories.

I long to be there. Don't go back too soon (to Mexico). That is what I am afraid of. C. says the ship will be ready for testing *Monday* (that is, the 14th), and I suppose we'll leave any day after that when we get good weather. It may be three or four days, which makes it around the 17th, 18th, 19th. I hate the way this date slips up but it is getting more certain all the time. We hope, of course, to arrive the same day that we leave here, starting about 5:30 and arriving about 10 (your time).

C. is planning now (a secret, of course) to stop in Saint Louis (a half hour) to refuel. The idea is that we haven't gas capacity to go at full speed the whole way. By going at a lower speed and using less gas we could make it nonstop. But C. feels (very sensibly) that the object of such a flight is not the nonstop element but simply the speed across the country. And we will make a faster record going full speed to Saint Louis and then full speed to New York. I like it better too because we'll get there earlier than if we made it nonstop.

The navigating (my job) is going to make it tremendously interesting. We will be able to tell, by looking at the sun through a sextant and knowing the time, just how far off course we are. It means very little work in the air—just looking at the sun, marking the time, and measuring off the position on the map. But it means quite a lot of plotting and working out beforehand. It is absorbing and interesting work and not hard. Only I *can't* multiply *at all* and I can only subtract dollars and cents. I'm no good at hours, minutes, and seconds.

I work all morning, all evening, and some of the afternoon at it.

I must stop and do up packages to send home. You know how neatly and swiftly I tie up packages and how they have a distinctive look about them when I get through!

It won't be past next week, Mother, it can't be. Think: today is Thursday, next Thursday I may be home![1]

TO C. C. M.   *Englewood, Monday [May 12th]*
The *London Daily News* has just called up about a widespread rumor in New York that the "heir" was born in April and something happened to it! It was all I could do, as "secretary," to answer calmly, "There is no information being given out."

Englewood, May 16th

Con darling—

For days your letters have been the one bright spot. There has been so much tension here, especially about Daddy, the campaign, and the Prohibition question[2]—Daddy bottled up in the little study from morning till night with Mr. Rublee[3] and countless strangers, Thomas rushing in little meals to them on trays. He has been very discouraged and worried—so much so that he couldn't sleep and Mother has been afraid of a breakdown and

---

[1] On April 20, 1930, the Lindberghs flew from Los Angeles to New York in 14 hours and 45 minutes, breaking the transcontinental speed record. They refueled at Wichita, Kansas.

[2] D. W. Morrow's election campaign in the New Jersey primaries for the U. S. Senate. He opened the campaign with a speech on Prohibition, advocating repeal of the Eighteenth Amendment and restoration to the States of the power to regulate the sale, transport, and consumption of liquor.

[3] George Rublee, Washington lawyer, legal adviser to the U. S. Embassy in Mexico.

Mother herself terribly worried and Elisabeth, although improving, and she looks awfully pretty and well, discouraged about having to keep quiet for so long. We would meet in Elisabeth's room for breakfast and say, "Well, here's a letter from Con," and then fight over it.

But yesterday, with the great success of that speech Daddy has struggled over, things began to look better. Daddy came home happy last night and slept.

I have not felt like writing anyone. Most of the time I am either tired, looking forward to a nap, or fuzzy, just having risen from one. I wish I could see you; perhaps I shall feel keen again when I do. Now I just feel tired and heavy and dull. I long to have my body obey me, in hard exercise and then sleek dives, to feel wonderfully young and slim and alive. Perhaps you feel this way when you're old. Your body won't obey you.

When are you coming back? I walk in the woods with the dogs every morning. Each spring I seem overcome with a new thing I hadn't noticed much before—this year, dogwood. It is so clean, such a dazzling chaste white. And there is a kind of restrained delicacy about it—it is not effusive, blurred. The lines are so restful: horizontal layers of cool white. It looks washed with rain and dew always, and gleaming in the sun.

Englewood [*May 25th*]

Con darling—

Aren't our long silences ridiculous on the telephone? Telephones should be used for business only. I can't tell you that the syringa is out or that Daffin is learning to *tolerate* Charles and will follow us on walks. Hasn't Daffin sweet curls on the top of his head? And the way he comes up to you, smiling with his ears wide apart, laid back a little, his head on one side. (But not like Peter,[1] wriggling and ingratiating, with his ears flattened against his head, ratlike.)

Someone said of Daffin that he was satisfied with being a dog,

[1] A West Highland white terrier belonging to E. R. M.

that he was very "dog"—in other words, chases squirrels, runs off independently exploring on walks, doesn't really enjoy sitting inside by the fire, doesn't like being a lap dog, is always three shades dirtier than any other dog. While Peter is *not* content with being a dog; he wants to be a human being. He wants attention *always,* whenever you come into the room. On a walk he won't leave you alone but puts a cold nose against your stocking every once in a while to remind you that he is there. If that won't do he barks and barks impatiently. He has the affection, the jealousy, and the possessive instinct of a human being. Elisabeth's fireside is His fireside and "Grrrrr" to him who intrudes on His private property and rights.

Of course Daffin is affectionate but it is the affection of a small, un-self-conscious, tousled-haired boy. It is hard to win that affection but it's very wholehearted and lasting. I could go on like this for pages. I have got to know them very well. Daffin is fond of me but he does not ever leap and quiver and dance with delight for me the way he used to every morning when he first woke *you* up. No—Daffin isn't easily won and he is steadfast in his hates and loves. I try to say *"cunning"* to him in just your tone of voice but it does not bring those electric wriggles of affection.

Today it rained all morning. Elisabeth had asked ten school-teachers here for tennis, swimming, and a picnic by the brook. It was too cold for swimming, too wet for tennis, and they all ate in the enclosed piazza off the ping-pong table, while Daddy conferred in his rabbit hole with important personages and Charles used up some energy clearing out the attic. Anna Fay and the Lamonts came to call. Mr. Rublee is staying here. I am feeling wilted. Charles is now trying to read peacefully. He is not peaceful—though patient—and I feel like biting my fingernails.

Well, "Said Tommy Snooks to Bessie Brooks
    Tomorrow will be Monday!"

[*Englewood*], *June 10th*

Dear Mrs. Lindbergh,

I wanted to tell you that we both feel that, considering the attitude of the newspapers—most of them—on this subject, they should be given no announcement. It is a hard situation and I think we do sometimes have to bend backwards on this private and public life issue and what the papers have a right to know. I do not know whether it will be *possible* to keep things quiet until after the baby is born and to give no information until the legal registering is given out, but we are going to try.

I wanted to arrange to send you a code message, from Hackensack or New York, and C. suggested a very business-sounding telegram. *For a girl,* "Advise accepting terms of contract." *For a boy,* "Advise purchasing property," both signed Reuben Lloyd. I don't know how we're going to remember them except that "*Advise accepting*" has two *A*'s, and the girl will be named Anne, we think. Of course there is no question about the boy—what he'll be named. That's been decided from the first: just *exactly* the same. Don't you think that is the only thing?

Oh, will you be terribly disappointed if it isn't a boy? I'm afraid C. will, though he is discreet and won't say so; he says it doesn't matter. I'm sorry—I can't do anything about it.

I want this to go to New York tonight so I'll have to stop here. Not that there seems to be any hurry. The doctor didn't say it was imminent, but I thought I'd better get the code to you anyway.

We're looking at some land on the Palisades—right on the cliff. C. likes it, says it's wild and rugged. I'm a little afraid the baby will roll off into the Hudson, but C. says being a *Lindbergh* it will have more sense than that!

Dear Mrs. Lindbergh—

I am so happy—was so happy when C. sent "Purchasing Property" and to get your return wire. Now I want you to come and see him and see us. Could you? We talked about it (C. and I) a long time ago, both wanting you so much to come after the very hectic days were over, like the primaries, and after today there won't be newspaper excitement about the baby. I hope you have not been bothered too much.

The house will be increasingly quieter from now on. My brother left this morning for Maine. Daddy leaves in a day or two for Mexico. Elisabeth and Con leave Monday for Maine—not that *you* need the quiet! But *I* find it very pleasant and a relief after the terrible atmosphere of a busy railroad station.

Charles said he would call you up and speak to you about coming in a day or two. Of course it won't be, perhaps, very much fun for you just because it *will* be so quiet, but I know it would mean a lot to Charles. And I am so anxious to see you and have you see the baby.

Now I'll have to add (indiscreetly) something about the baby. When I first saw it I thought, "Oh dear, it's going to look like me—dark hair and a nose all over its face." But then I discovered what I think is Charles' mouth, *and* the *unmistakable cleft in the chin!* So I went to sleep quite happy.

Please come soon and see it.

It has taken me forever to write this—in little patches—but I wanted you to know about that chin.

[1] The baby was born on June 22nd, A. M. L.'s birthday.

1 9 3 0

My darling Elisabeth,

I have read your letter over twice and I ache inside.[1] I want to see you terribly—have a long talk with you. I think it was a very brave letter; it wasn't even a discouraged letter but it made me ache inside because it made me feel that you *had gone* through the most terrible discouragement, the most terrible loneliness, and then had come out sane, calm, and determined. I don't like to think of your fighting through all that alone. I know you didn't say any of this and it was *really* a strong letter, only the very strength made me realize what you had been through.

Oh, darling. I have thought a great deal about you. I want to tell you first that I am convinced you have strength behind you. I just feel convinced—no one could shake that feeling —that you are *really*, were meant to be and will be a strong, healthy woman. Of course you give people that impression. No one ever thinks of you as weak or ill; that, I know, is just the spiritual side. But I feel a *conviction* of your inherent strength— used up temporarily, sapped too much—but I feel sure it is there, the foundation to be built upon if we only can find out *how*. Only a doctor, or *doctors* (I do wish Dr. Foster would consult someone else just to get another view on things, a fresh start), can tell us how to do it. Perhaps it will be some kind of regular exercise or rest or food, some kind of *positive* regimen.

I don't think it need take very long. Amey is wonderful about time: she says young people look on half a year or a year as a long time and it's nothing compared with one's whole healthy life. And I don't know that it would necessarily interfere very much with your school (you might take a passive part for a short time).

[1] E. R. M. had a damaged heart valve, owing to rheumatic fever contracted in childhood. At that time she had what was called "a murmuring heart." Although she suffered occasional mild attacks of heart failure, as in this case, and her activities were much restricted, the seriousness of her condition was not then recognized.

About C. Yes, it is true: it is wonderful to have him there and he has been understanding, patient, dear beyond words. And I have been happy—very, very happy all the time since the baby has been born. This setback[1] hasn't really mattered, or fever, or pain. I have been fundamentally happy—because of the boy, of course, but more, C. (but of course they're both mixed up together so it's silly to discriminate). And it is the most glorious thing there is. But you *will* have it—I know you will.

You are standing your illness all alone without that deep well of happiness to draw from. But you *will* have it, and you will have so much more to give than I have. The very fact that you've done things like the teaching, and now the school, shows you are a bigger, stronger person and have more to give, and that makes it richer. You will have it.

Darling—

I'll have to add a line or two because I'm up today and sitting outside in the shade next to the babe. It is so beautiful and brilliant outside—my eyes can't get used to it; things look blurry and I can see best the small crickets in front of my feet, and clovers. The oak leaves glisten and a wind rumples them so that they seem to ripple like water. Tomorrow I go *into town* for my dressing. Saturday Miss Cummings[2] leaves and I'm pronounced cured except for an occasional dressing.

Mother is planning to go up very soon,[3] and I want to go for weekend after next—I'm not sure yet. I'm glad Mother is going, for herself as well as you. I have felt guilty having her here. Though she has been wonderful. The baby developed a small trouble (very small, but of course it made me weep to have a *thing* come up), and Mother took him in to the baby doctor and was able to talk to him and reassure us.

[1] A. M. L. had a breast abscess that needed lancing; her condition kept E. C. M. in Englewood.

[2] The nurse, Miss Marie Cummings.

[3] To North Haven, where E. R. M. was recuperating.

Oh, he is such fun now. Every day I hold him once or twice and talk to him, and his eyes—very big and blue—look (wide open and curious) at me and then he smiles and opens up his face as Charles does. Soon I will wash and dress him and give him his bottle. He is gaining well. He is now lying in the familiar Highland Fling position—one hand above the head, one across his chest!

Yesterday I devoured from your bookshelf (but I'll put them back) *The Montessori Mother; The Everyday Child and Its Everyday Problems* (Thom). I really read more of Thom about *anger, jealousy, thumb sucking,* etc., and got years and years ahead of Charles Jr. and read about Alice age six etc. They all follow Watson[1] pretty much, though with discretion and sympathy. I think Thom has good (heavy) common sense, and that the Montessori ideas are enlightening and opening.

They all seem frightfully hipped on the overfondled child and its hard life. I don't want to *"fondle"* it at all, so perhaps there is something wrong about me. I do like to talk to him and get his attention. And he doesn't like "fondling" but kicks and knocks his fists about, so perhaps there's something wrong with him! A new mother-child complex for Watson! But he enjoys being talked to and he is curious and attentive!

Falaise, Port Washington, L. I., Sunday [August 3rd]
(Monday I see the baby again)

Con darling,

At last I am around and "alive" again. Today is a day blue with heat. Looking off from the porch, you can't see where the sea ends and the sky begins. It's blurry and blue with mist just where they meet. Still, one feels cooler just *looking* at the water and white bright yawls in the distance. There is a nice hum of motorboats at a distance and the wash splashes softly on the rocks below our window.

[1] John Broadus Watson, American psychologist and exponent of behaviorism.

It is such fun to see interesting, charming *new* people again (not that my own family isn't, but the newness is stimulating). To listen to Mrs. Breckinridge[1]—decisive and sparkling on education, bringing up children, etc.—is exciting, and how delicious just to sit in the same room with the grace—true, *true* grace of body and spirit of Mrs. [Carol] Guggenheim. And to hear intelligent, broad, internationally minded men talk; rich, firm conversation, like mellow fine-grained wood, nicely cut.

I just sit blinking blindly at the world, languid and slow as when one has just been waked up. I say nothing, but enjoy myself.

C. is in high spirits, shown by: 1, not allowing me to enter the house with my hat on (we had an absurd, hysterically funny, giggly struggle over it).

2. Tipping over the canoe when Colonel Breckinridge and Mr. Guggenheim were mildly paddling out to sea in it.

3. Trying to get me to wear no stockings.

This week we hope to go down to Princeton.[2] Mrs. Breckinridge says there are the most beautiful old trees there.

Englewood [August 20th]

Dear Mrs. Lindbergh,

It has been a long time again and I have so much to tell you, but I jumped from bed into a plane, almost. As soon as I was well we started flying and have just come back.

The baby is gaining much better than he did when I nursed him. But perhaps the abscess in the breast had something to do with that. Anyway, he is splendid and doesn't look thin. *Also,* his hair *is* coming out and lighter hair is coming in. His eyes are very big and blue. I don't think *quite* as dark as mine but not exactly Charles-blue. And when you talk to him he gives a wide smile that reminds me of Charles.

---

[1] Wife of Henry Breckinridge, lawyer, Assistant Secretary of War (1913–16); legal adviser and friend of C. A. L.

[2] Looking for land on which to build a house.

There are so many things to tell you—I don't feel quite free to write; I shall have to see you—about finding a hill we like. We're going to look up what is for sale there tomorrow, I hope.

Charles said more definitely last night we might stop in Detroit in the (fairly) near future. He has spoken of it before but now he thinks we might link it with a possible short stop at the [Los Angeles] air races. Anyway, whether we go to the air races or not, he has planned to go to Detroit sometime. I will bring the medal,[1] too, because I think you will think that the bas-relief is very beautiful and true of C. But we can't take the baby to the air races. Can't you visit here again, perhaps later? We're all alone and it isn't too hot.

Did you see the dreadful thing I did in Washington? Right in front of the camera and movie men, with hundreds of cameras focused on my legs, I made a dreadful fool of myself getting into the plane. It was too big a step for me and I had on a dress I'd had to wear at the White House for lunch—when I needed trousers—and the result was a great deal of laughter from the crowd and delight from the movie men for such an amusing reel.

[Englewood, September 9th]

Dear Mrs. Lindbergh—

I thought of you that night—the foggy night [flight back from Detroit]—but Charles feels strongly about telegrams. However, I am glad—although I was terribly frightened—to have had that night. You see, we have *never* turned back because of bad weather, and I kept feeling that we might someday run into a mountain because of not turning back. But now we *have* turned back so I feel much safer. He *does* know when to turn back and when to go on safely. He said we were never in a dangerous position but we might have been taking a chance if we pushed further.

---

[1] The Gold Medal of the Congress, presented to C. A. L. by President Hoover.

The baby is *twice* as big! Really he is, and getting a lovely sun tan.

We have almost located some land. A hill with a lovely rolling view, big oaks, woods, a field right in front of the house (the imaginary house), facing the prevailing breeze, only . . . we don't know yet whether it's available.

TO E. L. L. L.   *Falaise [September 29th]*
I have so much to tell you because so much has happened in the last week or two.

Now we are with the Guggenheims and old Mr. Dan Guggenheim[1] has just died. He was such a wonderful man—did you meet him? Charles compared him in caliber (though he says they were very different) to [Ambassador Myron T.] Herrick. And Mr. Guggenheim thought everything of him. It was of course inevitable but nevertheless very hard and shocking especially as he really *lived* up to the last.

I have wanted to tell you about Princeton. Everything has happened suddenly. We have bought that hill with the brook and the fields and the woods of old oaks![2] But C. is still looking for more, so he wants to keep it a secret. It is nineteen minutes from Princeton and faces the prevailing breeze and a nice rolling view. Also we have *rented* a small farmhouse about five minutes from Princeton with a field big enough to land on, in front of it. And we expect to go down in a week or two. Our own home—imagine it! I want—C. too, of course—you to come and visit us *as soon as you can,* if you don't mind the house not being well furnished or run. It is all so new to me and I have to buy blankets and sheets and towels and kitchenware etc.

The fast commuting train (morning and evening) takes one hour and five minutes from New York, and we take, motoring,

[1] Daniel Guggenheim, leading figure in the mining industry. Founder of the Daniel Guggenheim Foundation for the Promotion of Aeronautics. Backer of Robert Goddard's experiments.

[2] Near Hopewell, N. J., later named High Fields.

about two hours (or an hour and three quarters). This house is out of town on a quiet road and back from the road and surrounded by big trees. Also, there's a garage. Isn't that perfect?

Then Miss Cummings (the Canadian trained nurse, you remember?) has said she will come back and stay with us this winter so I feel quite happy (that is, *safe*) in leaving the baby with her.

The baby is wearing your dress now, and on his new big crib is using the silk quilt. It fits perfectly.

Won't you come soon and tell me how to run a house? Tomorrow I am going in to Macy's to try to get everything in one day. I suppose that's impossible. So we shall just start living in the house with lots of things missing.

Yesterday we went to Princeton to talk to a man about selling land. He was very nice, with a fine son and daughter and a nice wife. His name was *Land*. And we discovered that he was a direct descendant of Robert Land and that his family came from Hamilton, Canada, and that Charles and he had the same great-grandfather. Isn't that amazing! Charles will want to talk to you about it.

Charles is well, and happy about the land and very interested in fixing it up and building.

TO E. L. L. L.   [*Princeton, November*]

We have been here several days, going back to New York almost every day or night, but now we're more or less settled, and it is a dear little house.

I wanted to write you the first night but we were so tired. I wanted to tell you what fun it was. It is a real farmhouse with buildings around that once held cows and chickens etc. While I was fixing the house Charles was gone for a long time. He came back quite dirty but happy with a basket full of eggs and some bran mash, and was quite excited about six little yellow ducklings he'd discovered.

The house is lacking in rugs, and I am remembering your two

lovely ones—or weren't they for us? (Perhaps they were presents for someone else—sometimes one changes one's mind about presents; you've given us so much.) Anyway, they were lovely and if you really feel like parting with them they would brighten up the house beautifully.

But that's not the main point, which is: *when* can you come and see us?

The guest room is fully furnished (with borrowed things) and waiting. Though we only have one guest room, there is an extra cot we can put up if your brother would come; that would be lovely. It's real country and quiet, and there's a great big fireplace.

The baby is much bigger, with long eyelashes like C.'s, and laughs out loud and makes funny sounds. It is *very* important for you to see him.

C. wants everything put on the table, farm-fashion, and *not* served, though we have a nice simple couple helping us.

I know you'd like it if you could come.

Princeton [*November 10th*]

Con darling—

All your football games! I got a whiff of the excitement in town the other day—a bright cold day and the yellow leaves blowing, people blowing too the same way, men with red feathers in their derbies hurrying girls across the street, and a band in the distance. The old ladies here get all of a flutter the day of a Big Game and social life bubbles: lunches and teas and a "pass" to the campus— "And we *must* not miss them marching in, my dear!"

When can you come and see us? Today I planted bulbs—yellow and red tulips—patting the earth down firmly around them, and little upstart crocuses.

My hands still smell of leaves and the dry brittle skin of bulbs and leafy dirt.

There is a very *touché* bookshop here and the man in it is just as ga-ga about Katherine Mansfield as we are—has read *every-*

thing, much more than we, all her things in the *Athenaeum,* an early school story, etc., etc. We talked and talked, he ejaculating every once in a while, "And that brute of a J. M. Murry . . ." Also has lots of gossip about her.

You must come with me.

I have not had a pen in my hand for a month; this seems so nice and restful.

About Thanksgiving: we three are going to be in Englewood a week before until just after Thanksgiving dinner, I think, but *not* for the following weekend as it is Mrs. Lindbergh's only chance to visit us and we are taking her down here. Of course I will see you Wednesday night anyway, but I don't suppose I could persuade you to come down to Princeton for a day, a night, or a meal? There's only one guest room but we could put a cot in one of the living rooms, string up a curtain etc.

It is really quiet here, and peaceful, and one can think and work and talk and enjoy people. (Do you remember what you said about Englewood and our never getting together there? Well, I'm sure we could here.)

I must go and get my fat lamb, who is sleeping in the barn, which has two big glass doors that let in the sun and keep out the draft. He has a blue sweater suit on and lifts his arms for you to pick him up, and laughs when C. takes him ceiling flying.

1931

[Princeton], *Wednesday night* *[January 28th]*

Sweet Con—

It was so good to hear from you. Did you win the prize essay? Why didn't you tell me? I feel terribly elated tonight—I don't know why, except that it's been springy for two days and I've been writing; and then that letter from you.

You know, the other night I went to a concert alone, because someone was playing César Franck's *Prelude, Chorale, and Fugue*. I am fascinated by it just now and won't be in six months, I suppose. You don't like it the first time you hear it. And then certain themes step out and you feel slowly the strength of them and the repetition of them and the pattern, and what a thrill when one day you realize that both themes are being played together at the end. Do you remember when Swann hears the "little phrase from Vinteuil"? Or didn't you read that far? It is in *Swann in Love*.

Well, I went and was tinglingly alone. It was *delicious*. I came early, and I sat drinking it all in—every bit (of the bustle and rustle and whisper and glint of the moments before the artist comes in). And I looked at the people who were not alone and I pitied them. For each person had to share his impression with someone else. And it would just be thrown away, like as not, and each person had to add, to superimpose on his impression the impression of his neighbor. Neither of them had the whole perfect fruit.

And then, too, it seemed that, for instance, an intimate couple would be too bound to their everyday life to be really free to sink into the evening objectively. She would be drawn away from the evening (back to everyday duties) by a fine thread, starting— well, from the back of his neck. "Really, John *should* have a haircut." And he by the scent of perfume on her arm: "Always getting a new perfume, and they're so damned expensive," etc.

151

Don't you think that the presence of another person immediately draws a circle which shuts you two in together and leaves the rest of the glowing world out? Well, I sat there tingling and thought there was no one, *no one,* that I wanted with me. And then I thought, no, that I would like you, and that I wouldn't lose my impression at all by giving it to you, but that it would strengthen it because to talk to you rather clarifies my thoughts (on the theory that audiences are creative) and I was sure that your impression would enrich mine, and yet not go contrary to it—just go *beyond* it. But I was not sure that *you* would feel just that way (I felt we would both be alone, together) so I refrained from asking my Djinn to whisk you there.

The baby is terribly dear. It almost breaks my heart when I get back from the city late, after six, and from the far corner of the main road I have watched for the light in his window to see if he is still awake, and I see that it is dark, and I know he has been put to bed and I will not get one of those eyes-squeezed-up smiles until ten o'clock.

TO E. L. L. L.   [*Englewood, March 5th*]
I am so grateful to you for the "meow" ball. It came just after the doctor had given the baby a vaccination and he was still howling. I could not distract him but the sound of that ball did. He took it and balanced it in one hand, turned it, found out what motion made the noise, and repeated it again with intense interest. Then of course he dropped it, but it didn't break. Did you know that the bath balls are absolutely unbreakable? His latest trick is to pick one up with the palm of one hand (I don't know how he does it—perhaps with the heat of his palm), hold it over the side of his chair until the suction fails and it drops with a loud bang. If you pick it up he does it right over again. He's in the big bathtub now and reaches for the ball and kicks and loves it.

Thank you *so* much. The baby has been inoculated now for diphtheria and vaccinated for smallpox. I'm glad that's over.

I think the trip out west is pretty close now. Perhaps this last snowstorm did it—made Charles want California.

P.S. Little Daffin (the white dog—the most courageous, gayest one—Con's and mine) was killed by sightseers—right here in the front court. They drove in (very fast), swirled around that court, left a howling crippled dog, and rushed right off—never stopped at all. It makes me boil with anger.

Englewood [*March 10th*]

Dear Con—

I felt just as you did and could not get it at first when Elisabeth telephoned. *"Who?* Who?"—"Daffin, little Daffin." But I did not see him dead, thank goodness; none of us did. He was unconscious by the time the vet got here (very quickly). They say he only let out one cry, when hit. The vet gave him morphine anyway to make sure he would not suffer. But he just died and did not come to at all.

Oh, Con, everyone loved him so. They say none of them in the kitchen could eat supper that night. There was an awful gloom on everyone. Everyone had something to say about him. Violet said, "You know, I washed Peter on Saturday but I thought I wouldn't wash Daffin till Monday (just before Mother and I came) because he'd just get dirty again. And now I can't believe he's not here to wash." That makes me smile and want to cry too.

But then it was only right that Daffin should die dirty! And today walking . . . (I couldn't *bear* to walk along those paths, as it was always for Daffin I went, every morning I was here, and all that spring before the baby was born.) But this morning I went, and I met George (the gardener) in the vegetable garden and he said right away in his nice Scotch burr it was too bad about "leetle Daffin." And he said how "vurra fond" he was of those dogs and how they liked him. I said he was just like a person. "Sometimes," he said with a sweet twinkle, "I think, betterr than a perrson."

Then he showed me where "leetle Daffin" was buried (I'm glad someone who loved him did it: George) by the path in the vegetable garden, where we always went for walks, and George had planted scillas—the little bright blue flower—all over his grave. Wasn't it *sweet* of him. Most men would have thought it "sissy" to do it, and yet George isn't sissy, he was nice and kind and Scottish. And he said, "You'll never find one to take his place." And he was just as angry as I was about the people not stopping.

Charles really wanted to shoot them. He was very angry and he said, "You know Daffin made me awfully mad sometimes, but I loved him."

And Peter has been so lonely. They say he stood watch over Daffin when he lay unconscious and growled when anyone came near. And when Elisabeth came back he wouldn't come downstairs to meet her but stood at the top and howled. And for the first three days he wouldn't eat anything. The house has been so lonely—I think of him all the time. He was part of home and of us, and he has just left every room I go into. I see the print his little body made in the chair he has jumped down from.

And when Isabel came back I couldn't bear to see her because I knew she loved Daffin and I knew if I spoke about him to her I would cry.

We have been looking for another dog, partly to take Elisabeth's interest (she was awfully depressed about it) and partly to cheer up Peter.

TO E. L. L. L.   *Tuesday morning* [*Princeton, March*]
I should really wait and write after the puppy[1] comes. I know we'll love him even if he chews things. He can't hurt anything in

[1] Wahgoosh, a fox terrier given by Mrs. Lindbergh.

this house except perhaps your rugs, which are the nicest things we have of a chewable nature. We'll hope he doesn't like rugs.

C. says we will probably stop in Detroit on the way out [to California], which will perhaps make up for missing your vacation if we do. That's what I'm writing you about. I wondered if you couldn't come here during your vacation or some of it—if you felt like it—even if we weren't here. Perhaps your brother could come too.

The baby would be here alone. That is what I'm worrying about. I think this Scotch girl[1] is very good and would take perfect care of the baby and know when to call for the doctor, etc. But, you see, she and Elsie and Whateley[2] have had very little experience with publicity and reporters etc. They have none of them been over here very long and so are not so familiar with many U. S. A. customs. The baby is not quite in the same position as most other babies. I am thinking of the emergency situations that arise out of publicity. The house is rather unprotected. The baby sleeps outside. Unless he is watched every second, anyone could walk in and photograph him etc.

Perhaps this is all very silly. I am thinking of the exceptional things, I know: people reading in the newspapers that we are away and taking advantage of it. People a little bit off, like that woman who wrote me, or a woman who came to the door here and said she *must* see that baby—life or death. Or, perhaps, rumors of our crashing (there were six in about two weeks' time once) and reporters rushing out to get a picture of the "maybe orphan" etc. I would like him under the hand of some responsible person who knew about such things and could take a firm stand, and be on the lookout.

That sounds as if I wanted you to be watchman while we're

[1] Betty Gow.

[2] Oliver and Elsie Whateley, an English couple engaged by the Lindberghs for the Princeton household.

away. And I don't want you to have it on your mind. Some of the time I thought the baby might be in Englewood. My grandmother, Elisabeth, and Mrs. Graeme[1] will be there *some* of the time. It is a little harder for people to get in there. But I would feel a lot happier about him here if you were here. I know you could deal with any situation like that. Perhaps your vacation doesn't fit in, or you would be too busy or too crowded. But anyway there is our (not very inviting-sounding) invitation.

I'm afraid you will think I'm coddling the baby, which I don't want to do. He is allowed to get bumps on his head and let cry when he has a temper—all those things that are in his baby world. But I don't want to expose him to difficulties entirely outside of his world that even older people find hard to cope with.

My, how I hate to leave that baby! I suppose that's it, at the bottom.

C. has been chopping trees on the new place. The road is well in now, and the digging for the foundations started![2]

TO E. L. L. L.   *[March]*
Wahgoosh is a perfect darling, and "the hurricane" only described his first hour, when, ecstatic to get out of his box, he *tore* around in a circle from the fireplace room up the steps to the desk room, through the hall, through the dining room, etc., round and round, leaving a pile of rugs heaped up behind him and on each trip rolling over puppy no. 2 (Scotch terrier aged ten weeks, came about same time). Then I took him out and he raced in the fields and came back quiet.

When Charles came in he seemed to know immediately that he was Charles' dog as he leapt on him and climbed up on his lap

[1] Mrs. Cecil Graeme, E. C. M.'s personal house secretary.
[2] For the Lindberghs' house in the Sourland Mountains near Hopewell, N. J.

and wiggled all over with excitement. C. was *terribly* pleased. I don't know exactly what he told you, but he set to work immediately playing tricks with him which the dog adored. The first evening he taught him to "lie down" (I suspect that you had taught him that already). Said he was a very intelligent dog—a *real* dog, a live wire.

Wahgoosh has followed C. faithfully since the first. He whimpers at the door when C. goes to town in the morning. He is a remarkably affectionate and sweet-tempered dog, much more so than the Scotty I picked out; never growls or bites. He is gradually learning not to be so enthusiastic over the baby. (He always wants to leap up and lick his face, and the more he cries the more Wahgoosh wants to comfort him.) The baby is not frightened but bewildered by him.

He is *perfectly* house-trained and learns quickly. The two of them play all day long, Wahgoosh never hurting the little dog, but the latter sometimes gets snappy. They have found to chew (in spite of our giving them the glove, mouse, and birds) electric wires, bath mats, bits of charcoal, suitcase handles, also shoestrings on the foot!

(I am writing this on the train going to New York.)

Charles chopped wood (trees) again this Sunday and he looks very well, I think. He is getting a lot of enjoyment out of the [new] place. It is now in the hands of an efficient, honest man and is going ahead fast. All the blasting out of rock for the foundation is done and the road entirely finished.

We are still hoping to get off this week, but there have been many airline meetings, and C. just told me it might be Monday. I want to go soon, so we'll be back with the baby sooner. I hope your letter means you'll come and be with him part of the time we're away. We'll talk about it when we see you.

Princeton, Tuesday, March 24th

Dear Mother—

The baby cut his second tooth Sunday and is round and rosy. He is outside so much and his cheeks really are like apples. He takes his milk quite well now from Dwight's cup. Saturday was just like spring. I grabbed Laura[1] and we motored down to Princeton. I wheeled the babe outside under the apple tree and sat and looked at him and felt completely happy. The Stevenses stayed over the weekend, and we chopped down trees, Sunday, on the new place.

The elm buds are just beginning to open and look crumby.

We've got *both* dogs now. Wahgoosh arrived from Detroit a day or so after we'd bought a nine-months-old Scotty. We call him "Skean"—"short sword" in Gaelic. Wahgoosh is the kind of dog who doesn't let you get into a room without leaping up on you and tearing your coat. Skean likes to nibble at your shoelaces.

We may get off the end of this week or the beginning of next (surely), the 29th, 30th, or 31st of March.[2] I think Mrs. Lindbergh will be here for the first part of our absence, then if Grandma or Elisabeth is in Englewood he'll go there for the end of it.

I had such a lovely talk with Laura. She is very happy and feels as though she'd got to an age where she'd stay for a while. But I don't: I feel older than I'll feel in another ten years. A sudden rather overpowering sense of time, and people changing and going and other people taking their place. The cycle speeded up, as though I were looking back on it. I suppose it's the baby makes me feel it.

I'm sitting here by the fire with Wahgoosh and Skean stretched out asleep. C. is still in New York, though it's long after supper. I suspect he's at the Rockefeller Institute.[3]

[1] Laura Brandt, married George Stevens, editor.

[2] A planned trip to California, later canceled.

[3] C. A. L. was collaborating with the French surgeon and biologist Alexis Carrel at the Rockefeller Institute for Medical Research.

Englewood [April]

Dear Mrs. Lindbergh—

I am so sorry about your not coming, and C. was very disappointed. But it is dreadful to be pressed and pressed to come; perhaps we did it too much. And we will see you in Detroit. I am sick of waiting to go and you must be even *sicker* of my letters saying "We expect to leave Monday (Tuesday, Wednesday, Thursday, Saturday, etc.").

It has been a great strain on Charles this last week—the investigations etc.; meetings lasting until 12:30 at night.[1] I hate to see him doing it but he dislikes the pressure of New York life so much that I don't think he'll let himself be pulled in by it. We have been in Englewood the last few days; the commuting has been easier.

This is a hurry letter. Here are some pictures I took of the baby about a month ago and one of Charles—not as good as his pictures, but I thought you'd like to see them. He smiles and holds out his hands for your lamb and then strangles him affectionately around the neck.

[Englewood], April 4th

Mother darling—

This morning, because I have heard that Mrs. Lindbergh cannot come for her vacation, I telephoned Whateley and had him bring the baby and Betty up here. Then Aunt Annie will be able to see him. And C. and I will stay here for Easter.

We hope to leave next week; the accident on the line has delayed us.

The strain of this last accident in a Western Air plane in Kansas (Western Air has just merged with TAT) has been hard on C. Apparently (though the reports are not accurate yet) this accident was not due to poor judgment on the part of the pilot

---

[1] Relating to a Transcontinental and Western Air Fokker crash, in which Knute Rockne and seven others were killed. The plane was en route from Kansas City to Wichita.

going through bad weather but to a flaw in the propeller, which broke, cutting a spar so that part of the wing fell off. It has never happened before, never been known to happen—a perfect freak of an accident. But it wiped out all the passengers. It makes me *sick* at the pit of my stomach.

Monday

Grandma, Aunt Annie, and Elisabeth came up for supper with Dwight, Charles, and me.

It was a very happy Easter. In the morning I took the babe out in his carriage and let him see the crocuses, and we sat by the brook in the milky sun and I was terribly happy and remembered how everything lay in gulfs before me last Easter. I could not have looked forward to such joy as this with Charlie.

Englewood [*April 19th*]

Dear Mother—

We are not going to California—not now, anyhow. We may take a trip in the early summer, but not a long one. I am glad, very glad to be with Elisabeth, and I am staying in Englewood for the time being. Nassau helped her a lot and she is happy and has new spirit, but it needs guiding and tact so she won't do too much. She has a new beau, which is all right, but also needs tact. I'm glad the summer and leisure hours and lots of time are ahead of her.

I don't think *motoring* in Brittany will be good for her. It is tiring for anyone and Elisabeth will press herself to go on. Why can't you establish a point of departure: stay in some coast town and motor out in different directions in a radius? Then Elisabeth would not always *have* to go. Two of you could go off and leave one with Elisabeth.

The baby is beautiful and big: pulls himself up in his crib and in his pen, smiles and plays with people a lot more, waves good-by when you wave. His hair is curly and golden and his skin tanned and flushed with these warm spring days. He distinguishes people much more—will not go to strangers but keeps a firm sweet hold on me or Betty.

[New York], *Saturday, May 2nd*

Sweet Con—

Life has been much too complicated to write—Elisabeth and a new beau. She is happy and gay and young, very pretty and sparkly: "When R. was a little boy . . . he had such a hard time, etc."

It is nice to see her like that again—if she doesn't get too tired. But it has been a great strain, trying

1. not to get her too upset physically so as not to get her too upset emotionally

    and

2. not to get her too upset emotionally so as not to get her too upset physically.

Get it?

I'm feverishly cutting ads out of the paper with a safety pin or a pen, for clothes for a new trip.[1] "Low heels? No, Ma'am—try our *growing girl* department."

"You wouldn't *want* a coat *just* that color, dearie, would you? I think the contrast's much smarter."

"No, but we can get it for you . . ."

"Not in your size . . ."

"Just let me get the fitter to pin it up for you, then you can tell better . . ."

(Oh, hell!)

I am reading Jane Austen to calm my nerves.

. . . .

[1] The Lindberghs were preparing for a survey flight to the Orient via Canada, Alaska, and Siberia (Kamchatka) to Japan and China, in their Lockheed Sirius monoplane.

Jo to me: "Why don't you wear your blue shoes to the lunch?"
Anne: "They scuff so easily. I'm saving them."
Jo: "*Saving* them! What are you *saving* them for?"
What indeed? What or whom. Wait till you get to this stage in
life, my girl. No one to save your blue shoes for . . .
When do you come home? I'll wear them to meet you!

Sunday, May 10th

Dear Mrs. Lindbergh,
Charles has been working me very hard this last week, flying,
every day out at the Aviation Country Club, Long Island. We
were there almost every night for supper and sometimes spent the
night. Some good days, some bad days, some scoldings etc. You
know the way it is. I've now had about two hours' solo work.
Eight more to go before I can apply for a private pilot's license.[1]
(Did you know that Colonel Henry Breckinridge had his?)
We've also been in Englewood—my mother and father just got
home—so it's been quite busy.

The baby, everyone agrees, looks more and more like Charles. I
know you said he would just look like himself and that was all
one wanted, but it does make me happy to have him look like
Charles. His hair gets curlier and lighter. He has a real twinkle in
his eye.

He crawls fast now—scrambles out of the room after you, pulls
himself up by chairs and tables. I *think* he understands a few
words like "more" (cereal, carrots, etc.), "no," and the names of
the dogs. Charles begins to be interested in him, and the baby
pulls himself up by C.'s knees.

The place is full of dogwood and more beautiful every time we
go there.

[1] C. A. L. was giving A. M. L. flying instruction on a Bird biplane (see
Introduction).

[*New York, July 17th*]

Mother darling—

Charles says we'll get away next week![1] I suppose it will be the end of the week—if we do. He won't say for sure that we can stop in North Haven, though he thinks perhaps we can. It would mean everything to me, and I have told him so. However, we can just wait and see.

We'll leave from the Edo Pontoon Company float on College Point (Long Island, near Flushing) and go to Washington. C. has to stop there before he goes, for a night, I suppose. Then perhaps we'll stop in Maine.

I should love to see the baby in Maine with you. I have in the back of my tense-not-wanting-to-leave mind a nice cool spot of relief, and when I analyze it, it is: "He'll be in North Haven with Mother." It makes me very happy not only because I know he'll be safe and well and happy and loved, but a kind of selfish joy—a feeling that part of me will be there with him, because it is Maine, and you.

Will you keep some kind of record of his actions and take a picture about once a month? Don't let Betty give him too many toys at once, just one or two, and change them about and don't let people fuss over him or pay attention to his little falls or mistakes, will you? I'm sure you'll do it all just right—I'm not worrying.

[*New York, July 22nd*]

Mother darling—

We are just about ready to go and are making out the maps. C. thinks we can stop in Maine on the way from Washington to Ottawa—though it must be a dead secret. He thinks we can leave for Washington Monday, spend Monday night (perhaps

[1] May, June, and July were spent in preparation for the survey flight to the Orient (see note, p. 161). A. M. L. received her private pilot license and was studying radio operation.

Tuesday night too) there, and then fly to North Haven for the *next night*. The babe will leave the minute we leave for Washington. Miss Sullivan[1] has already gotten tentative tickets for a drawing room for "Betty and Mary" Monday night. I will wire you that "Betty and Mary have left on Bar Harbor Express" and you will know that means the baby. I am very anxious for no one to know, to get him up there quietly.

I will send a good map up there with him for you. Tokyo and then Shanghai are the only places I know where mail could reach us, and Tokyo is the surest.

[*The Lindberghs landed in The Thoroughfare, North Haven, Maine, on July 29th and spent the night at Deacon Brown's Point. The entire trip is described in A. M. L.'s book* North to the Orient.]

Aklavik, August 6th

Mother darling,

This is the first place I could send a letter from. An air mail leaves here once every two weeks. It probably will go out day after tomorrow. Mother, it has been the strangest trip—terribly exciting and new. I feel as though I'd been gone for months. The other night, flying, I dreamt about the baby and it was like another life—I couldn't believe I had one. I love to think of him with you.

I've got too much to tell you. *Ottawa:* seeing lots of people, fliers who told us not to go the way C. wanted to. They talked to him like grownups to a little boy who wanted to play with firecrackers: "Now these Roman candles are just as exciting and much prettier, and you'll get just as much of a kick out of them as from the firecrackers."

"Now this route, sir, will be quite wild enough for you, and there are camps all along it."

"But we don't like to go along organized air routes."

---

[1] Miss Katherine Sullivan, E. C. M.'s personal secretary.

"Oh, sir, it's no organized air route. It'll be plenty wild enough for you, sir, and just a few miles longer."

"Well, *you* all got back here, didn't you?"

It was awfully funny. Then C. ended up slightly peeved—smallboy: "I won't play-with-you-I'm-going home."

"All right, if you don't want us to take that route we won't, we'll go back and go over Greenland!"

Lots of long faces. "Well, that's worse."

Finally they came around and said one by one to C., "There's just one thing, sir, I'd like to tell you: I hope you don't change your route a bit!"

Then a flight to Moose Factory over hundreds and hundreds of lakes, absolutely flat, and tall thin pines.

Moose Factory: a few white houses on the green bank of a slow, glassy river. A stiff white church with a red roof, stiff red-roofed houses (like New England), about nine or ten, a white flagpole flying a British flag, whitewashed picket fences, closing in "front yards," whitish gray tents on the shore, fish hung up to dry.

Absolutely still except for the sound of a put-put from a canoe cutting through the glassy water. Thin sharp pine trees against the sky on every horizon.

Indians came down to meet us and Hudson's Bay Company men; about four white women. We stayed in one of the Hudson's Bay houses, very old—one of the first Hudson's Bay posts, about 1650.

The house was made of great thick boards and there were huge old locks on the doors. A nice Mr. and Mrs. West of Aberdeen, Scotland (Hudson's Bay man), took care of us: gave us a good meal of fresh moose, lettuce (grown on the island), canned raspberries, and canned pound cake and tea. It was quite warm and mosquitoey. But the firm houses—bare, whitewashed—suggest winter; great stoves all through them, storm windows, etc.

After supper we called on the Mounted Police (all through

Canada, to guard the game laws etc.—fine, straight, tall men) and on the Mission School (Anglican). An Anglican priest and two Canadian women teachers keep a school for Indians (boarding school), wash, feed, and keep them. The Bishop of the Northwest Territories was there and two women (one quite young) who were going far north to Baffin Land for five years, one to teach, one as nurse.

The young shy nurse had never been north before. It made me quite sick to think of five years up there: a boat once a year and no other women—a missionary, a Mounted Police, a trading post, and Eskimos. She did not say much and I couldn't think of anything encouraging to say except that she would be doing wonderful pioneering work. A slight flicker of satisfaction on her face at that.

They spread out tea for us at ten in the evening, and very sweet cookies. The women—some of them—have not been out for several years and their dresses are quite to C.'s liking: up to the knees. It's much more convenient and comfortable. Some of the people there came by boat straight from Scotland or England and have not seen anything of Canada except that spot. The eager priest showed us the church which they have to anchor down with great wooden pins when the snows melt in the spring. He knew the Indian language, Cree, and showed us a hymnbook in Cree: it looks like this: ⟨triangles⟩ "Lead, kindly light" etc. translated into triangles.

He was proud of his larkspur, growing very high and blue. He showed us the tablet to the former priest and description of his work which had inspired him to work there. An eager fire in his eyes. I don't see how they do it.

Mrs. West had a six-year-old boy in Aberdeen who was born in the Hudson Straits. She had left him with her sister and said he was quite happy and called her sister "Mother" and her brother-in-law "Daddy." It was not comforting to me but evidently was to her.

A long flight to Churchill. The pine trees gave out and we flew for miles and miles over islands of swamp, along the coast of Hudson Bay. Once on the trip we saw a camp of Indians on the beach, a tent and a boat. They waved madly at us. And once we saw a two-masted schooner in a harbor of a river. Otherwise, swamp and wastes—*nothing*.

We got to Churchill in the evening—a rocky projection in the bay and the river on the other side. A tall grain elevator (amazingly incongruous in that bleak land) and quite a number of white houses. It was a clear bright afternoon. We got in about 6:30 their time. It was a little snappy, like fall, and felt more like the North. The cold bright light on the white sides of those bleak houses looked like Edward Hopper's paintings.

The North Star was getting more and more right on top of us, and we saw the first streak of northern lights. No trees here—low brush and flowers.

Flying over the river mouth we saw huge fish jumping through the water like dolphins—white whales, we were told.

We got to Baker Lake in late afternoon. It was raw and damp. A glassy lake, and gray bleak shores; no growth except gray moss; about four houses and a church on the bare shore. All the men (there were eight) came out to meet us, and a larger group of Eskimos.

No white woman had ever been there before, so I was quite a freak (and a disappointment, I guess, with my trousers on). The first thing you saw, stepping on that bare shore, was a white shack with neat lettering on it: "Revillon Frères Limited, Furs"— Revillon Frères making me think of sophisticated, roaring Fifth Avenue. There could not have been more contrast.

We walked through mosquitoes into a small white bungalow where the Revillon men lived. One trim rosy little Scotchman who operated the radio, and an Englishman, two Hudson's Bay men and the Mounted Police and a Canadian surveyor and a trapper, an English priest and a Roman Catholic priest all came in and sat around a big table and looked at us. The one that had been there the shortest time had come in a year ago. The boat only comes in *once* a year with provisions for all year, and mail. Some had been there for six years or more without going out.

"What's it like outside?" they said. They all talk about "outside." They were rather short on some things, as this year's ship was due in a fortnight or so. No cigarettes, no books, papers, of course. And they hadn't had fresh meat or vegetables or fruit or any liquor for a year. C. and I were shocked to think we hadn't brought in anything. We thought there were planes that dropped in now and then. But we had three plums and a pear left over from a picnic lunch at Ottawa, and four meat sandwiches, which we gave them, while we ate delicious fresh salmon caught in the lake, and canned raspberries and bread made there, with a sour taste.

They had a radio with which they got Pittsburgh all winter and they play rummy and bridge in the evenings. But the Anglican parson won't play cards, so he breaks up the second table. The Roman Catholic priest both plays and will take a drink. There were only about two tents full of Eskimos. I don't know how they divided up the converts.

We had a comfortable room, and I don't know how they did it. Everyone here is so good to us. They were very jolly too, and the next morning they all got out their cameras and took a picture of us with the Eskimos. I looked up and found the Mounted proudly taking "the old lady" down the bank on his arm. She was small and wrinkled and toothless but smiling. She had an old calico petticoat on, but a little high up, around her shoulders! She made funny moans of joy and giggled when you looked at her.

Must go, darling. Kiss Charlie for me and run your hand across his curls.

Aklavik, August 8th

Mother darling—
We left Baker Lake late in the afternoon. It was sunny; the ground, though it has no bushes, is covered with small flowers— short-stemmed fireweed and a kind of yellow poppy. We took eleven letters from the men to post here. We had quite a time getting off because it was rough, and since the self-starter broke on the plane, Charles has had to crank it by hand. I have to sit in the front cockpit and switch the ignition on and off and work controls, and that means a swift acrobatic act when it's started. I have to crawl out and back along the wing and up into my cock-pit, and C. has to jump up into his cockpit, all while the plane is taxiing across the water.

Point Barrow, August 10th

From Baker Lake we flew all night—almost twelve hours—but it never got dark. For hours on one side of us a sea of fog with the sun setting into it; on the other side, stretches and stretches of dead gray flat land, scattered with lakes—a blue-gray light like dawn. The sun did go down at last but it was twilight until we got there [Aklavik]. About halfway, near Coronation Gulf (below Victoria Land), I sent out messages "blind" to a station, Coppermine, also on short wave to New York. The message to Coppermine got through, though I couldn't hear *him*.

Aklavik is on a huge delta, more water than land, hundreds of rivers and streams snaking in and out, crossing and recrossing, like so much tangled thread. The tree line comes up here again and it is warmer.

We landed (very sleepy) in that strange gray dawn on a bend of one of the glassy rivers between pine-treed banks. There was another plane pulled up on the mud, quite a big settlement of houses (twenty), two churches, radio masts, etc. A group of enthusiastic people all dressed and waving. On the bank, lots of Eskimos with "parkas" on—fur-lined and covered with bright calico. The girls wear long skirts with ruffles on the bottom.

People rushed out and took pictures (at three in the morning!). We pushed up onto the muddy bank and turned the motor off. There was a terrible noise we hadn't heard before: a bedlam of howling dogs, not barking but howling like coyotes—the "huskies" they use for dog teams in the winter. They were all chained to posts and leaping and straining to get loose. They're very wild, most of them, and will leap at strangers, or a whole pack will turn and fight another team.

We walked up the muddy bank into a small bungalow. I pulled the black blind down, trying to create a little feeling of a deep black night I could sink into. Daylight is so shallow, I hate the feeling of going to sleep in it. I want depths and depths—endless depths of black night to sink into—for sleep.

We stayed with the one doctor for miles and miles around. Some of the places he cares for he can only get to once a year, in a little boat or by dog team in winter. He pulls teeth, delivers babies, operates for appendicitis, treats tuberculosis, etc.—*everything*. He and his wife—a very sweet girl who is about to have a first baby—took us in and gave us their bed. There was one other bed in the house and they had a friend staying with them. I don't know yet where *she* slept. Perhaps in the bathtub! For there *was* a bathtub, the only one in town—a tin bathtub (unporcelained), filled with a teakettle. I had a wonderful bath.

They were lovely to us and gave us everything. It means a lot because their supplies come in by boat—three boats in the summer and two or three dog hauls in the winter. Then there is air mail two or three times summer and winter.

There were both Eskimo and Indians here. The Eskimos *always* smile at you whenever you meet them, and such darling babies on the mothers' backs underneath the parka and held in by a waist cord. Sometimes when it's cold you can't see the baby at all, just a lump on her back.

The afternoon after we arrived we heard all the little Eskimo children screaming and all the dogs howling, and coming out of the bungalow we were told excitedly, "The boat's coming, the boat! See—the smoke!" You could see the smoke coming up from the trees miles away. The boat was winding slowly up the river. By the time it got in sight every man, woman, child, and *dog* was down on the mudbank to see it. It was tragedy not to be there. "Oh, poor Kay, she's on duty at the hospital and won't see it!" someone said.

An old white boat (like the Hudson excursion boats), the water wheel churning foam, was towing a big barge. Everyone speculated:

"Perhaps my shoes will be on it!"

"Doesn't look like much gasoline—hope there's more inside."

"Look at those new huskies—lot of police in those dogs. Don't look as strong as the others."

"Perhaps Mother sent me some fresh tomatoes."

The mission (Roman Catholic) school marched down, all the girls wearing magenta bandannas on their heads, led by full-skirted, white-capped Sisters (the Gray Nuns of Montreal).

Everyone trooped on board very excited and looked over lists of packages.

"*We've* got a bathtub! You won't be able to lord it over us any more—a regular bathtub."

"That's the new tank for my motorboat. They've sent the wrong kind! Look, Lenny, they've sent the wrong kind—and I sent them all the specifications. Can't use it—have to wait till next year."

Our friends, Dr. and Mrs. Urquhart, got a huge keg of Mission Dry Orangeade, and boxes of cookies and things; also a crib and a bathinette. And the next night at supper with the Mounted Police we had fresh tomato salad.

There are two small hospitals here: the Anglican mission one and the Roman Catholic one. Only two nurses in the Anglican one to do all the nursing and night work and the scrubbing up besides. One girl I talked to was so discouraged and tired. She hadn't had more than five hours' sleep for a month, and often less.

There were several children in the hospital, and one fifteen-year-old Eskimo girl with her *second* baby. And they go right on having them. (At Barrow I saw some pictures of a Mr. Brower's children and asked innocently, "How many children has he?"—"Seventeen—and some people say it's twenty-five.")

The Roman Catholic mission school-hospital is a big old rather rickety building swarming with boys and girls. The Sisters, with full gray skirts reaching to the ground and big poke-bonnet hats, had bright smooth-skinned faces. They were most of them French (French Canadian) and quite gay and jolly.

We saw the girls' schoolroom where the children had made, and hung over the room, birds' nests and paper chain decorations and paper lanterns, all decorating colored pictures of Christ. In the boys' room, hanging from the ceiling, was an old forget-me-notted, pink-rosed valentine—an airplane carrying Cupid.

"The boys are so interest een airplans," explained a sweet-faced Sister.

In a playroom were a group of girls making dresses—good dresses, too. They teach them dressmaking and shoemaking. They asked the girls to sing. They were very shy and finally looked away stiffly and began in high sweet nasal voices, "Wailcome, wailcome, we wailcome you to day."

Then one of the Sisters picked a sweet pea from a window box (almost nothing grows outside) and gave it to the smallest child to give me. All the others pushed around to see and she tried to hide under the big Mother Hubbard skirts of the Sister. I got down on my knees and finally she came out and gave me the flower.

Then out into the yard to the fish-drying house. The Eskimos feed their dogs, and themselves too, often on dried fish, and the Sisters teach the children cooking, sewing, and the boys, hunting, fishing, and also fish cleaning and drying. The Sister in her gray eighteenth-century skirt and poke bonnet rubbed her hands after opening the smelly shack. "Eet ees hard for us to learrn—that."

I liked them all so much. They have adapted themselves well and were sweet and gay with the children. The sweet pea baby adored one Sister, hid in her skirts and lifted her arms to be lifted up. "She was afraid of my bonnet at first," the Sister laughed, "but now she likes me."

It was rather bad weather to Point Barrow. But it was a thrilling day for the radio. I was terribly pleased because the radiomen at Aklavik had been so considerate and helpful. I was in contact with them and then Herschel Island and then Point Barrow. The Barrow radio led me in; I got weather right along from him and he got our position. When we got almost to Point Barrow it was darkish and misty. I noticed that the "land" ahead of us was chopped up with queer shadows. I thought, seeing irregular blocks, the half-light striking them, it was Barrow, a group of houses. Looking again, I saw it was the ice pack, as far as we could see rough blocks of ice on top of each other, a rough sea of it, grim and gray.

Petropavlovsk [August 17th–18th]

Mother darling—
I wish I weren't so far behind, because I want to give you things in the right order.

But I must tell you about Point Barrow. It was so real and poignant to us. We got there, very grateful and cold, through the fog about one at night but it was still light—a cold gray unearthly light that seems to grow right off the ice pack; a barren corner of land on one side of the ice pack as far as one could see, on the other a lagoon, surrounded by fog so that I felt the little settlement (a red-roofed church, four or five houses, tents, and another small group of houses on the other side of the lagoon) was an island.

It looked wonderful to us because it was a hard trip and we had hit the actual point of Point Barrow first—a long spit of land, ice pushed up against it, small lagoons cutting into it; about four shacks and a few tents. My heart sank as I looked at that deserted group. How *can* it be Point Barrow? A radio office? *No!* No radio mast. It *can't* be Point Barrow.

Then we followed the spit inland until we found the larger and newer group of houses—red-roofed—and two radio masts, and an American flag flying. We landed on the lagoon and pushed up toward the beach where a group of people huddled. We opened the sliding cabin covers and I took off my heavy socks and put on shoes. It was bitterly cold, like a raw November day. My feet were numb before we got ashore.

As we looked at the group—all in parkas, fur around their faces, sealskin boots on—I thought suddenly, "They're *all* Eskimos!" No—the radioman came out in a khaki mackinaw. I was so grateful to him. I had to shout to him immediately and thank him. He kept contact with us all the way and told us what the weather was like at Barrow. C. said he wouldn't have gone on if he hadn't known.

And even when I couldn't send—when we were flying too low for the antenna to be out the right length to send but I could drop it down enough to receive—he went right on sending weather and information. It is wonderful and heartening to get when you are cold and isolated, flying through the fog. He was a nice big jolly man, Mr. Morgan. I liked him very much.

As we climbed up the bank the Eskimos drew back and a great cry went up—not a shout exactly, but a slow deep cry of welcome. There was something about it akin to the bleak land and the ice pack, and I felt terribly touched.

An oldish man in a great overcoat came out—Dr. Greist: Presbyterian preacher, doctor, teacher, everything for that settlement —welcomed us and helped me up the bank, where I met the four white women of the "island," all in fur parkas. Mrs. Greist, very sweet, kind and unselfish and motherly, took me over the tundra, soggy and wet with icy pools, to their house. It was warm and bright with gas lamps. The kitchen door was open to a bright living room and it smelled of sweet potatoes and new muffins. She showed me upstairs to our comfortable room, lit the lamp and stove and showed me soap, hot water, powder, toothbrushes, etc., etc., and an *inside upstairs toilet!* (No plumbing, of course, but it *looked* as though there were.)

A big table was laid downstairs, filling the whole living room. A window box with growing nasturtiums and a tomato plant with one green tomato. I noticed it coming into the room. Mrs. Greist smiled. "That tomato won't ever ripen. It hasn't enough sun, but the leaves grow and we can smell it. Even the smell of green vegetables growing is good to us."

Then the whole settlement "family" came in, Mr. and Mrs. Greist, host and hostess: their boy (fifteen) David, the radio operator, Mr. Morgan, and his wife and little girl (about eight or nine), the government teacher, Mr. Trindle, and his wife and little boy (twelve), a Miss Bailey, trained nurse, and an old Scotch trader, Hopkins, who hadn't been "out" for thirty years— never seen telephones, automobiles, etc.; had married an Eskimo and had dozens of children.

We sat down to the most *marvelous* American Thanksgiving dinner: fruit cup (canned), sweet potatoes (canned), peas and beets (canned), reindeer meat, goose (wild goose killed and kept in the meat cellar; if you dig down a few feet you strike ice, so they dig a cellar and keep their things there), salad of canned celery and fruit and ice cream (canned cream).

Mrs. Greist told me there was no more tea, no more coffee, no more flour left in the village. Their boats (yearly) hadn't yet come in because of the ice pack. All their provisions were running low, and they went around and pooled their things for the dinner. Mrs. Morgan had a few eggs (not fresh, of course— packed, preserved ones) for mayonnaise. Someone else had grown a little parsley in a window box. They can't grow anything outside. Mrs. Greist has brought up dirt from Nome for her window boxes.

The ice pack is last winter's ice. It never melts but with the right wind it is blown back away from the shore and the boats get in. On the boat were a new nurse and a new teacher and all their provisions, packages, letters for the last year.

Anyway, they gave us a dinner that lasted until 3:30, when C. fell asleep at the table (a little bit on purpose, I'm afraid).

The next morning Dr. Greist, a white-haired, active man with the grit and spirit of Calvin, showed us around the house, which he built himself—really built himself. A son "outside" had planned it with him. They'd shipped up everything, but Dr. Greist had had to measure, plan, fit every board and nail while Eskimos helped him. It was planned for insulation, ventilation (all the windows—double storm ones—were nailed in. You could not open them, so there were no cracks, but they had a kind of funnellike ventilator in each room which let in air but not snow or rain), heating especially planned for the Arctic. He had made the water tank and heated it from the stove and fixed pipes so they had running hot and cold water downstairs. At the same time he preached every Sunday, had a Bible class Wednesday nights, was the one doctor, and was trying to keep his boy up in studies. Mrs. Greist is a trained nurse and teacher too.

I felt as though my life didn't count for anything against the terrific sternness of that life. And terribly sad. They had been there so long and were old and tired and they dreaded sending David out. When they first went up there there was no radio, only the one boat, and they heard about the death of one of their sons four months after he died.

They lent me "mukaluks," sealskin boots, to walk around in; otherwise, your feet were always icy wet. We walked over the tundras after a big herd of reindeer the Eskimos were chasing in to kill their year's supply—real reindeer with great heavy horns on their heads—treading with deliberate delicate steps quickly over the moss.

"Hi! Hi!" the Eskimos would shout, running after them to herd them in—little Eskimo boys with bright cheeks and bright slit eyes in their fur caps. The Eskimos here were so friendly. You had a warm family feeling about each one you met. Old "Solty" in bright green calico, who, when she ran, heaved from one side to the other like a bear. She was always laughing and I could tell her laugh in a crowd. We went out walking on the ice pack and she padded ahead of me, never letting me get on a soft place.

On Sunday we went to church. Charles and I sat in the front row in the little white church packed with Eskimo men, women, children, and babies. There was a general shuffling and crying of babies all through the service, but they leaned forward in their seats eagerly to hear.

It was so strange, terribly strange, to hear Dr. Greist explain the Bible to them.

" 'We have gone astray like sheep.' Like the reindeer who have scattered on the tundras."

" 'The power of God.' Force—like dynamite that blows up the ice sometimes and lets us get a ship out—the dynamite of God."

" 'That your garners may be full . . .' Your meat cellars will be full of reindeer meat."

" 'Your oxen will be strong.' Your dogs for your dog teams will pull hard."

Then they sang in a queer kind of wail (very sweet, a little like Negro songs) in a slow singsong way: "Glory for me, glor-ee for me . . ."

Whenever a baby cried too much (they let them go until no one could hear anything else) the mother would get up reluctantly, hitch her bundle higher onto her back, and pad out clumsily.

Dr. Greist asked Charles to speak to them and he said he

would at a meeting in the evening. He spoke slowly and through an interpreter, comparing dog team and airplane speeds, what the airplane might bring them, and thanking them for all they had done for him.

We stayed at Barrow about three days, waiting for the fog to clear, and finally left quite late one afternoon. I really hated to leave them and felt that I got into that small close group, and I felt terribly grateful for all they had done—given us their last good butter, their last coffee and flour—and I went away with someone's "mukaluks" keeping my feet warm and dry.

Mr. Morgan followed us with radio for two or three hundred miles. We flew over the *Northland,* their marooned ship. Then I got Candle, from the Seward Peninsula. It was getting dark and there was fog on the mountains, and C. suddenly shouted to me, "You tell him we're on the north side Seward Peninsula and there's fog on the mountains ahead, that we'll land for the night and come into Nome in the morning!"

The ship was then diving down, and I tapped the message out very fast about three times and tried to get an "R" back from Candle (R = received), but the static was bad and I couldn't. I had to reel in the antenna in a hurry.

We landed in that blackness and came to a standstill in the middle of a big lagoon. We could just make out the dark outline of the shore and, to our great surprise, a light far off in the distance: an Eskimo tent fire, we thought.

C. poled down to see how deep it was—only about four feet! We decided we'd better anchor there and, taking parachutes for pillows, stretched out on our baggage in the front compartment (our warm flying suits on), feeling very lonely and faraway but safe.

About three o'clock in the morning I heard a funny put-put and voices.

"Hello!"

"Charles! What's that?" We both woke with a terrible start.

He jumped up, pushed back the cover, and saw two boats covered with skins, a small light in one, and dark faces.

"Hello," said C.

"Hello. We . . . hunt . . . duck."

"Oh," said C., "that's nice." It was rather surprising in the dead of night out in the "sticks."

"You . . . land here?"

"Yes," said C. "We came in for the night. You see many of these around here?"

"Yes . . . yes," said the man vaguely, not understanding at all.

"Get many ducks?" (What was one to make conversation about at 3:30 in the morning off Seward Peninsula?)

"Yes—get ducks."

"Well, guess I'll go back to bed." And they went off. The next morning we found we had spent the night in Shishmaref Inlet.

We had good radio communication all the way into Nome. We crossed our first mountains coming into Nome. The Bering Sea shone very blue beyond them and the ground was green. (We had gone quite far south from Point Barrow.)

We landed in a lagoonlike harbor—Safety Harbor, about thirty-five miles from Nome. There we got into a *car* and drove on a *road* into Nome. Such nice people met us—a Mr. and Mrs. Grant Jackson.

There were lots of flowers along the road: fireweed and monkshood and yarrow and deep purple iris. But they cannot grow vegetables there except in window boxes. Nome, right on the Bering Sea, is a little town of gray board houses all leaning one way or the other, like a cardboard movie set about to fall down. The houses were never painted, just weathered a sea gray, many of them completely deserted and boarded up after gold-rush days. Yet it had a busy, cheerful look: several stores with moccasins, ivory, drugs, provisions, etc. One big show glass window was *all* nasturtiums, a wall of nasturtiums! I thought they were paper decorations but they were growing vines from a window box inside.

Mr. and Mrs. Jackson took us into their four-room apartment in the tin bank building and gave us everything, including a running-water hot bath in a porcelain tub (!) and fresh milk (from a cow there in summer only). Mrs. Jackson used to sing over the radio and teach dancing. She said quite sadly that no one was interested in music or dancing in Nome.

Eskimos from King Island come up in big sealskin boats to Nome in the summer. They tip over their boats and make tents out of them. They have small sealskin kayaks, too, all covered up except for a hole where the man sits. They put on a race for us in the kayaks. The chief of the King Islanders won. He is a little taller and stands better and is stronger and dances better and hunts better than anyone else in the tribe. When he ceases to, he ceases to be chief. He also can turn a side somersault in his kayak in the water. I talked to his brother about the dance they gave. They wore eagle-feather caps on their heads or, part of the time, wolf's heads, and bangled gauntlets on their arms, and their movements were elastic and sudden like animals. He looked very pleased and then said gravely, *"My!"*

"My?" we asked him. "What do you mean?"

"My!" he said emphatically. *"My* brother, *my* son, *my* nephews —*my!"*

Nome to Karaginski Island was a long flight: all day long, the first part over fog, then, along the coast of Siberia, we flew over jagged mountains—volcanic, with glaciers on their sides. I didn't see much of the country because I was talking to Saint Paul Island all the way, every half hour, and part of the time to a Russian station and part of the time to *S.S. President Cleveland.* Charles shouted "Here we are!" and I just had time to pull in the antenna and look out.

It was quite green, with bushes growing and jagged mountains in the distance. Four well-built timber houses with peaked chimneys looked quite foreign. A small crowd (twenty-five, perhaps) was on the beach. Some, the conventional Russian picture—a blue smock over knee breeches, bearded face, cap, and high boots; some, native Eskimo (only they don't call them that)—two women in baggy blouses and short skirts. A little brown bear was following them around like a dog. A very nice-looking bobbed-haired young woman came out in the heavy flat-bottomed boat and greeted us in French.

Before I had time to finish *"Je comprends le Français et je parle un peu"* she said gaily, "Oh, I spik English." It was hard to understand at times, though. For instance, "The mother bear was kiled" (to rhyme with *child*) and then, "He will grow quite quite willd" (to rhyme with *killed*). It *is* illogical, isn't it? She was the only one who could speak English. She introduced us to her husband, tall and fair, and to a gruff unshaven man who stuttered fiercely and his wife, shy and smiling with sleek brushed hair tied into a knot on the back of her head.

They took us into a dark hall covered with skins, in through a skin-covered door, through a kitchen with a big stone oven, into a small room where we sat down after much bowing and gestures and smiled at each other. Then the sleek-haired one brought us fruit and fresh milk from a cow there, and meat and bread. Such good fresh food. And we took out our lunch basket, filled at Nome, and passed around meat sandwiches and butter cookies and milk-chocolate candies. They seemed to like that. They talked to each other, the girl trying to translate. Suddenly the two men went into gales of laughter. The girl laughed and asked us what day it was when we left Nome (the same day, of course— that morning). "Friday!"—"Yes, yes!" they laughed again. "It is Saturday here!" We had passed the 180th meridian and lost a day.

The bear, smelling food, nosed his way into the kitchen and stood up on his hind legs next to the table. Great shouts: "Oh, Dunya! Dunya! Dunya!"

They couldn't quite push him off because his nails were long and he was beginning to be a little unmanageable. So a boy rushed in with a piece of meat, held it to Dunya's nose, withdrew it, and the bear followed clumsily, shaking from side to side, out the door. But he grunted angrily outside when he discovered he couldn't get any more.

We slept in that room. A bunch of ermine were strung up on a hook on the wall, pictures of a favorite cat and a piece of embroidery of gnomes in a pine forest; a big chest-dresser for plates and food, the dining-room table, and a narrow bench. They brought a cot in for us—canvas stretched across boards—and we used the blankets off our bundles.

In the morning the bobbed-haired girl told me she was a zoologist studying the animals of the island for the summer. She lives in Moscow and has a little boy there. I said I had one too. They were very interested (both women) and asked how old, and where was he? Then, after discussing it in Russian together: "Have you a photograph?" shyly. So I took them out. They were sweet and gay about them—"Oh, oh"—and spread them all out on the table in a row and made big circles with their hands to show his big eyes. Then they pointed to the one they liked best, to the one that looked like Charles.

Tokyo, August 29th

Mother darling—

Before I start on Tokyo I want to tell you a little about Petropavlovsk. It was so interesting and different. A gem of a harbor set in steep green volcanic hills: gray roofs growing up the side of one of them, quite a large town with lots of construction work going on and a busy little harbor, a toy harbor, small but *very* deep. Big boats are hardly able to turn around there.

A terrific number of men met us, some in uniform (army), and we walked through crowds of workmen to get into an old but comfortable open car. They were cordial and gay and very considerate—I somehow had been prepared (Hindus' book[1]) for no

[1] Maurice Hindus, *Humanity Uprooted.*

courtesy at all—helping me over the muddy places, then we bumped up the steep dusty road that wound up the hill.

There were no crowds along the streets; lots of busy people walking back and forth on the wooden sidewalks minding their own business. With terrific speed we zigzagged across the road avoiding children, pigs, and bumps. (The children—also the pigs!—were healthy and happy-looking.)

The people on the whole were *very* healthy and happy-looking; not well dressed—simply, in old clothes, the women in baggy shirtwaists and *very* short skirts. The houses lining the road were all old, rather ramshackle but with great charm, the eaves carved and some painted. And all *packed* with busy people. The town hummed, except for the white church with boarded-up windows and high-grass-grown yard where some workman was stretched out for an afternoon siesta.

We went into the Government House, a big, rather old wooden building several stories high; through the hall, papered with large posters of tractors and laborers, also propagandist posters about capitalists; up into a nice corner room where they had put *three* cots—one screened off with an old Chinese embroidered screen—for Charles and me and a mechanic! Also two razors laid out for the two men and a bottle of perfume for me.

We had running water (from a gravity tank into a slop jar) and a basin right in the room. Then, after washing up, I took one of your (sweetened with note) headache powders—the first one I've had to take. (The trip from Nome to Karaginski was a hard, long one and we went right on the next morning.) Then we were brought a good meal of "black" bread, which C. has got very fond of (I always have been), pork, and lettuce and radishes in sour milk (which is delicious), and *very* sweet tea in a *glass,* and Russian chocolate and cookies.

The next night in Petropavlovsk they gave a dinner in the government building. All the officials of the town were there, and two women—the first I'd met.

The bare walls of the room were pasted with large posters and photographs of Lenin and other leaders (there are pictures or busts of Lenin in *every* government room). No one was dressed up at all; many of the men unshaven. Such nice men, though, gay and cordial. I sat next to the President of the committee—a quiet, good-humored man. He had previously worked for twenty years in a metal factory and now was head of the local governing committee.

We had a lavish dinner; plenty of everything, especially wine. And the great game was to make us drink by toasting everybody imaginable. Again and again C. and I would lift our glasses to our lips and yet the same amount remained in our glasses, which amused them beyond words. The most ardent and pressing person was a gay buxom girl who lifted her glass to me every moment: "Your son!" "Your mother!" "Your father!" "Your trip!" etc., etc., with sparkling eyes.

There were two or three people who spoke English, and I walked around town with one girl looking at schools, shops, etc., and asking questions. There were three schools in that little town. At thirteen years they begin to teach *anti*-religion. They are (according to the person who told me) afraid to start earlier for fear the child will ask, "Who is God?" and get an irremovable impression.

If a scientist needs extra money for experimental work he writes a request to the Zav (the local representative of the Communist Party—we did not meet him—he was away) and he is freely granted the expenses, though *not* allowed to travel. My charming guide with delicate humor explained to me that in the old days there was a high priest and he lived "up there," pointing to the best house in town, and the Governor did not dare do anything without running up the street to ask his blessing. "Now there is no priest but the Zav, and when the President of the local committee does not know what to do he quickly runs up the hill (pointing to the same house) to ask the Zav if he is doing right!"

We had quite an adventure the night before we left. We woke up to loud shouts about four in the morning, sharp staccato shouts falling abruptly one on another, and then a crash of breaking glass. C. leaped to the window. "That's a real shout. Either something's happened to the plane or there's a fire!" We could see the plane—safe—from our window. More shouts and the smell of smoke. Fire! "Quick, get dressed! Help me put these things together in the blanket—here, near the window—so we can throw them out if necessary." Windows open, curtains rolled up, all our things in blankets near the windows. "I'll come back!"

Then he opened the door. Clouds of smoke rushed in. He went out, back in a minute for a wet towel for his nose and mouth. "I'll come back. You can still go down the stairs, but . . . very easy jump—one story—out window."

I looked out at an easy drop, and one could catch hold of the sill below for the drop. Men were running down the hill toward us, carrying buckets.

It seemed like half an hour, then steps running down the hall; a loud knock. "Come in!" A frightened-looking man flung open the door and hesitated a moment. "O-pen win-dows!"—"Yes, I have," and he ran away, shutting the door.

Another wait. The voices subsided below in the street. Charles came back, laughing. "It's out." We pulled down the curtains and got back to bed. "A fire in one of the files downstairs; didn't get far, but this house would go like kindling if it got started."

In a few moments we were wakened by a "ting-a-ling" in the street below and the rattle of a cart. We looked out. A one-horse cart pulling a wound-up hose and small tank drew up to the door. Two men leaped out dramatically. They had brass bee's-nest helmets on their heads and shouted orders.

The fire engine!

Darling Mother,

How I love your letters. I haven't had time to write yet and I've gotten two from you. I've never wanted letters like this and never enjoyed them so much. I read them over and over, and take the last ones around in my purse everywhere and put them by my bed so when I pop into bed they are there to read before I turn the light off.

What you say about the baby sounds fine, so well and gay. I like everything you tell me about his playing, exploring your room while you write at your desk. I love to think of that, and crawling over the lawn with his blocks. And describing his curls coming out from his blue cap. All just what I want to hear. I *love* your dancing him at night. Oh, Mother, don't worry—I am very happy thinking about him with you. I know you will do just what is right for him.

I don't believe I can possibly catch up with myself in these letters, so I'll just have to hit the high spots. And you are getting more than I realized from the newspapers—only much exaggerated. We didn't have a bad time at all off Ketoi Island, and he tried to get down several places unsuccessfully and landed in *thick* fog finally—quite wonderfully.

He says we were never in danger, but I was so grateful to be down safely that nothing else mattered, except that I worried until we got communication—there was over an hour (two hours) there when we were taxiing, trying to find a quiet spot for anchorage, out of communication, and I didn't want them to get out a "crash" rumor. Really, it was a *glorious* relieved feeling to be safely anchored, to have gotten radio communication and to hear him, as I cut off, rushing on the news of our safe arrival.

Then we spread out the baggage smoothly in the baggage compartment up front (quite a big compartment where they took out a huge gas tank), then the soft flying suits on top, then the sleeping bag unrolled on top, and we stretched out into the front cockpit (C.'s feet had to go around a few corners) and slept *very* soundly (after a meal of sandwiches and chocolate).

We had made a radio schedule for the next morning, and in the middle of it we discovered the *Shinshiru Maru* alongside of us! Four jolly singing sailors with round navy caps rowed the radio operator out to us. He spoke broken English and was *terribly* nice and good to us, despite the fact that he touched the antenna climbing onto the plane and got quite a shock.

He was a smiling, apologetic little man, anxious to help, and really apologized for *being hurt*. He then asked C., "You a—a—have—a—a—cohhee?" which C. misunderstood for *"cooky"* and handed him some of our soft crumby yesterday Petropavlovsk cookies, which he ate very politely smiling and then patiently tried again, "You—a—a—have a—a cohhee?"

C.:?

Radio operator: "Cohhee on *sheep"*—pointing to the *Shinshiru Maru* and smiling. Finally we got it and clambered out, all smiles. (I've just had this read by C., who says it's none of it true and that he offered the cooky to be polite and also thinking that it might suggest breakfast to him.)

The *Shinshiru Maru* was quite a small boat—like a large sailboat with one good cabin—but it looked wonderful to us. We climbed down the steep ladder into the nice warm cabin where the handsome captain and two officers sat. Here the smiling radio operator left us to talk with our hands and went back to his work.

However, we managed very well. They seemed to understand everything before we spoke: hot water in a brass basin, towels, a comb, and cold cream, and (magically down the ladder) hot coffee and toast. You know most of the rest. We couldn't start the engine. The anchor rope broke and they rescued us from rocks. We wanted to save our battery (the engine charges the battery for the radio), so we used the *Shinshiru Maru's* radio for a while and had to be towed to a safer anchorage.

We had one rather rough night with quite a wind and we tossed around. It was raining and blowing—a bad night. About three o'clock in the morning C. was woken by a shout. We got up, swore a little, and peered out. There, tossing up and down on the wild sea, were the singing sailors holding up a telegram. C. snatched it from the staggering sailor and read something like this: "The Japanese people anxiously hope for you and wish message from you—signed, the *Nichi-Nichi* newspaper."

C. swore again, but answered it politely. The next morning we discovered that they'd come over to fix a stronger cable on us. The telegram was just thrown in extra.

The first night we slept on Japanese soil was at Buroton Bay, a little harbor with steep green volcanic hills on every side. It was still and twilight when we were towed in and we stepped onto the pebbly beach in front of the one house, thatched roof, a one-story bungalow with sliding doors to get in.

The host—keeper of a fox farm—bowed us in and served us unsweetened green tea out of handleless bowls and then offered us the one room, with lovely clean mats covering the floor (like the Chinese matting we used to have in our nursery). He took his shoes off and stepped up into the raised room, pulled out of a sliding-door closet three quilts (Japanese mattresses) which he laid one on top of the other for us. Then we took off our shoes and stepped up. There was nothing else in the room except a wooden box full of sand and charcoal (the stove). We pulled to the sliding papered doors and had a beautiful sleep.

The next morning we worked on the engine, the singing sailors helping us. When we finally got it started I was so excited I didn't look back till we got in the air and then turned back to see them all waving their arms off.

We set off for Nemuro again. This time we were warned (by radio) of bad weather before we got there and so landed at Shana in a lake full of water lilies and wild iris.

At Shana we stayed at our first Japanese inn. As you enter the sliding door there is a big step where everyone sits down to take off his street shoes. On top of the step are shuffly slippers—mules with no heels—to step into. The innkeeper and all his family and household are down on their knees bowing to greet you. Then you shuffle down halls, over boards that are just like satin—not a high polish but soft, as if rubbed smooth by many feet. The innkeeperess (in kimono, of course) shuffles ahead of us with quick little steps. Then she pushes back a sliding paper door, drops her slippers, and steps up onto the matted floor of our bedroom.

There were three people in the little town of Shana who spoke (very broken) English. Charles tried to ask, that night, for boiled rice, but they couldn't understand and wouldn't bring him any (we'd already been greeted at the town hall with cider and apples—and toasts). They brought in chairs and a table for us and some sweet pink cakes and coffee that tasted like weak cocoa. People serving you always bow before coming into the room. After this they spread out the quilts—with giggles putting *two* end to end for Charles!—and slid to the paper doors on all sides of us. They left cotton kimonos for us; all hotels provide these lovely cool clean kimonos.

The next morning we had a Japanese breakfast, sitting on our knees on the cushions. They brought little trays with legs on them (little lacquered tables) that just fit in front of each person. The tables are already set with five or six little dishes of food. All the dishes have covers and they are all sizes and shapes. We had (among other things I don't remember) fish soup in lacquer bowls, pickled beets and cucumbers, baked fish, and last of all a bowl of boiled rice—all eaten with chopsticks.

We left hurriedly that afternoon for (again!) Nemuro but came down in bad weather on a lake near a thatched-roof hut. It was raining hard and a man sculled out in a flat-bottomed boat. He wore very old ragged Western knickers. He helped us pull our ship up into the marshy grasses and tie it to a willow tree.

Then he motioned us to his hut. We pushed between the grasses up to his hut, took off our boots, and walked in: a hearth in the middle of the one room. By it sat an old man (in kimono) smoking a long pipe and a young boy (in kimono) carrying fresh fish.

We radioed our position after C. took out his map and got the man to show him where we were: Kunashiri Island. We tried to say "America," and pointed. Couldn't understand. Then we said New York, and a light came on the young boy's face: "New York!" They all talked together and smiled. Charles drew a map: "New York—Canada—Alaska—Siberia—Kamchatka—Chishima (Kurile)—Kunashiri," of which they only got New York and Chishima. Then we put our wet feet up against the fire and all smiled, the rain beating outside.

Charles drew a picture of a fish and pointed to his mouth. They laughed and started to cook fish and potatoes, which they gave us with their own chopsticks and rice and a little tea (quite precious). The old man took his pipe out of his mouth and offered it to us. I took my little list of words out of my pocket (I got someone at Shana to help me) and tried to say *"oishi"* (delicious!), which with my smiles and pointing to the fish could hardly be mistaken.

Again reading off the paper I said, *"(T)s(u)kareta"* (We are tired), *"toko"* (bed), *"hikoki"* (airplane), pointing out the door. They smiled and understood. We bowed our way out, trying to say *"Arigato"* (Thank you), but they couldn't understand. We said it consistently until we left the next morning and finally hit on the right pronunciation, and they understood just as we left!

During the night we were wakened by shouts. Some people had rowed from the nearest village with *six* bottles of beer for us, and some fruit.

The next morning again off to Nemuro after finding out (by radio) the weather was good. This time we got there in twenty-eight minutes. A big town—big harbor, lots of boats—and a huge crowd along the shore and docks. All the schoolboys with shaved heads and gray uniforms waving paper flags. The officials, Mayor, etc., out to meet us, and a Captain Swift—stationed at Sapporo—who was a tremendous help. Bouquets, cameras, reporters, crowds, as we pushed up the cobbled street to the Japanese hotel where we had a pretty corner room upstairs: sliding paper doors leading to a porch on two sides. Everything is so fresh and cool in a Japanese room, uncrowded, clean matting, bare paper walls, unpainted woods, and a place for one lovely *kakemono*. This one was an old Chinese poem (which no one could translate for me) and a few iris underneath.

First we asked for a bath. We hadn't had one since we left Nome—nothing but basin washing once a day in public, which is not very efficient. That bath was too divine. We poured basins of nice hot water over each other and washed everything—hair, teeth—and soaked under the water to get fleas off! And then felt renewed. Oh—marvelous!

At Nemuro we had our first Japanese dinner, given by the Mayor. We sat around in a square on cushions in a large matted room, C. sitting in front of the *tokonoma*, the place of honor. Then geisha girls, very gaily dressed (trailing kimono and stiff headdress), pass wine, dance, and generally entertain the company. They brought us each a little table with dishes of different sizes and shapes, and covered with a bird-cage to keep off flies. (You drink green tea before and after every meal and whenever you call on anyone, even if it's right after breakfast.) I think I counted over twenty different dishes, all strange to me. Your sauces are in separate little dishes.

Then the geisha danced for us: strange, posed dances, the face doll-like, without expression. The dance is with the hands and long kimono sleeves rather than with the feet, all in time to slow minor chants, quite beautiful. They never open the fingers, so you are not distracted from the simple gestures—swift and direct like the flight of birds.

At Nemuro we first had that strange impression of waking up

in the morning to the sound of many wooden geta shuffling along the cobbles. It sounds like hands clapping—a strange, almost musical sound.

[*September*]

Dear Mrs. Lindbergh,

I have never seen anything like the reception we got at Tokyo when we first arrived. Perhaps the early days when he came back to New York—were they like that? The car *pushed* through crowds of shouting people. First you'd see their eager peering faces, then lit up with a wild joy. Their hands would go up above their heads and shouts, *"Banzai! Banzai!"* (*"Banzai"* means, as you perhaps know, "ten thousand years!"—that is, "May you live ten thousand years!") In the beginning I got *Benjo*=toilet, much-used word, and *Banzai* mixed up. I'm afraid it gave the innkeepers quite a shock to see me shuffling down the corridors in a kimono and mules whispering to every person in the hall a questioning "Ten thousand years?"!

Charles has made a great hit by preferring Japanese food to American: rice (plain), unsweetened tea, raw fish, and eels all go down without a murmur. And they are amazed at the way he uses chopsticks; he even cuts lobster with them. (He learned eating on the boat *Shinshiru Maru*.)

I'm not as good and I only eat one piece of raw fish with each Japanese meal.

However, from now on we are only eating cooked foods and boiled water; they are not as careful in the south and in China.

As far as we can tell, we are going from here to Fukuoka (you'll read it all in the papers) and then straight to Nanking and then somehow to Peking. After two weeks or so in China we hope to go to the Philippines. After that we don't know, though C. says (only to me, and you) that we'll probably fly around home by way of either the Azores-Bermuda route or the South Atlantic route, Africa to South America—probably the latter.

This is the best-weather route and the most traveled, and we'll have radio communication all the way. If we do this we'll probably visit (or go through) the countries in South America that we haven't been in before: Brazil, Argentina, and up the West Coast. Of course this is tentative still, but I thought I'd tell you anyway.

I hope very much that if the house at Princeton is ready you could visit the baby there. I don't like him to be in Englewood all the time, and yet I don't quite like him in Princeton alone. I know there is your school and I don't like to press it. Of course the ideal thing would be if there was no school and he could go to Detroit and live quietly—very much like our life in Princeton —and crawl around your secluded garden. Or else if you and your brother would come and live in Princeton. I spoke to Elsie and Whateley about the possibility. Don't you think you could both arrange nervous breakdowns and need a complete change?

I'm not wishing one on you, but I'd feel very happy if you were there with him.

This is a fretful letter. I'm afraid I'm rather wanting to be back with the baby now. I rather counted on being back in the fall. But I can't fuss too much before Charles—it is such poor sportsmanship—when this *is* a marvelous experience. But I *am* thinking a good deal about that baby now summer is over. They're calling for us any minute: more sightseeing. Much love and *please* see the baby.

Kyoshintei Hotel, Hakata, Kyushu, September [18th?]
Mother darling—
Tomorrow early we leave for Nanking. I'll never catch up in letters. I wanted to tell you about the unofficial things in Tokyo. The fun I've had with Mrs. Neville,[1] wife of an Embassy staff member, in having a lesson in Japanese garden-making, in flower

[1] Mrs. Edwin Neville, wife of the U. S. Consul in Tokyo.

arrangement and its philosophy, a visit to the museum, being told about the tea ceremony by the very charming and cultured curator. Mother, please get and read in half an evening *The Book of Tea,* by Okakura Kakuzo. It is the essence of the Japanese philosophy. To read this and also to learn it from some of the people I've met here has been the most thrilling thing to me about this trip.

And then a morning through a park, where we watched the little boys chasing dragonflies with bamboo poles (stickum on the end) and crickets that they catch and sell in the stores for music (like canaries!). I have written down a very poignant poem told me about a mother whose boy is dead. It runs over and over in my mind.

> How far in chase today,
> I wonder, has gone my hunter
> Of the dragonfly?

Nanking, September 26th

Mother darling—

C. and I are crazy about China, from just coming onto it. For miles out in the China Sea you see mud from the Yangtze river,[1] then suddenly you are on China, and you gasp at the flat fields stretching as far as you can see, and the great flat river. Somehow it was intensified after leaving Japan, which is all accordion-pleated, coming to the great expanse of China. There is something magnificent about it. A feeling of its grandeur and age; every bit of land is cultivated in small narrow strips, not at all like our great plains in the West. Through the Middle West, where there is so much farmland, you get the feeling of space and few people. But here it is almost terrifying: no trees, no wild land, nothing left but narrow, back-yard strips of fields, and mud huts representing thousands of people as far as one can see. For

[1] The Yangtze river was in major flood.

what ages have they been there along the banks of that old massive river!

Nanking was quite a shock to me: it's really just a country town that's been made into a capital—very few modern buildings. The first thing you notice is a great wall that surrounds the whole city, and *twice* as much fields as city. They expected us to land on the river. The buildings and huts were flooded up to the doors and all the people had gone out to the docks in sampans. We landed, though, on a lake just outside the wall— quite a lovely spot, with willows and lots of sampans poling around—and walked into the city through an old gate.

Nanking is the strangest place. You keep wondering just *where* it is. Most of the old city (except the wall) has been destroyed by wars, and they are just beginning to put up new buildings and widen the streets. But there is a lot of color and character in the people. Everyone seems to wear blue (it is the cheapest dye). There is the fierce strong blue of the rickshaw driver's ragged coat (*lots* of rickshaws here). His coat flaps in the breeze and his glistening brown skin makes the blue even stronger. He really "trots" down the street pulling his black or red rickshaw. All workmen on the roads and everywhere wear this color, their trousers rolled halfway up their bare legs.

We have walked through some of the streets of the old city, so narrow two rickshaws could hardly pass, cobblestoned, with open shops on both sides: clay brick buildings, *dark*, no windows, bright signs on the fronts. The street is a bustling line of rick- shaws ringing their warning bells, of long-gowned men and women, of vendors balancing a pole carrying a small stove on one end and a basket of food on the other—traveling restaurant. They sing their wares or knock on a hollow bamboo stick to attract passers-by.

In the open shops a man will be standing on a counter waving the rippling lengths of silk out toward the crowd and *singing* (really singing) the praises. The shops are full of such strange assortments: golden-oak chiffoniers, Chinese carved teakwood stands, flowered European spittoons, silks, all kinds of paper, beaded bright headgear and ornaments (for weddings, funerals, and births), a bar with great green porcelain jars of liquor of some kind.

Along the bridges over canals they spread out wares in open markets: fish and eels in a tub, vegetables, lotus roots, fruits, and sprays of sweet-smelling wild olive; a little boy here with his tiny silver fish squeezed in his palm, trying to sell them.

We met Chiang ("jang") Kai-shek (President and Generalissimo) and Mrs. Chiang the other day. He is a keen, straight, quick, military man and his wife a Wellesley graduate, quite beautiful and very clever, not at all second fiddle to him.

I dream about the baby every night, almost, and am quite homesick for you. But I want to see Peking before I start home.

September 28th

This letter doesn't say half enough about this place, or why I love it and want you here. I am reminded of Mexico all the time: poor dirt houses with thatched roofs and dirt floors (they do use stools, though, instead of the mats of the Japanese). Children with runny noses and sores on their heads, and the terrific labors the men endure—bearers of poles carrying two heavy baskets, or four big sacks of grain on one man's shoulder. But the streets do somehow remind me too: a man patting out dirty-white doughy cakes, a man stirring chestnuts in a big bowl of hot cinders, a woman washing lettuce in a copper bowl (the water looks soapy, as though used for many other things first), a little boy going to the john.

A carriage, stopped in the center of traffic while the passenger and driver argue about fare. Its stopping causes the rickshaw behind to collide with the pole of a cotton carrier. The rickshaw driver drops the shafts of his cart to harangue with the cotton carrier. Up swing the shafts and back goes the silk-gowned passenger onto the street. You can't hear him shout, there's so

Anne Lindbergh with Charles, Jr., Princeton, N. J., autumn, 1930

Mrs. E. L. L. Lindbergh with Charles, Jr., Princeton, N. J.

*Learning to fly in
Bird airplane,
Long Island Aviation
Country Club,
May, 1931*

Anne Lindbergh and Charles, Jr., Next Day Hill, summer, 1931

Charles, Jr., summer, 1931

First birthday of Charles, Jr., June 22, 1931

Packing equipment before take-off from Ottawa, Ontario, August 1, 1931

AT LEFT, ABOVE   *Anne and Charles Lindbergh and Bird biplane, Deacon Brown's Point, North Haven, Maine*

AT LEFT   *Anne and Charles Lindbergh at College Point, Long Island, en route to Washington, the starting point for their trip to the Orient, July 27, 1931*

After landing at Aklavik on flight to Tokyo, August 5, 1931

*On a bank of the Mackenzie River, preparing for the flight
from Aklavik to Point Barrow, Alaska*

Point Barrow, Alaska, August 9, 1931.
Dr. Greist on Colonel Lindbergh's right

Eskimos welcome the Lindberghs on their arrival at Nome,
Alaska, August 11, 1931

Charles, Jr., at North Haven,
with Peter, Skean, Bogey, Pim, summer, 1931

much noise already. He's in such an undignified position that he has to laugh getting out. Lots of little boys (with heads all shaved in different ways, each way to ward off some disease) stand around and gape at him. Then a high-squeaking wheelbarrow shoves them on.

Flying from Wuhu to Hankow, September 30th

Mother darling,

I am sitting in the baggage compartment this time because we are carrying a Dr. Borcic of the Rockefeller Institute to various places in the flooded area, and he surveys the land from my seat. It is quite comfortable and I can see out of the baggage compartment hatch hole.

Our first surveys we did alone,[1] I doing the flying and C. the sketching and mapping. The first day was terribly shocking: the area east of the Grand Canal from Nanking to Peking flooded by both the river and the grand canal—you just can't believe the extent. Looking as *far* as you can see on all sides, nothing but water and the tops of trees, collapsed thatched roofs, and here and there a smear of brown on the surface, where a mud village or house was, or a road.

They estimated that the square miles we covered that day would equal the state of Massachusetts—as though you put Lake Superior down on top of Massachusetts. And there is *no* higher ground, therefore no large collections of refugees easily reached and helped. We passed thousands of small groups: two or three mud huts, pathetic little mud dikes frantically built up around them to keep the water out. They have usually pulled their grain stacks in with them, though often these are halfway in water.

They got one harvest, and C. says probably still have enough to

---

[1] On landing at Nanking, the Lindberghs learned that millions of people were homeless and starving, that it was essential for relief organizations to know the limits of the flood, and that theirs was the only plane in China with enough range to discover these limits. They relaid their plans and began charting in on a map the extent of the floodwaters.

live on—those who weren't drowned. But there is not much hope of the water *really* going down before spring and certainly not in time this fall to get a winter crop. They *can't* all be reached. There are no roads left, of course, and no rivers for big boats; miles and miles of water to be covered only by sampans. (Some whole families are living floating in sampans.)

There are too many individual groups: isolated thousands. It seems quite hopeless.

We have just left Wuhu (to rhyme with Boohoo!). The flood is very bad around there but people are not so far from help. It is hilly country and there are uninjured towns and crops near. We landed on a field—or several flooded fields—and the sampans and *tubs* full of people gathered around. I thought they were large wooden washtubs at first, but apparently they are made for some kind of fishing. A man squats inside and with one paddle (like butter-ball patters) in each hand he steers along. A woman in a sampan kept shouting at me and then, seeing I didn't understand, made a cup out of her hand and with the other imitated using chopsticks; she wanted food. But C. wouldn't let me—we had only a sandwich or two—as we would have been mobbed.

The other day he and two doctors landed outside some completely flooded city [Hinghwa]. Sampans gathered. One doctor got out and then they handed out a bag full of medicines—antitoxins, serum, etc. The minute they saw the bag they thought *"food!"* and mobbed the doctor and the bag. His sampan sank, the bag sank, and they started climbing over the plane. C. had to (this is not for publication) get out a revolver and fire once into the air in order to get the doctor (who was Chinese and talking as hard as he could) back and get away. They will have to send provisions and supplies in an armed boat.

However, at Wuhu, relief work is being done. There are free food-distributing places. Later in the afternoon we took off and were able to land in a flooded field next to the hospital, which is built on a high hill. (The Chinese don't live on hills but in the valleys near their fields. The hills are covered with grain, usually.)

We got into a sampan and started for the hospital over a flooded field, across a broken dike—the river water was still rushing through it with such current that they couldn't pole the boat through. So we all got out and stood on the mud dike until they pulled the boat through. Across another field, up a flooded road (where the sampan scraped the bottom) to the bottom of the hill where we could walk up. A group of modern brick houses there.

Dr. and Mrs. Brown (head of the hospital) took us into their home, where we met all the American staff of doctors and nurses and some missionaries.

Their fine big modern hospital is, of course, full. The majority of cases are tubercular and dysentery. Most of the surgical cases, I was surprised to hear, are people shot, burned, or tortured by bandits asking for money or food.

The streets of Wuhu are flooded, but people go along in sampans and rickshaws and the shopkeepers put boards across their chairs and tables and go right on selling things or, if the flood gets higher, build a hasty second floor above the dirty water. You walk above the water in the streets on planks stretched above wooden horses.

In all the flooded fields there is fishing (which is saving many lives). The Chinese say the reason one can always find fish in a field that's just been flooded is that in a dry year the grasshopper eggs become grasshoppers, but in a wet year they become fish!

En route to Shanghai, H. M. S. Hermes [*early October*]
Elisabeth darling—
I am breaking all regulations by being the first woman passenger on board the British airplane carrier *Hermes.* The Admiral who gave permission is a darling and his name is Colin MacLean, which I'm sure has something to do with it.

It is a great holiday feeling, and I feel about fourteen, quite deliciously shy and thrilled with the bugles and salutes and uniforms, and running up and down ladders. Can you remember how we felt on our first trip abroad—or no, in Panama, only (praise be) I am *not* really shy and Charles is always there. But I find myself hanging on to him as I did to you in the cabin. "Oh, Charles, please don't go up without me. If I go up alone someone will feel they'll have to talk to me and . . ."

Last night they had a celebration: the anniversary of their commissioning. Speeches and toasts with funny quips, and explosions of laughter periodically from different parts of the room. And I longed for you so that we could get together as at fourteen and sixteen and sit on the edge of the bunk and whisper, "Which one do *you* like best?"—"Oh, *do* you? So do I! You *would* like the same one I did, and he moved over and sat next to you, too. He likes you best."—"Oh, I don't know. *You* were talking to the one they call 'The Queen Bee.' "—"I liked the one that played the guitar too. Did you hear him say . . ."

And so on, far into the night.

All this is because we turned over in "the treacherous Yangtze" and the *Hermes* has very gallantly offered to take the plane and us to Shanghai for repairs. We haven't seen any reports of the accident. I wonder how it got back—probably exaggerated. It was not really dangerous, though exciting. The current in the Yangtze is very swift and strong. It seems to be *tearing* by an anchored ship. The plane got its wing in the water the day before. If it gets a little crooked in the current then the crane is pulling it one way and the current another.

This day C. put me in the back with a life preserver on—a collapsed one. You are supposed to turn the lever and the carbon dioxide bottle inside breaks and inflates it. Two men stood outside on the top of the plane hanging on to the pulley. (They both had life preservers on; men working on the ship all wear them.) The pulley dropped us from the deck beautifully straight facing the current, but then the engine or the current pulled us out away from the ship. The men could not release the cable, and the pontoon and wing were drawn down into the water. The current then pulling *against* the cable started turning us over.

Charles shouted, "Look out there in the back!" And I pulled my belt open.

"Jump!" (The wing in the water was acting as a pivot and turning the ship over.) I stood up.

"Jump quickly."

So I went—strangely enough, without the slightest hesitation or fear, and yet thinking calmly as I went under, "I am jumping up-current and the ship is falling over in that direction. I'll probably get hit."

The next second I was up and *down*-current from the plane— I'd slipped right *under* it. My life belt was flapping at my sides ignominiously, but it was surprisingly easy to swim; no feeling of fear or choking or anything. I knew how to swim and felt at home. Charles had watched me jump and go under and then dove. When he came up, "There was little Anne Pan, perfectly happy paddling along like a little mud turtle."

I looked back and saw him, mouth closed, smiling and coming toward me—also the other two men. We reached the tender and climbed up (a few seconds), all four at once, and all saying, "All right"—"All right"—"All right." The first thing I thought of was, "Think of the weeks I have been brushing my teeth in boiled water and then I swallow buckets of this Yangtze mud!"

Then I looked back and saw bits of the wood and fabric breaking off the wing that was in the water and felt quite sick for that dear old plane—to come all the way across Canada, Alaska, Siberia, the Kurile Islands fog, just to be smashed like a matchbox in a few seconds in the Yangtze current. The plane was about upside down now, but still held by the cable. Something dropped out. "There goes a parachute. Let's save that," C. shouted, and I thought, "I suppose that's all we *will* save."

Then, dripping, I was led down to the Captain's cabin and given someone's shirt, someone's shorts, someone's long white cotton socks, and a hanky and some hot tea and hot Bovril and offered brandy and castor oil to kill the germs of the Yangtze inside me!

It took quite a while to get the ship righted, but they did it very skillfully with not much more harm done to it, and hoisted it on deck. There was a good hunk taken out of the wing, and the cables had torn part of the fuselage out when it snapped right side to. But the plane looks surprisingly whole, and *nothing* was lost; my coat, the package of radio papers, even a nicely done-up lunch all came out intact, soaked, of course, but all there. The radio still worked.

I felt quite exhilarated because I have been afraid of an accident, and of being dragged out of life terrified. I don't want to die that way—screaming. But I don't think you do—you are spared that. There is no time for fear or much consciousness in an accident. It is over in three seconds; even if you can realize the danger, as I did, it does not frighten you at all—you are outside of it. C. says, though, that even if I'd been hit I wouldn't have been badly hurt. It wasn't as dangerous as it seemed for a moment.

But I'm still wondering about what flashed through my mind. One of the first things: "How long will it take to repair, and *when* will we get home?"

En route to Cheyenne, Wyoming, October[1]

Darling Con,

Yesterday at Victoria I got a package of mail, and as soon as it was light enough to read in the plane I started in: two terrific

---

[1] The Lindberghs planned to have their plane repaired at Shanghai, but on October 5th, while still on the *Hermes*, A. M. L. received a cable from her mother telling her of her father's death. They then decided to go home by ship and to send their plane back to the Lockheed Aircraft factory in California for reconditioning. At Vancouver A. M. L. received the first

letters from Mother and Elisabeth, then a warm one from you, which I needed.

But I wanted the details terribly. All the way back I have been tortured in feeling that I *cannot* touch the reality of his death (or death at all); perhaps I never shall. I tossed between an uncontrollable physical emotion, a temporary spasm, and long numb periods when I could look at it all from a great peak in time and space, as a statesman in England now who did not know him might deplore the loss of a great man in the world, or as someone might say reading in history, "If only Dwight Morrow had lived to take hold of such and such a situation."

And always between me and reality lay either the veil of emotion or a veil of time. The letters helped a lot because they brought it to me passionately, but not completely—too emotionally.

Not to realize, not to think, works very well when you're out with people or working. But you keep pushing and pushing it back in your mind until it recoils and jumps back at you—not true, clear, calm realization, but the pendulum swings too far, and it's just an emotional spasm.

It has been so much easier for me, with Charles, and then strangers to steel me to a calm. I cannot conceive of what it must have been for you and everyone at home. But I won't go over it, though it does seem to me strange that Daddy, who would be the most magnificent about death, cannot be here to explain and show us its reality. He would look at it calmly and deeply and sanely. I can only try to look at it as some kind of great cycle turning in the earth—a broad, impersonal cycle of birth, life, and death. Do you know Masefield's poem that ends:

> ". . . and we, who pass like foam,
> Like dust blown through the streets of Rome,
> Change ever, too; we have no home,

---

family letters about D. W. M.'s death, to which this letter, written in the air, is an answer.

Only a beauty, only a power,
Sad in the fruit, bright in the flower,
Endlessly erring for its hour,

But gathering as we stray, a sense
Of Life, so lovely and intense,
It lingers when we wander hence,

That those who follow feel behind
Their backs, when all before is blind,
Our Joy, a rampart to the mind."

Englewood [*November 12th*]

Dear Mrs. Lindbergh—

I have not written for so long and there's so much I wanted to tell you. Perhaps I should tell you first that in one of the early (code) cables from home they told me you were coming to the service for my father. The service meant a great deal to Mother, and that you should come meant more than you can realize. Any tribute to him they appreciated terribly—we all do.

It is good to be home—and oh, the baby! He is a boy, a strong independent boy swaggering around on his firm little legs. He did not know us but was not afraid of us—not at *all* afraid of C., which pleased C. tremendously. He began to take such interest in the baby—playing with him, spoiling him by giving him cornflakes and toast and sugar and jam off his plate in the morning and tossing him up in the air. After he'd done that once or twice the boy came toward him with outstretched arms. "Den!" ("Again!") C. admits the boy is "good-looking" and "pretty interesting." We gave him one of your red apples to play with, thinking he'd just play ball with it. Not at all; he knew it was much too good an apple to play ball with and immediately dug his four front teeth into it!

Did Mother or Elisabeth tell you that he takes your lamb or pussycat (*always* holding it by that nice tail) every night to bed with him, especially the lamb (he can say "Baa"), which he hides under the bedclothes and then brings out with glee—a game of hide-and-go-seek. The first time he saw the duck he laughed; he was a little afraid of the noise when C. pulled it after him, but he couldn't help laughing at it. We've not yet got him to pull it.

I am so happy about Thanksgiving. I can't wait to have you see the boy. I wonder if you will say he looks as C. did. C. himself says his hair was *just* like that. They say the house will be done by then—of course that means papering and painting—but not the curtains or anything, and all the furniture is borrowed and temporary, but I think it will be fairly comfortable. It will just be you and C. and the baby and I. We spent a weekend down there before they started painting. Wahgoosh looks weightier and *much* better. He was *sweet* with the baby, who was not afraid of him and ran up to him saying "Bowwow."

C. is going to Panama but he'll be back in Miami on the 23rd, he says. I'm not going, but staying with Mother.

Cleveland [November 16th]

Dear Con—

We are in Cleveland, Mother and I. I feel as if I had stepped out of life into a quiet backwater, the way you feel if you step from a roaring city street into a small park where there are only children rolling hoops and nurses slowly wheeling baby carriages and old people sitting watching and time is a long peaceful sigh.

Oh, Con, you should see Charlie going to school.[1] The first day he went the children all made a great fuss of him, crowding around, and the littlest boy who hitherto had had a fuss made of him punched him in the back. Charlie sat down and cried. He was utterly bewildered; that anyone should hurt him *purposely*—that hadn't entered his life before.

The teacher and children tried to keep Donald from Charlie,

[1] The Little School in Englewood, which was started by E. R. M. and Constance Chilton.

but he ran around and as soon as Charlie stopped crying he would hit him again, take his shovel away from him, and pull his hair. I saw him do it *five* times. They're all fascinated by his curls. One little girl tried to scrape them off like effervescent golden froth with a trowel. Consequently Charlie cried most of the first three days.

When I suggested he might be too young (he's a month and a half younger than Elisabeth takes them, and six months younger than any child there) the whole staff of the Little School got on its mettle, working on schemes to give Charlie individual attention. Four teachers stood out in the yard watching him and a conference was called with Dr. [David] Mitchell.[1]

Finally it was decided that he should play alone in the sandbox for a while, "getting accustomed to his environment" before the horde of children burst on him "to make social adjustments." In the meantime Charlie is perfectly happy playing in the sandbox or rustling in the leaves, completely and superciliously unconscious of his social obligations.

Con, I am crazy to have you see the house. I have enough modern papers to shock the architect and am now looking for some *modern* chintzes. I don't think I can stand any more bunches of flowers, especially roses; there's something about a cretonne rose that sickens me—bulbous and insipid.

Englewood [*December*]

Dear Mrs. Lindbergh:
I have been in bed for over a week with a kind of ptomaine poisoning. I am better. But that's why I've not written about Christmas and you've had no word. I *was* planning to be in Princeton by now, getting things ready, and I'm still in bed. There has been some doubt whether I could get down there for Christmas, but I think now I can, though things will be pretty helter-skelter.

[1] Consulting psychologist for The Little School.

C. says your vacation begins the day before Christmas, so perhaps you could just get there for Christmas. I think it would be lots of fun. We're not going to make much of Christmas, except for the boy. We will stay down there, as long as you can stay with us. I am so crazy to have you see C. Jr. The doctor says there's nothing wrong with him except he needs a haircut! But I don't want to cut his curls off till you see him. He has great fun with his father now. C. says "Hi, Buster" to him whenever he sees him, so the other day when Charles came into the room the baby looked up and said "Hi! Hi!" and the other day when C. left the room the baby said, "Hi all gone."

HOUR OF LEAD

Introduction

For other sections of my diary and letters I have tried to fill in by an introduction a factual background of the events of my life at the period. This section (1932) hardly needs any explanation. The bare facts are that on the evening of March 1, 1932, our eighteen-months-old child, Charles Lindbergh, Jr., was taken from his crib in our home near Hopewell, New Jersey, and a note was left on the window sill from the kidnapper demanding a ransom for his safe return. After ten weeks of negotiation and contact with the kidnapper and the handing over of the demanded ransom, the dead body of the child was found in the woods a few miles from our home. Newspapers of the time are full of accounts of the tragedy and books were written about the crime. In this period my diary reappears, and a series of letters to my mother-in-law, written almost daily after the kidnapping, give a full account of the progress of the case as we lived through it.

What needs to be explained are not outer facts but certain inner mysteries. How could I have written those letters which I have only recently recovered? I had not seen them since the day they were written. They were carefully put away among my mother-in-law's papers. When I first reread them, I was shocked and bewildered. How could I have been so self-controlled, so calm, so factual, in the midst of horror and suspense? And, above all, how could I have been so hopeful? Ten weeks of faithfully recorded details have the emotional unreality of hallucination. It was, of course, a nightmare, as my mother wrote at the time from Hopewell. "It changes but it is still a nightmare." The letters to my mother-in-law confirm the impression: "It is impossible to describe the confusion we are living in—a police station downstairs by day—detectives, police, secret service men swarming in and out—mattresses all over the dining room and other rooms at night. At any time I may be routed out of my bed so that a group of detectives may have a conference in the room. It is so terrifically unreal that I do not feel anything." Here is one key to the mystery.

Another key was hope. After the first shock, we were, to begin with, very hopeful for the safe return of the child. Everyone around us—friends, advisers, detectives, police—fed us hope, and it was this hope I tried to pass on to my mother-in-law. ("In a survey of 400 cities, 2000 kidnapped children returned." "Never in the history of crime has there been a case of a gang bargaining over a dead person.")

Not only was I surrounded by hopeful people, I was surrounded by disciplined people. The tradition of self-control and self-discipline was strong in my own family and also in that of my husband. The people around me were courageous and I was upheld by their courage. It was also necessary to be disciplined, not only for the safety of the child I was carrying but in order to work toward the safe return of the stolen child. As in war, or catastrophe, there was a job to be done. The job and hundreds of dedicated people working with us for the same end kept us going.

Also, as in war, the case, like a great bubbling cauldron of life itself, threw up both evil and good. Greed, madness, cruelty, and indifference were countered by goodness, devotion, self-sacrifice, and courage. There were people who fluttered around the flame of publicity, politicians who came and posed for pictures next to the kidnapper's ladder. There was one city official, acting as self-appointed investigator, who woke me in the middle of the night and asked me to re-enact his theory of the crime, which ended with the imaginary throwing of a baby into the furnace. And there were friends who left their homes and lives and slept on the floor of our house in order to help us. We were upheld by the devotion, loyalty, hopes, and prayers of many.

But after six weeks of unsuccessful efforts, after the ransom had been paid and no child was returned, after the clues began to run out, hope dwindled. I found it necessary, while trying to keep a surface composure for my husband, my family, and those working for and with us, to give way somewhere to the despair banked up within me. For sanity's sake I went back to writing in my diary, two days before the body of the child was found.

A second mystery, however, both for myself and the reader, is why publish this material at all? Why expose the pain and horror of a tragedy forty years ago? Tragedy is the common lot of man. "So many people have lost children," I remind myself in the diary several weeks after our own loss. So many, I might have added, have lost husbands, wives, sweethearts, parents, whole families.

Horror, perhaps, is not as universal, and yet, looking back over the last forty years, what horrors have been experienced not only by individuals but by masses of people in the world; the holocausts of war, of civilian bombing, of concentration camps, of torture, of gas chambers, of mass executions, of Hiroshima and Nagasaki, of lynchings and civil rights murders, and "simply" of street crime that has risen in our cities to unheard of heights. Does not this vast accumulation of horrors dwarf out of any meaning a single crime that happened long ago in a period when crime was not as frequent? Its rarity, along with the blaze of publicity that surrounded it, was one reason why it shocked the world.

The first answer to the question, and the simplest, is that this tragedy is such an inextricable part of my story that it cannot be left out of an honest record. Much that was written about the crime in the newspapers of the time was concocted of rumors, gossip, and fabrication. Consistent with my original premise in releasing this autobiographical material, I believe a fuller personal account of the experience should be left.

But a deeper reason moving me to publish is that suffering—no matter how multiplied—is always individual. "Pain is the most individualizing thing on earth," Edith Hamilton has written. "It is true that it is the great common bond as well, but that realization comes only when it is over. To suffer is to be alone. To watch another suffer is to know the barrier that shuts each of us away by himself. Only individuals can suffer."

Suffering is certainly individual, but at the same time it is a universal experience. There are even certain familiar stages in suffering, and familiar, if not identical, steps in coming to terms with it, as in the healing of illness—as, in fact, in coming to terms with death itself. To see these steps in another's life can be illuminating and perhaps even helpful.

What I am saying is not simply the old Puritan truism that "suffering teaches." I do not believe that sheer suffering teaches. If suffering alone taught, all the world would be wise, since everyone suffers. To suffering must be added mourning, understanding, patience, love, openness, and the willingness to remain vulnerable. All these and other factors combined, if the circumstances are right, *can* teach and *can* lead to rebirth.

But there is no simple formula, or swift way out, no comfort, or easy acceptance of suffering. "There is no question," as Katherine Mansfield wrote, "of getting beyond it"—"The little boat enters the dark fearful gulf and our only cry is to escape— 'put me on land again.' But it's useless. Nobody listens. The shadowy figure rows on. One ought to sit still and uncover one's eyes."

Contrary to the general assumption, the first days of grief are not the worst. The immediate reaction is usually shock and numbing disbelief. One has undergone an amputation. After shock comes acute early grief which is a kind of "condensed presence"—almost a form of possession. One still feels the lost limb down to the nerve endings. It is as if the intensity of grief fused the distance between you and the dead. Or perhaps, in reality, part of one dies. Like Orpheus, one tries to follow the dead on the beginning of their journey. But one cannot, like Orpheus, go all the way, and after a long journey one comes back. If one is lucky, one is reborn. Some people die and are reborn many times in their lives. For others the ground is too barren and the time too short for rebirth. Part of the process is the growth of a new relationship with the dead, that *"véritable ami mort"* Saint-Exupéry speaks of. Like all gestation, it is a slow dark wordless process. While it is taking place one is painfully vulnerable. One must guard and protect the new life growing within—like a child.

One must grieve, and one must go through periods of numbness that are harder to bear than grief. One must refuse the easy escapes offered by habit and human tradition. The first and most common offerings of family and friends are always distractions ("Take her out"—"Get her away"—"Change the scene"—"Bring in people to cheer her up"—"Don't let her sit and mourn" [when it is mourning one needs]). On the other hand, there is the temptation to self-pity or glorification of grief. "I will instruct my sorrows to be proud," Constance cries in a magnificent speech in Shakespeare's *King John*. Despite her words, there is no aristocracy of grief. Grief is a great leveler. There is no highroad out.

Courage is a first step, but simply to bear the blow bravely is not enough. Stoicism is courageous, but it is only a halfway house on the long road. It is a shield, permissible for a short time only. In the end one has to discard shields and remain open and vulnerable. Otherwise, scar tissue will seal off the wound and no growth will follow. To grow, to be reborn, one must remain vulnerable—open to love but also hideously open to the possibility of more suffering.

Remorse is another dead end, a kind of fake action, the only kind that seems possible at the moment. It is beating oneself in a vain attempt to make what *has* happened *"un*-happen." ("If only I had done thus and so, it might not have been.") Remorse is fooling yourself, feeding on an illusion; just as living on memories, clinging to relics and photographs, is an illusion. Like the food offered one in dreams, it will not nourish; no growth or rebirth will come from it.

The inexorably difficult thing in life, and particularly in sorrow, is to face the truth. As Laurens Van der Post has written: "One of the most pathetic things about us human beings is our touching belief that there are times when the truth is not good enough for us; that it can and must be improved upon. We have to be utterly broken before we can realize that it is impossible to better the truth. It is the truth that we deny which so tenderly and forgivingly picks up the fragments and puts them together again."

Undoubtedly, the long road of suffering, insight, healing, or rebirth, is best illustrated in the Christian religion by the suffering, death, and resurrection of Christ. It is also illustrated by the story of Buddha's answer to a mother who had lost her child. According to the legend, he said that to be healed she needed only a mustard seed from a household that had never known sorrow. The woman journeyed from home to home over the world but never found a family ignorant of grief. Instead, in the paradoxical manner of myths and oracles, she found truth, understanding, compassion, and eventually, one feels sure, rebirth.

But when all is said about the universality of tragedy and the long way out, what can be added to human knowledge or insight by another example? I can only say that I could not bear to expose this story if I did not believe that one is helped by learning how other people come through their trials. Certainly I was strengthened by the personal experience of others. It is even helpful to learn the mistakes made. As the reader will see, I am familiar with the false roads: stoicism, pride, remorse, self-pity, clinging to scraps of memories. I have not named them all; they are legion. I tried most of them. The fact that, in our case, horror was added to suffering does not change its fundamental character. The overlay of crime, horror, or accident on loss *does* increase suffering, but chiefly, I have come to feel, because it delays healing. It separates one from "the long way out," the normal process of mourning, of facing reality, of remaining open, and of eventual rebirth.

My own recovery, I realize, was greatly furthered by the love, understanding, and support of those around me. But I was also indebted to many unknown friends who had gone before me and left their testimony to illumine the shadowy path. In return I leave my own record, bearing witness to my journey, for others who may follow.

"It is, after all," as another writer has stated, "the only treasure, the only heirloom we have to leave—our own little grain of truth." Truth that is locked up in the heart—or in a diary—is sterile. It must be given back to life so that "the hour of lead"—of others—may be transmuted.

A decade later, when our tragedy was behind us, buried and overlaid with new life, I wrote a poem which described this transmutation, as I had experienced it. It was one of those poems that shoot up whole, a spear of insight, from some deep unconscious level. Although it outdates this diary by many years, it says in essence what I have tried to cover in these pages, and is, perhaps, a fitting end to my introduction.

SECOND SOWING

For whom
The milk ungiven in the breast
When the child is gone?

For whom
The love locked up in the heart
That is left alone?
That golden yield
Split sod once, overflowed an August field,
Threshed out in pain upon September's floor,
Now hoarded high in barns, a sterile store.

Break down the bolted door;
Rip open, spread and pour
The grain upon the barren ground
Wherever crack in clod is found.

There is no harvest for the heart alone;
The seed of love must be
Eternally
Resown.

1932

Mother darling,

I have been wicked not to write, but most of the writing has been on the trip.[1] It goes slowly, but one chapter I like, the stop in Maine. I have hardly mentioned the family or anything that happened, have not described good-bys, but I simply let myself go emotionally in writing it, hoping somehow that pure description written under emotion may somehow be tinged and heightened by it—as Amey says the sides of old barns in Edward Hopper's paintings have an emotional content. Perhaps it ought not to go into the book but I had such complete satisfaction in writing down and expressing some of the joy, the *supreme* joy I had in that twenty-four hours.

Isn't it wonderful that it should have meant so much to me at the time,[2] instead of looking back now and saying, "If only I had appreciated it." I *did* appreciate. It was one of those rare times when not only are you fully aware emotionally of your joy but somehow all the appreciation of a lifetime is balanced miraculously on that pinpoint in time—like a bee tasting a whole summer in one honeysuckle! I tried in writing to re-create that feeling and went to your drawer to get out the letter written from Ottawa, hoping I had put some of it down. Do you know what I put down? Only that poem:

"But gathering as we stray, a sense
Of Life, so lovely and intense,
It lingers when we wander hence,

[1] A. M. L. had started writing an account of the previous summer's flying trip which eventually was published under the title *North to the Orient*.

[2] A. M. L. is referring to her good-by to her family in Maine at the start of the flying trip to the Orient. It was the last time she saw her father.

That those who follow feel behind
Their backs, when all before is blind,
Our Joy, a rampart to the mind. . . ."

[JOHN MASEFIELD]

Isn't that strange.

[*Hopewell*], *Sunday* [*February 7th*]

Dear Mrs. Lindbergh,

C. Jr. is trying to stand on his head and look at me upside down through his legs! I have been dreadful about writing chiefly because any writing has been taken up in two things. 1) Charles was asked to speak over the radio for the China Flood Relief and he wants me to do it. Of course it will be very short and purely descriptive, and I'll read it. But it gives me a nightmare to think about. 2) Charles has been (both of us, in fact) urged to write about the trip and he wants me to do it, so I am trying to, though no one knows it and we've promised *nothing* to anyone. If I get enough written, soon enough, and it isn't too bad then we'll talk to publishers. In the meantime I've absolutely let go for a while answering letters of condolence, etc. But it is easy to write to you, only I have too much to tell.

C. Jr. talks a *great* deal more; he says everything after you. As I've been *so* much better (all well now) I take care of him more and do not take Betty[1] down to Princeton so that he'll know me better. It is such a joy to hear him calling for "Mummy" instead of "Betty"! And she understands just how I feel about it and helps me. He says a very firm "uh huh" (for yes) which sounds quite tough and apparently he gets from me and a *very* firm complacent "naw" when he doesn't want to do something. It is slightly nasal and not angry at all, but he's perfectly *sure he doesn't want what he doesn't want.* I say it's a very determined Swedish *no.* I wouldn't be surprised to hear him add on to it, "I tank I go home." C. Jr. and Sr. have a wonderful time together.

---

[1] Betty Gow, Charles Jr.'s nurse.

Sr.: "Want to go up?"

Jr.: "Uh huh."

Jr. (high in the air): "Down! Down!"

Sr.: "Again?"

Jr.: "Naw!"

Sr.: "Want to swing?"

Jr.: "Uh huh."

Charles puts him down after swinging.

Jr.: "Den! Den! Den!"

They had a pillow fight the other day, at least Charles threw pillows at the boy and knocked him down but he only laughed (which surprised Charles very much and he was quite proud of him) and picked up a pillow clumsily and tried to throw it at his father.

C. says we can't go west for two weeks and that it will be a short trip. Then we'll come down here for good. I don't know about the summer—Mother and the girls are going abroad. I shall have to be in Princeton or Englewood for all of August and perhaps July too.[1] I don't mind but I don't like to keep Charles Jr. in heat and possible danger of Infantile. Of course, I don't suppose there'll be an epidemic *this* year. But it was bad around New York last year.

The other baby seems so unreal. I can hardly imagine it, and I took your lovely blankets immediately up to Charles Jr. When I realized he was still using three of yours it suddenly occurred to me that you might be thinking of the other baby. If you were, they are the first things I have for him (or her!).

Did you know that Walter Winchell announced over the radio that I was going to have a baby three or four months ago? Before there was anything in it—because I did not go to South America with C. I did not go because I did not want to face all that publicity right after Daddy's death. And it would have made it embarrassing for the Company if I had gone under those circumstances.

[1] A. M. L. was expecting a second child in August.

Wahgoosh and the baby play together wildly, chasing one another around the room. Wahgoosh is *just* like a person.

The baby can wind up your music box by himself. He is more interested in the elephant and says something that sounds like elephant, but he still prefers the gray pussycat with the flat tail to take to bed at night.

Charles is still "Hi." Perhaps we'd better stop it and get something more dignified. The other day a car ran into us from behind, in New York City, smashed our taillight, mudguard, etc., put a leak in the gas tank. All the bags in the car (we were on the way to Princeton) fell forward; I grabbed the baby. We stopped traffic for a second while irate drivers came out trying to justify themselves. Charles walked out of the car and slammed the door. At this a small calm high voice chirped from the back of the car, "Hi—all gone!" No one was hurt and that was the only part in the incident that the child thought worth commenting upon.

(Charles asks me whether I'm writing a book. Sorry!)

TO E. L. L. L.   [*Hopewell*], *Wednesday, March 2, 1932*
                        (Better destroy after reading.)
I am going to write you this first afternoon all that I know and some you may discover in the newspapers; however, they are trying to keep *some* items from the press, so I know you will keep all this private, as you always do. I will write everything as I would like it told me and as I *cannot* tell you on the telephone. Oh, it was dreadful just giving you the bad news last night and nothing else. But C. thought immediately of you and wanted me to get you—he and the detectives were busy around the place.

At 7:30 Betty and I were putting the baby to bed. We closed and bolted all the shutters except on one window where the shutters are warped and won't close. Then I left and went downstairs and sat at the desk in the living room. Betty continued to clean the bathroom etc. until some time between 7:45 and 8:00, when she went in to the baby again to see he was covered. He was fast asleep and covered. Then she went downstairs to supper. C. was late in coming home, not till 8:20. Then we went upstairs. He washed his hands in the bathroom next to the baby's—we heard nothing—perhaps because of the water. Then downstairs to supper at about 8:35 to 9:10 (at this time Betty was still eating her supper—we were all in the west wing of the house). At 9:10 C. and I went upstairs. C. ran a bath, then went down again. I ran a bath. No noise heard. From about 9:30 to 10 C. was in his study, right next to the window under the baby's; no ladder could have been put up *then*. Betty and Elsie were upstairs still in the west wing.

At ten Betty went in to the baby, shut the window first, then lit the electric stove, then turned to the bed. It was empty and the sides still up. No blankets taken. She thought C. had taken him for a joke. I did, until I saw his face. Evidently they got about one and a half hours' start. You know the rest except the bits of evidence which have *not* been released.

1—A well-made small pair of ladders, found to the left of the house, evidently built and planned for that exact height window; 2—mud on the sill of the window with the shutters unbarred; 3—and a letter on the sill telling us that the baby would be taken good care of, that they wanted several thousand dollars, divided into three divisions, that they would let us know in four days where to leave the money. Experts found the ladder, bedclothes, window, and letter had been handled *with gloved fingers*.

Also footsteps below the window. Their knowledge of our being in Hopewell on a weekday. (We have not done it since *last* year and only stayed down because the baby had a cold. However, Tuesday, and Monday too, he had *no* temperature and was *cured* Tuesday really. We planned to take him to Englewood Wednesday.) Their knowledge of the baby's room, the lack of fingerprints, the well-fitted ladder, all point to *professionals,* which is rather good, as it means they want only the money and will not maliciously hurt the baby.

I was afraid of a lunatic. But the well-made plan knocks *that* out. C., Col. Henry [Breckinridge], and the detectives are very optimistic though they think it will take *time and patience*. In fact they think the kidnappers have gotten themselves into a terrible jam—so *much* pressure, such a close net over the country, such sympathy for us, and the widespread publicity, every police force on its mettle, that their one hope is to get the baby back unharmed.

That is all I know, I have written fast so someone can take this out. C. is *marvelous*—calm, clear, alert, and observing. It is dreadful not to be able to do *anything* to help. I want *so* to help. I know you do, C. knows it too. Thank you for all I understood over the telephone—what you couldn't say.

Forgive this brief account for I send much love to you.

[*Hopewell*], *Thursday morning* [*March 3rd*]
Dear Mrs. Lindbergh,
I wish I had more to tell you. We are waiting for the move of the kidnappers who said they'd let us know where to put the money in two to four days (all this private, of course). They think now that they are not *real* professionals, that real professionals would not walk into such a hornets' nest, that the phrasing of the letter is not hard-boiled enough for professionals. Also the amazing knowledge of the country around here, the house, situation, etc., points more to a local gang. They think that the terrific pressure may force them to give in very soon, i.e., work for negotiations, or else it may frighten them so they don't dare negotiate. But the general impression is that the longer they keep the baby, the worse position they're in.

We've gotten several fake postcards etc. about the baby's position, but they got a telegram this morning that looks as if it might be genuine, (addressed) to me, saying that the baby was under the care of a trained nurse and in good condition. All the papers said he was "ill" when he left but he *wasn't*. He was just over a cold and was dressed extra-warmly that night, with an extra shirt on under his regular shirt and then the wool cover-all sleeping suit on top.

Charles got a short nap yesterday afternoon and a good sleep last night. But he is very tired. But marvelously contained, and acts with such swiftness and judgment. He was pleased to see in the newspapers that you were going on with the teaching.

Wahgoosh was in the opposite wing of the house that night and did not bark. He couldn't have heard through the howling wind all that distance. He has been barking ever since. This house is bedlam: hundreds of men stamping in and out, sitting everywhere, on the stairs, on the pantry sink. The telephone goes all day and night. People sleep all over the floors on newspapers and blankets. I have never seen such self-sacrifice and energy. The chief of Jersey police[1] has not been to bed or to rest since the thing started. Col. Henry looks gray—under a great emotional strain. The press have moved down to Hopewell [the town] and are not photographing around the place any more. Which allows us to go out and walk. That is a great help to me. Wahgoosh follows C. around the grounds and I think it distracts and pleases Charles. There are planes overhead now.

I wish I had more to tell you. It is so hard to wait and do nothing. I know it is a terrible strain on you. It is easier to be in the place where things are happening, even though you can't do anything. I am in that position.

[*Hopewell*], *Thursday afternoon* [*March 3rd*]
Dear Mrs. Lindbergh,
The newspapers are not at all indicative of the progress of this search. That is, I suspect that the detectives only give out the clues they have already proved false. Also while all this open and almost "stock" running down of clues is going on there are three or four other lines that are being followed privately. One of these

[1] Colonel H. Norman Schwarzkopf, Commander of the New Jersey State Police, in whom Charles and Anne Lindbergh had complete confidence.

lines last night suddenly opened up and things are *really beginning to move* on that line. Definite moves toward negotiations with the kidnappers and (as much as is ever possible) therefore definite assurance that the baby is safe, and so a much more hopeful outlook for a safe return. I can't tell you any more than this.

Perhaps I should not tell this much, but as long as I know it and know how you must wait for news, I can't help sending it to you. It is of course a very very delicate situation—may take much time and endurance and patience. But if you could see the difference in C. tonight, from last night. He is tense and worried still, but excited and buoyant; Col. Henry, also. They are definitely moving toward the goal of the safe return of the baby.

This must go off. But please don't be discouraged by the newspapers, for the most hopeful things are going on quietly.

C. looks better today, got a pretty good sleep last night and has thrown off the cold he had yesterday. I feel much better.

I hope you haven't written C. or me because there are 700 letters or more coming in every day—eventually we'll see them. But now detectives go over all. You could write, though, in an envelope addressed to Mother[1] with your name plainly on the front.

[*Hopewell*], *Saturday* [*March 5th*]

Dear Mrs. Lindbergh,

I can only tell you that everything I wrote yesterday seems to be corroborated and strengthened. Even Charles (who will not give me *anything* that I might build false hopes on, he is so afraid that I will count too desperately on something that looks plausible but might fall through) talked to me with almost assurance today. We seem to have pretty tangible word that the baby is safe, and *well cared for.* "Of course," he said, "you must never count on anything until you actually *have* it but the news looks good." The progress is slow, but we *are* progressing toward recovery of

[1] E. C. M. had moved to Hopewell to be with A. M. L.

the child. We are all quite hopeful tonight, more than last night and *much* more so than during the first two days.

I can tell more from C.'s actions and manner than from his words. The first two days he looked like a desperate man—I could not speak to him. I was afraid to. But these last two days he is quite himself, only stimulated more than usual.

It is impossible to describe the confusion—a police station downstairs by day—detectives, police, secret service men swarming in and out—mattresses all over the dining room and other rooms at night. At any time I may be routed out of my bed so that a group of detectives may have a conference in the room. It is so terrifically unreal that I do not feel anything. Betty was terribly pleased by a note from you this morning. It came just at the right time, for she has had so much grilling and criticism and is such a loyal girl. C. got good sleep last night.

[Hopewell], Sunday [March 6th]

Dear Mrs. Lindbergh,

Yesterday I wrote you not to believe anything the newspapers said and this morning they came out with very accurate and hopeful news, much more fully than I could tell you by letter. So this letter only corroborates the fact that we have come to an understanding with two of the biggest men of the underworld—men who have tremendous power with all gangs, even though they are not in touch with them and are not responsible for their actions. We do not know where the baby is or who has him, but everyone is convinced it was the work of professionals and therefore can be reached through professionals, and they seem to be convinced that the baby is safe and well cared for. It may take a good time to get him back because they naturally are *not* going to run any risks of being caught and the police and press will *have* to quiet down—the headlines *must* go before they will move.

Charles is buoyant and had good rest last night. I met the two underworld kings last night. Charles, Col. Henry, and I feel convinced they are sincere and will help us. Isn't it strange, they showed more sincerity in their sympathy than a lot of politicians who've been here. Whateley and Elsie and Betty are working like dogs—we all are, but they have been so fine.

[*Hopewell*], *Monday* [*March 7th*]

Dear Mrs. Lindbergh,

This morning the newspapers say "go-betweens fail." That is an unfair statement. The newspapers would not know if they failed or not, perhaps will never know. It is too soon to tell now. But they are really anxious to succeed—we are convinced of that. As I said in the last letter, we do not expect any culmination of this until the publicity dies down a little but we continue to have corroboration of the baby being safe. But even feeling pretty sure of this, it does not make it less tiring to wait and wait. I feel as though it had been years and years—I feel old and tired and numb. But C. and Col. Henry continue very hopeful and active. Things are moving—we must be patient.

Please do not let the newspapers worry you about C. or my health. C. and I both had very bad colds, but C. has thrown his off almost entirely and has slept every night except the first. He is tireless working, but he seems buoyant and alive. I am much better and otherwise all right. Everything is so unreal. I am glad it is unreal, I do not want to realize anything. I don't think there's any danger of a miscarriage or any complication about the other baby. I am past the time when there is danger of miscarriage and I'm eating and sleeping fairly regularly and have no unusual pain—have not even felt nausea—and things are quieter now.

TO E. L. L. L.　　　　[*Hopewell*], *Tuesday* [*March 8th*]

I hardly see C. at all. All day he is locked up with detectives, by the telephone, at night talking late. Last night he slept in Col. Henry's room while Aida [Mrs. Henry Breckinridge] came in here. She has acted as general buffer to the outside world, sometimes acting for me over the telephone. I have never in my life seen such selfless devotion and energy as is being poured out here by every trooper, officer, and detective etc. working on this thing. Col. Henry has hardly slept for six days. I am worried about him and C. counts on his judgment. It is a very hard time right now; everyone is under a terrific strain, the first stimulus has worn off, and the men who have worked hardest are on the verge of breaking. C. has gotten more sleep than most by choosing his time, not wasting strength on petty things, and is now a general managing his forces with terrific discipline (which is necessary in such an emergency) but great judgment.

Conditions are just as before. It is a slow hard game, but they all have faith in the ultimate success. They know what they are doing.

[*Hopewell*], *Wednesday* [*March 9th*]
Dear Mrs. Lindbergh,
I can only write you that we're all waiting. The newspapers are quieting down a little, there are many fewer police here, everything is holding off. We are just waiting. It is a very hard time because there is nothing to do, but the men do not feel less hopeful. We must wait till things are fairly quiet and rest on our assurances that the baby is safe. This lull is good in a way for the men, for they can get sleep and exercise. C. slept late this morning and went out for a walk. Our colds have vanished. The house is being tidied up a little. Elsie and Whateley and Betty have more time. The police force have sent up a chef. Wahgoosh is the pet of the New Jersey police force!

With this lull the papers, especially the tabs, bring out wild stories every hour—none of them true, as you know. I am so afraid you get false clues and hopes every hour. They say the New York tabs bring out an "extra" every night to say the baby is found. But here they think it will be a slow unspectacular regular business "deal"—the return of the child—and it will not happen till things are quieter and safer for the kidnappers. The sympathy and indignation of hundreds of people all over the country, as shown by the thousands of letters, the newspapers and the editorials, is very inspiring.

[Hopewell], *Thursday* *[March 10th]*

Dear Mrs. Lindbergh,

I think you'd better send the letters to Mother direct, that is, addressed to her, because apparently the post office (now) only reads my name and then sends it to Hopewell along with the other thousands.

But perhaps it isn't worth the trouble.

Nothing seems to be. I have been trying to make up the baby's record. I haven't kept it since November, partly because I felt so miserably in December and January. I know that I did write *some* letters to you. I don't know whether you keep any letters. I don't usually and I never can find them again. But if you happen to find any having facts about him during November, December, January, and February they might refresh my memory.

Everything here is going on as usual—nothing has changed.

[Hopewell], *Thursday* *[March 10th]*

Dear Mrs. Lindbergh,

There *really* is definite progress. I feel *much* happier today. It does seem to be going ahead. Yesterday things began to move again and it was a great relief to everyone.

C. is resting now and says I *must* come in. We seem to work most of the night and now are working out a system of sleeping by day.

But it is a slow long negotiation and takes such care and patience.

C. is in much better shape and handling things wonderfully.

[*Hopewell*], *Saturday* [*March 12th*]

Dear Mrs. Lindbergh,

C. was up most of last night but slept most of today. He is in good condition, as I am.

Did you hear that in Madison Square Garden last night they stopped a big boxing match or hockey game and asked everyone to stand for three minutes and pray for the safe return of the baby—and that whole great square full of people stood quiet (just as they did for C.'s flight)? I think it is thrilling to have so many people moved by one thought.

[*Hopewell*], *Wednesday* [*March 16th*]

Dear Mrs. Lindbergh,

It is a heavenly spring day. I have been out all morning and feel better for it.

They keep assuring me that they are certain the baby is safe and will be returned. But we must play a game of patience. Everyone seems to lay this length of time only to the extremely hazardous position the kidnappers are in. They must, one can understand easily, have every assurance before they will act. It takes such endurance and patience just to sit and wait, especially for a person of C.'s active nature, but he is splendid. And I do trust the people that are handling things. I have never seen such a spirit of wholehearted sacrifice as is exhibited by everyone working on this.

I hate to think of the reporters following you and watching you. It is such an extra strain. Here it has been quite marvelous in that the reporters have stayed two miles off the place! Of course the police are guarding this (C. says to tell you to ask for a guard if you want it, to do whatever is easiest for you. It might cause *more* fuss or it might clear things up). Even so, the decent papers have been considerate and helpful. It has been remarkable, quite unlike any other case.

Charles is not discouraged. Three to four thousand letters come here a day.

Darling Elisabeth,

I am sitting in Mother's room (the back nursery, Betty's room). I like to sit here. I have never lived in this room, so it seems like another life. I try to analyze why this room *is* Mother immediately, as soon as she starts to live in it. It is comfortingly and reassuringly "Mother." Small bunch of flowers (little flowers—forget-me-nots, etc.) on the bedside table. Traveling clock, bottle of ink, glove box for a pen tray, full of pens, pencils, etc., blotter, pads, matches, candle, and lamp—all on this table (which is a red-legged nursery school one of yours).

Recent papers all in a neat pile on one suitcase, letters all in tidy bunches, held together in neat piles by elastic bands sorted on the other big table. Mother's address book and a little list fastened with a blue rubber band also on table. All toiletries neatly assorted on this table with the pink powder box and Mother's piece-of-chamois powder puff in it.

In the closet is stored a bottle of port; on the shelves, neat piles of old papers and folded-up pieces of wrapping paper, saved. Also a shelf of special provisions. I forgot to mention on the big table with the toiletries, Mother rescued an empty cellophane ginger container in which she has pins and hairpins. Also a little dish of saltines.

Mother has put a tack up on the wall and hung a hand mirror on it (just like camping out west), as there is no bureau or mirror in this room.

I love to sit in here with Mother. She has been so wonderful, never trying to comfort me when I felt I might cry. Always here, always understanding C. and the situation. And of course knowing when I'm tired before I do. She is so utterly unselfish that you never never are allowed to realize it.

We are all living a very regular life now, regular sleep, meals, and walks. Mother and I both take naps in the afternoon. The afternoons are so long and nothing happens.

I realize nothing emotionally except when some other small immediate annoyance sets off the blaze. It is possible to live here and realize nothing about the baby. This is so removed from him. Does that sound hard and unfeeling? I feel that I am willing to barter *anything* for my self-control right now—because it is so necessary, just like sitting through church that day and drawing squares on the back of the hymnal to keep the flood of memories of Daddy and old Sundays from seizing my emotions and making me lose all control at that moment.

C. and Col. Henry, etc., are working with great zeal—with infinite patience and caution but with cheerfulness.

It is strange, but I didn't feel that it was your birthday yesterday. Time has not continued since that Tuesday night. It is as if we just stepped off into one long night, or day. And I have a sustained feeling—like a high note on an organ that has got stuck—inside me. The time since then has been all in one mood or color, no variation, no come and go *fundamentally*. It is just that night elongated. Of course, it has superficially been different. Every second, like a dream, the whole scene swings, melts, changes. Personalities change from black to white, faces look different, tones are different, the tempo of the activity speeds up and slows down, but always that high note that got stuck in the organ Tuesday night!

Also there is no sense of continuity, as in a dream or as they say in the minds of mentally upset people. You cannot remember what happened before what. You know the feeling that "something has happened before," when you get your impressions mixed up and cart-before-the-horse? It is like that all the time.

I sometimes think that perhaps our minds are too weak to grasp joy or sorrow except in small things. Joy in fresh fragrance of flowers, or warmth of a fire, or a handshake. Sorrow in fading flowers, a lost dog, a fretful child's cry. In the big things joy and sorrow are just alike—overwhelming. At least, we only get them bit by bit, in tiny flashes—in *waves*—that our minds can't stand for very long. I felt that way about Daddy's death, most of the time numb, or unimpassioned sorrow, as though from a height. And then great uncontrollable gusts of feeling that I could not realize for any length of time.

What a long letter, but I am relieved to write it and I hope you don't mind.

TO E. L. L. L.　　　　[*Hopewell*], *Wednesday, April 6th*
We had quite a bad fire here yesterday; started down in the fields to the right, beyond the tree line you see looking out of the south windows. There was quite a wind and it swept up very fast across the long dry grass. However, the ground is rather damp and the woods too, so it did not catch trees, just ran along the surface. It leapt up to a few feet of the house and we shut all windows and doors to keep cinders out, though C. shouted that there was no danger of the house catching fire.

I was certainly thankful we had a stone house (C. was right about that. I wanted wood!). It swept over about two hundred acres, but C. says practically no damage done to trees and it'll be good for the soil. But it is a danger I had not thought of. C. went out, and the troopers, and fought it with bushes and brooms and shovels. Whateley was *wonderful*, cutting young cedars for brooms to beat it out, using his head with great coolness in emergency.

The exercise was really good for C. and took off the tension. We have had some very disappointing setbacks and think we've got a long wait ahead, but the consensus is that the child is still safe and well.

TO E. L. L. L.　　　　[*Hopewell*], *Friday* [*April*] *8, 1932*
All the papers here lately say that there is "an air of great optimism" etc. and predict a speedy return of the child. I don't know where they get that from. We have been rather gloomy lately though the best opinion here is that the child is still safe and all

right. We are now living from day to day but realize we must look forward to weeks.

Last week was one of tension, this week a letdown that is always hard to bear, but on the other hand it has given C. a chance to rest.

The troopers have cut out a shooting range in the woods back of the house and C. goes out with them and has target practice.

Our letters have fallen off to a hundred or so a day and there are many fewer calls. The troopers have made out an approximate listing of the letters up to April 5th. They have been sorted as to contents.

Dreams	12,000	
Sympathy	11,500	(This list does not
Suggestions	9,500	include *personal* mail)
Cranks	5,000	
Total	38,000	

Isn't it surprising the number of people who have written their dreams to us? Also the demands for money have been very shocking, the number of people—like the man who came to you, with no proof, no guarantee for us, no logic of any kind—who say if we will hand over such and such an amount they will deliver the child. (They are, though, all investigated by police.)

Charles always says when I quote from a letter of yours about some rumor or something that has come up, "Mother will know how to deal with that" or "That won't bother her," etc.

I have pieced together a pretty good account of the last three months for the baby's record. Your letters have been a great help.

The *Herald Tribune* of Wednesday 6 had a short good editorial by Walter Lippmann, called "Let Lindbergh Alone," quoting C.'s statement about feeling that he did not have to report every action of his and that he should be left free to carry on his actions privately. The *Herald Tribune* and the *Times* and others have been very good, but the tabloids I believe have cost us this terrible delay and waiting and we don't know *what* in the future. I think such papers are really criminal outside of their inaccuracy.

TO E. L. L. L.   [*Hopewell*], *Sunday* [*April 10*], *1932*
You now know from the papers all I could not tell you: that we have been in communication with the kidnappers (properly identified as such), that after five weeks of bargaining we finally took the chance, on the best advice of criminologists, detectives, etc., of giving up the money *first*. If we had not done that—and we were urged to do it *immediately*—we would have blamed ourselves forever for not trying what works in most cases.

You know what happened. We were told a location—the baby was not found. We informed the kidnappers of this and waited for further communication and have gotten none. We then were attempting to trace the bills. It was of course criminal that this information should have leaked out: it makes a difficult thing (tracing the money back to the kidnappers) impossible. We tried to get the newspapers to "kill the story." One paper broke faith with us and with all the others, and it splurged the whole thing in headlines over the front page. Of course the publicity makes it almost impossible for them to get the baby to us. There will probably be terrific delay.

C. does not think (nor do others)—though of course there is always that possibility—that the baby has been killed. They say it is harder to dispose of a dead baby than a live one. There is the chance that he died, but he was over his cold and was a strong baby. C. doesn't think there is much chance of that. He tells me not to be discouraged. I have told you all that (which has all been in the papers) so you will know just how we stand. It has of course broken very badly for us. That we can't keep anything private is most discouraging. Although things are bad they are not hopeless.

I wish I could say more. Things are quiet here now and we are waiting. It looks as though we were starting all over again with a worse start than we had six weeks ago. But of course that does not mean that things are hopeless.

TO E. L. L. L.   [*Hopewell*], *Wednesday* [*April 13*], *1932*
You must know now from the newspapers—I will just corroborate—that the negotiations have been hitherto carried on through letters and through the go-between[1] who was chosen by the kidnappers, apparently chosen through his offer in a newspaper to act as go-between. While the kidnappers can write us (and we can identify the letters unmistakably by comparison with the original note left in the nursery) we have had only one way of communicating with them: through the newspapers. That is unfortunate as anything as obvious as that is almost sure to be suspected.

We are at a standstill now of course until the publicity dies down. It is still front-page headlines here.

In the meantime all tips from telephone calls, letters etc. are followed up daily. They never seem to come to anything, but there's always the chance one may. You know the kind of thing: Child seen in a boat somewhere and evidently did not resemble people caring for it, or child seen in a hotel window of a room whose blinds were usually pulled down, etc., etc. They investigate all of those.

C. knows what a terribly hard position you are in in Detroit, and neither of us able to give real information to the other over such distance when every means of communication is tapped. But I don't know what we can do just now.

I think you have been very patient and wise.

[1] Dr. John F. Condon, a retired teacher, who had offered himself as neutral go-between and through whom the ransom money was passed.

TO E. L. L. L.   [*Hopewell*], *Monday* [*April 18th*]
I begin to think everyone talks too much. Of course we have a
very high standard as few people have had C.'s press experience and I always measure other people's contacts with the press
by him.

There have been terrible rumors here. I don't know what
comes out in Detroit. There are probably entirely different
rumors there. So I feel it is useless to call you on them—for
instance, last night that C. had shot himself. That made him and
me very angry.

Did you see in the papers about a Greta Gray of Minneapolis
who came here with supposed information and said she knew
you?

Preliminary telephone conversation between C. and Greta:

C.: "This is Col. Lindbergh's secretary. You say you knew Mrs.
Lindbergh?"

G.: "Yes, in Minneapolis."

C.: "Oh, then that was when she was living in Minneapolis?"

G.: "Yes, that was it."

C.: "Did you know her very well?"

G.: "Oh, not very well, but I used to see her quite often when
she lived in Minneapolis."

C.: "But, you know, she never lived in Minneapolis."

G.: "!!! Oh, I wish you hadn't asked me that question."

She finally admitted she didn't know you and she had no
information.

No news yet, but they are not discouraged here. We follow
everything, never knowing what calls, or what strange-appearing
person, may be from the kidnappers, to test us out. Only of
course when a person starts by asking for money we are suspi-
cious. We demand absolute identification before we will hand
over any money. They go off for "identification" (that is, definite
proof that they are in touch with those who have the baby) and
they never come back.

Apparently there are very often in kidnapping cases double payoffs—that is, two or three gangs plan it from the beginning to make the victims pay twice. C. talked to some parents the other day who had that experience. Child returned OK after second payment.

Also I was glad to hear the other day of a case of a little boy (aged two or three years) kept four months and returned in good shape to his family at the end of that time.

Your "Love to you three" makes me quite sad but I like to hear it.

TO E. L. L. L.   [*Hopewell*], *Wednesday* [*April 20th*]
C. has not had time to call. So many cases have come up here: a man says he is in touch with the kidnappers but needs expenses paid somewhere to investigate. Usually he is a hijacker.

Everything is quite busy here now: lots of fairly good leads, all different and from different sides. I wish there weren't so many. I'd have more faith if we just had *one* good lead, but with so many contradictory ones you are apt to discount them all. C. is well. More good news from my doctor yesterday.

Hopewell, April 25th

Dear Sue,[1]
I'm afraid it is too late to write Mexico. I should not have delayed so long but I have had a curious sense of time having stopped. Because of our extreme absorption and isolation in this case. For weeks I talked about "this weekend" as though the weekend of the kidnapping had never ended but was just stretching out interminably. I am glad you are coming back. It would be nice just to sit and hear you talk about Monte Albán, just as it was good to read how richly you were drenched in that world.

I am afraid, though, that I will have nothing to offer. Having

[1] Sue Beck, see notes pp. 20, 99.

read nothing but tabloids and insane letters and having thought about nothing except criminals and having talked nothing but crime, I cannot get my mind to work on any abstract problem— in fact, it does not work at all.

But part of it is because I'm having a baby—that drugs you somewhat. Being drugged that way—the strangeness of this life isolated with detectives, state troopers, and the monotony of waiting—is a help. It is completely unreal. I don't know how long I can keep that impression.

TO E. L. L. L.   *[Hopewell], Friday [April 29th]*
I know so well that discouraged feeling in having a clue fall through completely. It is impossible *not* to build hopes even though you reason and reason that you shouldn't. I know I am counting too much just now on Reuben's[1] lead, and by the time you get this it will probably have fallen through. It has less to recommend it than the majority we follow, and everyone I respect (except Reuben, who is slightly more hopeful) thinks it is a lot of "hooey," an absolute waste of time, and that the sooner they get Reuben clear of it and started on something else, the better.

There are one or two other moves to make, thank goodness. I suppose I should look ahead to them, but I can't help hoping for this nearer lead of Reuben's and I know I will be terribly disappointed. He has been gone almost ten days but checks in by telephone from time to time.

About C.'s article: yes, it is true. I am sending you the clipping from *Time*. C. has been working in his spare time for about a year at the Institute.[2] I have never seen him as happy as when he is working quietly there or watching the other men at work.

[1] Code name for C. A. L.

[2] The Rockefeller Institute for Medical Research, in New York, where C. A. L. was working on the design and development of an apparatus for the perfusion of organs, and related projects, in Dr. Alexis Carrel's department of experimental surgery.

He has many friends there. I did not take it very seriously at first, not understanding the worlds of physics, chemistry, biology, etc. Also he has been *very* secretive and shy about it. However, two or three times when you've been down here I've heard him discussing certain scientific problems with you which I realized later were along the lines of their work. I remember some questions about the coagulation of blood and then some about the properties of wax, and then about certain types of glass, do you remember? Those vague statements show the state of my mind.

There *has* been a definite leak in the organization here, someone working for Col. Schwarzkopf. The leak was proved and traced and *removed bodily*. I suppose that is the "high New Jersey official" the papers talk of. Though he certainly was *not* that. C. trusts Col. Schwarzkopf absolutely, and he has been wonderful to deal with. He has had hundreds of complications and difficulties, pressure of the press, petty jealousies, interference of politics, etc., etc.

I love some of the police lingo: "She's a wheel" (mental case— "see the pretty wheels go round"); "just another butterfly" (clue that leads nowhere). It seems to me there have been an unreasonable amount of "butterflies!"

Mother, by the way, did *not*, of course, go to Washington to see Hoover about freeing Capone,[1] as all the papers said, but to attend the opening of a library which my father did a lot to get started. She felt he ought to be represented.

I should love to have the baby turn up in Detroit, in your quiet home. Of course anywhere would be wonderful.

TO E. L. L. L.   [*Hopewell*], *Saturday* [*May 7th*]
We keep getting messages from Reuben, one last night late, one the night before. Apparently the lead has not yet fallen through and is progressing satisfactorily. Reuben keeps expressing faith in

---

[1] Al Capone, the notorious gangster, in jail for income-tax evasion, had proposed to help find the child through his contacts with the underworld.

it, though *never absolute faith*. Still he has been rather encouraging, for him. So I suppose we must trust his judgment and believe that he knows more than we can know here: things which convince him that it is worth while going on and seeing it through anyhow. I have, of course, great confidence in *his* judgment but I do not dare hope too much, especially in the face of the tremendous body of evidence which seems to say, "Don't trust these people." In the meantime there is nothing else here.

The place looks so beautiful now. I wish you could see it, such a great deal of dogwood. We have never seen this place in the spring and it is a wonderful surprise—the hill behind the house is massed with white and pinkish dogwood which shows up against the dark cedars. Then there is the very light green of the new leaves of tulip trees. Against the wall by the entrance to the court is a lovely little pink dogwood. Then facing it, inside the wall is a little white one. There are occasional wild cherry trees that show white in the hedgerows as one looks down the hill from the terrace. And walking around the fields I have found old deserted apple and cherry trees blooming still. The woods are full of violets.

I wish C. were here to see it with me. He got such pleasure out of this place and saw that it would be beautiful long before I did. Perhaps we will all still be here together in the spring sometime—and happy.

TO E. L. L. L.   [*Hopewell*], *Saturday* [*May 7th*]

Yesterday I forgot to answer your question about the boat C. was searching for in Buzzards Bay a month ago. They had definite instructions as to where to find it and a definite description of it. They went to the spot assigned and also all over that region by air, two days in succession, and there was no sign of it. Also men have been up there since by boat all over the region.

About the Englewood rumor, Col. Schwarzkopf has been moving more and more men away from here as the base of operations has been chiefly New York and environment. Trenton is the usual headquarters so there are always men there. Everything that can be done around here has, as far as possible, been done. He tells me that C. is seriously considering moving to Englewood to be nearer the base of operations. However, C. has not told me anything about it yet. I can see how it might be a good idea but I rather dread doing it. There is more to do here in my own house and woods, even though just futile routine.

Apparently we have had no definite contact with the kidnappers for a month. If you had any letter or message, no matter how ignorant, demanding ransom and sounding like the work of a reasoning mind (if one can say that of criminals) you would send it on, wouldn't you? Or telephone. Of course I know you have reported several things like that before so it is silly to reiterate this, but I feel they *must* communicate before long.

DIARY   *Englewood-Hopewell, Wednesday, May 11, 1932*
Woke from a dream of the return of the baby and someone saying, "Why, she hasn't even kissed him yet!" I thought, "They don't understand—I don't want to kiss him but just put my hand over the top of his curls."

Call from Col. Henry. Nothing developed from number. Dead end again.

Break in the newspapers about Curtis[1] in boat off New York, also reasons for failure at Norfolk; no word of C.

Long ride down—very blue. The eternal quality of certain moments in one's life. The baby being lifted out of his crib forever and ever, like Dante's hell. C.'s set face, carved onto Time for always.

The peculiar ephemeral quality of this last development. The people in the stories (told second and third hand) change their characters and melt into one another like faces in a dream. "You thought I was a face? I'm just a doorknob!"

We try to test one story by another story to prove both true.

[1] John Hughes Curtis, who had come with the story of a gang involved in the kidnapping, supposedly operating from a boat, the *Mary B. Moss.*

But we do not know how much of each story is a lie, intentional or unintentional. We argue along quite nicely: "This checks with that, that checks with this," until you come across the inevitable "according *to their story*," and all your ground falls from underneath you.

Long talk with Schwarzkopf encouraged me. His word is of bad weather; must remain in harbor.

Hopewell, Thursday, May 12, 1932

The baby's body found and identified by skull, hair, teeth, etc., in woods on Hopewell-Mount Rose road. Killed by a blow on head. They think he was killed immediately with intention of hiding all evidence. They took the sleeping garment off him to use to extort money.

The hardest thing to bear—Mother's "The baby is with Daddy." Called Mrs. Lindbergh. She is much braver than I. C. not able to be reached for several hours. But the weight on Mother is unbearable—wanted Baby to come back on a Monday, wanted to take the sting out of *Monday*.[1]

Everything is telescoped now into one moment, one of those eternal moments—the moment when I realized the baby had been taken and I saw the baby dead, killed violently, in the first flash of horror. Everything since then has been unreal, it has all vanished like smoke. Only that eternal moment remains. It *was* then and it *is* now.

I look at it now as a police case, a murder case, and I am interested in it as such and can and *have* to ask and talk about it. Soon it will be personal, but I do not face it yet.

I feel strangely a sense of peace—not peace, but an end to restlessness, a finality, as though I were sleeping in a grave.

It is a relief to know definitely that he did not live beyond that night. I keep him intact somehow, by that. He was with me the

[1] The day on which D. W. M. died.

last weekend and left loving me better than anyone, I know that. But all that is merely selfish and small.

But to know anything definitely is a relief. If you can say "then he was living," "then he was dead," it is final and finalities can be accepted.

TO E. L. L. L.   [*Hopewell, May 12th*]
(After telephoning)

Dear M.,

I know you thought my voice meant good news—we seemed so near it—and so it was doubly terrible for you. But I know how Charles and I feel about bad news: we feel we must tell each other immediately. The newspapers have it already, so I felt I must call you. I will tell you all I know now.

The baby's body was found in the woods near the road from Hopewell to Princeton. It was identified by the homemade shirt Betty and I put on it. Also the teeth and hair. There seems to be no possible doubt. The child was evidently killed by a blow on the head—killed instantly undoubtedly, and, from the state of the body and from its being so near here, a long time ago, perhaps in panic during the first blast of publicity.

Charles is off on a boat somewhere off the Jersey coast between Cape May and Atlantic City. He telephoned us as late as 7 o'clock this morning but then they evidently went off to try to effect this contact with the gang that Curtis has been working with. Oh, Charles felt *so* encouraged and hopeful. I cannot bear to think of the news coming to him. They have not reached him yet though they are sending planes, cruisers, etc., to try to get him. What that gang is doing I can't see; perhaps they have another baby on the boat.

This is all I know now. They have just told me—at least perhaps a half hour to an hour ago.

I have never known such courage as you and Charles have. It is a wall to lean upon. I am grateful for both of you. You have and always will help me in that. I wish I could help you. You know how I am feeling for you. And we must both help Charles.

Later—7:30 P.M. C. has been reached and will be here in two or three hours.

DIARY   *Hopewell, Friday, May 13, 1932*
He has already been dead a hundred years.

A long sleepless night but calm with C. sitting beside me every hour, and I could see it all from a great distance. His terrible patience and sweetness and silence—terrifying. "We look on Death as . . ."

Then a long day when everything personal flooded back over me, a personal physical loss, my little boy—no control over tears, no control over the hundred little incidents I had jammed out of sight when I was bargaining for my control.

C. to Trenton—the cremation—the blanket. C. going through that—even in the brief news account—is unbearable.

I am glad that I spoiled him that last weekend when he was sick and I took him on my lap and rocked him and sang to him. And glad that he wanted me those last days. . . .

Impossible to talk without crying.

Immortality perhaps for the spark of life, but not for what made up my little boy.

TO E. L. L. L.   [*Hopewell*], *Friday* [*May 14th*]
Dear M.,
Charles got home last night about 2 A.M. and was, as you know he would be, wonderful. He spoke so beautifully and calmly about death that it gave me great courage. He asked about you when he came in and said he was glad I had telephoned.

In the conversation about the whole thing two or three things came up that are not exactly consoling but keep us from remorse.

They think the baby was killed that first night. And so nothing we did could make any difference, not if we had tried to keep it secret (we couldn't have anyway), not if we could have kept the publicity down, not if the ransom bill list had not leaked out. From the blow on the head, the baby must have been killed immediately. C. said, "I don't think he knew anything about it."

Of course it makes the kidnappers of the lowest brutality—I cannot conceive of it. I think it is well they did not have the baby long.

I know this is not real comfort—nothing is—but it is something definite for one's mind to settle on, and that is a relief—I only write hoping it will be some to you.

C. did not even lie down last night. They are, of course, working on tracing down all evidence. But he says that he will sleep tonight.

My letter sounds strange and unfeeling. I can't express what I'm feeling. C. is inarticulate too. But very courageous, as you are.

DIARY   *Hopewell, Saturday, May 14, 1932*
(Curtis sitting dejected, broken, on the running board of C.'s car all day, being questioned.)

A long night—spasms of emotion, uncontrollable, all pictures, memories—and I begin to realize I must reconstruct all of him, every incident, every act, every word—I must go over it all emotionally—before I can accept this grief and incorporate it into my life.

"But not all at once," C. says.

Today Mrs. Lindbergh arrived, sweet and natural and lovely, understanding. I am very tired from not sleeping and the drugs. But I feel that perhaps he gave enough in his short life, amazingly—to Daddy for a year, to Mother when Daddy went, those first three or four months, to me, to Mrs. Lindbergh, to C., to my grandmother. C. and I have never been so close as at his birth, except now, at his death. He has made something tremendous out of our marriage that can't be changed now. And for the world, too, perhaps, the sacrifice will bring something.

C. trying to comfort me, "Perhaps there will be a spark of him . . ."

Today I have more control but heavy as lead and tired and sad and old.

No other child can take his place, but he has perhaps made a place—a union more complete—for their environment.

Hopewell, Sunday, May 15, 1932

Mrs. Lindbergh and the Breckinridges leave in evening.

C.: "We must find some way of making Time go backwards."

Walk with Mother and Elisabeth. We walked off the road a little. A bough of white dogwood, dazzling, bent over us. I looked at it and felt that something would break inside me. We talked fully, emotionally, for the first time. I am glad he did not live beyond that night. He was such a gay, lordly, assured little boy and had lived always loved and a king in our hearts. I could not bear to have him baffled, hurt, maimed by external forces. I hope he was killed immediately and did not struggle and cry for help—for me. I look over the pictures. There are none like him, none recent enough. It is very cruel. C. and Mrs. Lindbergh are wonderful. I think she is relieved to be here, and it really helps me. She is so calm and brave and I do not feel constrained with her. We speak of the new baby and C.'s scientific work—two things of hope.

Hopewell, Monday, May 16, 1932

C.: "And the security we felt we were living in!"

We sleep badly and wake up and talk. I dreamed right along as I was thinking—all of one piece, no relief. I was walking down a suburban street seeing other people's children and I stopped to see one in a carriage and I thought it was a sweet child, but I was looking for *my* child in his face. And I realized, in the dream, that I would do that forever. And I went on walking heavy and sad and woke heavy and sad.

I have to wait as long for that new child as Charlie has been gone.

They seem to think that murder was not the intention, that something went wrong. I feel as though I could hardly bear it. I would rather believe in crueler mankind than in such a cruel god of chance—chance that we came down that weekend and without Skean,[1] chance that the baby caught cold and had to stay over, chance that I was not taking care of him alone, being overcareful as I usually was without Betty, chance I didn't send Elsie upstairs during supper as I had the night before—and then finally chance that the baby was hurt or killed being taken out the window.

Then C. comes back from the spot where the body was found with stories of search of a shack which would perhaps mean he was *not* killed that night. I don't believe I can go through suspense, worry every night, with no object. I want the truth when they find it and I will face it and Justice should be pursued. But to face a new reconstruction of the murder of our child every night, with no object but a little more horror for this solution, a little more comfort for that one: it does not help me be courageous or build a new life. It is just the same thing I have been going through for eleven weeks, with no object on my side. Justice does not need my emotions.

Hopewell, Tuesday, May 17, 1932

Late Monday night Curtis confesses whole story a hoax to get publicity.

We talked a long time trying to get something constructive to do. We will have to be around New York till the baby is born. It

[1] The Lindberghs' Scottie.

is the only thing I look forward to. I feel we can't start anything until we have that new baby. Anything to do with that I want to do. Perhaps I could sort out clothes, perhaps make some. There are two nonintrospective things I could do that seem nice: flying, and piano. Just enough to play nursery songs—I wish I could have done that for Charlie. Writing is too introspective. A certain kind of reading perhaps I could do.

C.'s grief is different from mine and, perhaps, more fundamental, as it is not based on the small physical remembrances. There is something very deep in a man's feeling for his son, it reaches further into the future. My grief is for the small intimate everyday person. How much of it is physical and can be allayed by another child? C.'s "And I hoped so I would bring that baby back."

C. says, to my remorse about the element of chance, "Everything is chance. You can guard against the high percentage of chance but not against chance itself."

"You have a right to expect in a civilized country . . ."

We both feel we are starting over again. I remember my second thought after the shock and the picture of the baby killed that first night. I thought, "If this is true, I'll never believe anything again." A complete wiping out of faith in the goodness and security of life. C. says, "It is like war."

C. up all night with Curtis: more confession.

Hopewell, Wednesday, May 18, 1932

I thought I would lead him and teach him and now he has gone first into the biggest experience in life. He is ahead of me. Perhaps when I have to go through it I will think of him—my gay and arrogant child going into it—and it will not seem so terrifying, so awesome, a *little* door.

They talk and talk, conferences, discussions. But I am so tired of the talking. What difference does it make now? *"Why* Tuesday night?" "What happened to the diapers?" To reconstruct his murder, to try to understand. I will never climb out of this hell that way. And yet perhaps it is better, more unreal here. Englewood will be a place every corner of which will bring back the physical dearness of my boy. But I want the image of my boy, a spiritual thing, I don't want to get any nearer to his murderers, to see their faces, the weapon they killed him with, the place where he was killed. It must be discovered, but not by me, not every night.

I cannot see his face, the meaningless newspaper distortions are in the way. But I can hear his laugh and see his lips puckered into imitation of the wind: "Oooh—"

Long periods of chill stupor; no realization at all.

Hopewell, Thursday, May 19, 1932
They have had a duplicate ladder up to the window and gone through the whole thing again. They reconstruct this: That the baby was put into a burlap bag (found near the grave) and passed or taken out of window. The ladder broke, fell against lower shutter (marks), and the man dropped the bag; the head of the child struck the cement window ledge. The man (having gagged or chloroformed the child) did not know how serious the injury was at first. They stopped at first place where there was water—where the thumb guard was found by the gate. They took off sleeping suit to find where the blood came from and the diapers to bathe it off. When they found the child was dead they buried it in the first possible place.

If this is true he died before he really woke up. I would like to think that. I hope they will not go through it all again for a while. C.'s mind works on it incessantly. But I am sick of this police-case end of it. Is this going to be the realest thing in my memory of my boy? This picture of his mutilated body and how it happened? I must go back to Englewood and find him again.

Even though I am afraid of it. Decent grief, no matter how great, is better than this distorted, prolonged, unreal horror. There is no reconstruction until this is over. We are building backwards, not forwards. I feel as if it were a poison working in my system, this idea of the crime. How deep will it eat into our lives?

Hopewell, Friday, May 20, 1932
Last night I sat a long time with my eyes closed and tried to see and feel, relive that last weekend, to reconstruct the baby. It was good to do. I found my fingers could reconstruct better than anything else. My sense of touch. But I've always, since the early train game as a child, been able to re-create sensation of touch, at least in my right hand. I can put my hand across the top of his curls and feel his hand in mine when I said, "Shall we go up-stairs, Charlie?" and his weight when I pulled him out of bed and took him to the bathroom at night. It was so lovely. I went to bed eagerly to be alone and quiet to think about him, as one waits to be alone when one is in love so that one can remember all He said and did and warm oneself with the memory.

Mrs. Neilson said when I told her I was afraid of living (at the time of Francis Smith[1]), afraid that I couldn't stand sorrow—she said it was easier to bear one's own sorrow. In a way it is. You are *inside,* at last. And it is not a terror. There is no fear, no nightmare in grief, no horror as I felt that winter. Then there is the strength that comes to you when you know that you have and can bear sorrow. I was always terrified, waiting for some terrible stroke—we had always been so happy.

They talk about this child as an "innocent babe, helpless," etc. I see him a *person,* not a baby, gay, full of power, sure of himself—untouched and untouchable by outside forces.

[1] A Smith student who committed suicide while A. M. L. was in college. See note, p. 78.

Hopewell-Falaise, Saturday, May 21, 1932
Amelia[1] landed in Ireland!

Last night I went into His closet, opened the door, a flood of warmth. His blue coat on a hook, his red tam, his blue Dutch suit, the little cobweb scarf we tied around his neck. I opened the suitcase and went over each suit. His two wrappers hung on a hook and a pair of white shoes and his bunny bedroom boots. In the pockets of his blue coat I found a shell, a "tee," and his red mittens. It was like touching his hand. In the drawers I found all the Hänsel and Gretel set he played with that last day and the little pussycat I pushed in and out of a little toy house for him. It delighted him so. It gave me a pang of happiness to find it again. Oh, it was so good to feel that intimacy of that memory. It was grief; but it was my own boy—real, alive in my memory, not a police case. I gave Mother the shell and tee.

C. and I talked about the feeling of insecurity in life. Never, never will I dare say of him, *You are mine* or, *I have you* now. While we speak, things change—slip from us.

Up to Falaise.[2] Elisabeth and Mother to Englewood after hard morning. It is still and cool, dark with lilacs, rain on the terrace and on the pearl-gray sea. The smell of wet ground, of the tide, and the quiet sound of waves. C. and I might be coming back from our honeymoon three years ago. It is so peaceful, like that evening—only I am old, old, but I understand nothing more.

Perhaps one can count only on the present instant or on eternity—nothing in between. These raindrops and . . . the planets.

Falaise, Sunday, May 22, 1932
A strong wind from the sea blowing in our window, the roar of waves—like Maine.

[1] Amelia Earhart flew across the Atlantic, alone, from Newfoundland to Ireland.

[2] The Guggenheim estate on Long Island.

We walk about the place—lilacs. Harry[1] finds an "umbrella in a case" (two rhododendron leaves curled up) for Diane.[2] I find a broken robin's egg for Charlie. Mrs. Guggenheim is gentle and calm. Her faith is whole, like a child's, and soothing. This place is beautiful and untouched and quiet as a cloister. I have come back from the war.

We talk of the future. We have an intense yearning for a quiet life, free from publicity—at any price. Nausea at the sight of newspapers. We are starting all over again—no ties, no hopes, no plans. C. grasps at the straw of research work. I feel as if I wanted nothing but a normal family life. A hunger for children, a home, and all that goes to make it physically, spiritually. I suppose I would need more than that, some work. But that's all I want now.

So many people have lost children. I must remember.

TO E. L. L. L.   *Falaise, Sunday [May 22nd]*
Yesterday we came up here. C. has been out fishing and out walking. It is very peaceful and beautiful and I think it has done us both good. He is studying now.

Mother and Elisabeth have gone back to Englewood, where I think they'll stay—I hope so, because there is no use living in the crime element of this any longer, that is what it is at Hopewell now. Constant reconstruction of the crime. I want to dwell on the boy's happy life, not on the crime that ended it.

I do not think the police will stay on (perhaps not past this week) in Hopewell. It is not necessary any longer and they would rather be in Trenton. C. wants to keep in close contact with them, because of course he feels the criminals must be caught and the police, who have been so good, should have all of his backing, even though our personal end is lost. I feel as if I

[1] Harry Guggenheim.
[2] A daughter of the Guggenheims.

would like to get away from it and Hopewell for a while (though I have grown to love the place strangely in these last months).

Still I don't think it is altogether good for C. to be completely absorbed in the case. I would like him to get back into the Institute work; it would be a definitely constructive thing for his personal life. It is quiet, absorbing work and he is happiest now when he speaks of it. C. would like to get away from both Hopewell and Englewood too for a while. But we must be near New York, both for the case and because of the new baby.[1]

C. and I have walked every day in the woods at Hopewell with both Skean and Wahgoosh. It has been very beautiful and I was glad to have him see what I have grown to love on the place. I think it surprised him. We found more maidenhair, and he cut the underbrush to clear the trails with his Mexican machete.

DIARY   *Englewood, Monday, May 23, 1932*
My boy is so far away, even here—until I went upstairs. I tried to steal up when no one would know.

As I walked into his room, before I looked at anything, everything came back. I looked at his toys, the rooster, the Swedish horse, the music box, spools and crayons, the little blue stool, his cart of blocks, my scrapbook.

The Johnson powder tin, sweet to smell. The pictures I tacked up on the wall for him, the white table and chair. Then the bureau drawers—each one so full of him. There was a new poignantly personal thing in each drawer. Jo's knitted red cap, the Peter Rabbit blue tam. And, mussed and crushed under blankets, the little blue knitted jacket he wore over his sleeping suit when he came downstairs to play every night. I put my face into it. In the crib were the linen dog and the gray pussycat with

---

[1] The Lindberghs moved to Englewood to be nearer the doctor as the time for the birth of the new baby approached.

the tail almost off. Just the familiarity of my hand on the crib seemed to put him back there. What is this thing that is presence and yet not presence? I went down crying but more satisfied. I did not click the gate—afraid.

I'm so glad C. is coming back tonight.

Englewood, Tuesday, May 24, 1932

Woke up to hear noise on the floor above, and had to remember it was not the baby and Betty. I used to hear them and go up the stairs. As he heard my footsteps he would strut out to meet me by the gate quite gravely. "Do you want to come down?" And he would put up his arms around my neck for answer and I would carry him down. "Shall we go in and see Tee?" I put him down and he ran into Mother's room ahead of me. She was not dressed but he heard her voice in the bathroom and stood at the door. In the little sitting room, C. and Elisabeth and I having breakfast, he would eye the trays and play, exchanging the sugar bowl (blue Canton) tops with the marmalade tops. Or C. would say, "Charles, would you like some cornflakes?"—"Uh huh!"—"What do you say?"—"Pease."—But I do not remember enough—hardly anything.

Dinner at the Breckinridges'. C. very tight and bitter. Henry deeply grieved and pitying. Aida very sweet, generous. I felt old and heavy.

> "We thank with brief thanksgiving
> Whatever gods may be"[1]—

Englewood, Wednesday, May 25, 1932

Sick about Elisabeth all morning—new [medical] report. She very very depressed. I feel helpless and appalled at the transitory quality in life. I look at her and think, Life is captive here—

---

[1] "That no life lives for ever; / That dead men rise up never; / That even the weariest river / Winds somewhere safe to sea." (Swinburne, "The Garden of Proserpine.")

now—soon it will go. Why can't we hold it, why can't we help it?

I sat under the beech trees and looked up at their pattern against the sky, each leaf outlined because they grow horizontally.

In the afternoon the baby was so far away, I could not bear it—that he is growing further and further away, the faded daguerreotype of a little boy who died, a long time ago.

TO E. L. L. L.   *Englewood, Wednesday [May 25th]*
I am so glad you feel just as I do about getting C. out of the close detail of the police work and I think he feels the good of it too. Monday, he went down to Hopewell but came back at night. I have not been back since but expect to go in a day or two. C. has been to the Rockefeller Institute and to the office and has been quietly reading all day today here.

You may have seen reports of our going abroad to have the baby. We are *not* going, though for one wild moment we *felt* like it, to get away from the American press. But it would all be too much fuss and not leave us better off for doing it. So we'll hope for the best here.

Elisabeth is going abroad Tuesday (secret) and Mother, Con, and Dwight a little later, around the 15th of June, I think (also a secret).

I hope that you will come on again after you finish school. C. speaks of it. We have such a long two months ahead, and we will be so quiet.

I am trying to make up the baby's record. I would like to give you some things of his—if you want them. Perhaps it is wrong and childish to treasure things like that. But I cannot help it. I will wait till you come on.

DIARY   *Englewood, Friday, May 27, 1932*
Elisabeth persuaded to go to [the Rockefeller] Institute for examination. We all felt miserable.

Englewood, Saturday, May 28, 1932

Cooler. To Uncle Jay's—so broken; there is no comfort in life for him and nothing I could say. I felt strong in comparison.

"The last time I saw him was just a few days before the kidnapping; he was down here (pointing to his feet) playing with the poker chips."

I hadn't been able to remember what it was he had been playing with and the joy and pain of remembering made me cry.

To the Rockefeller Institute. The report. Elisabeth so happy to come home for [Mother's] birthday. Mother and I talking on that porch,[1] the tiled floor, the river, the boats slowly going by, the potted plants, the quiet—the loss of hope settling down again, with the same weight.

People coming and talking to us, unspoken pity, unlooked pity. Mother's face in the car coming home.

Elisabeth in the white polka-dot chiffon dress, soft, cool, green, white, with a green girdle, [like a] white columbine—no, a spray of blackberry blossom.

Con home—blooming.

Englewood, Sunday, May 29, 1932
Mother's birthday

Amey and Chester out for lunch. Had presents under new gaudy blue and yellow umbrella.

Terribly vivid dream about the baby, condemned to die—saw him running, hair all curly and tangled, and I (not realizing what I know awake and yet conscious he had been away) said, "Betty, I cannot remember how you combed his hair." Then I was raging, raging like an animal, against the people who were

---

[1] The doctors told E. C. M. that E. R. M. had suffered severe and irreversible damage to the heart valve, owing to rheumatic fever, and therefore had high vulnerability to infectious diseases. The life expectancy at that time for patients with her condition was not over five years.

going to take his life. The dream—a certain reality in memory as though I'd just seen him—stayed with me all day, warm and delicious like a remembered tune.

Monday, May 30, 1932

A quiet day, cool and sunny. C. and I walked in garden, played with dogs. Elisabeth and I on the terrace talking. We agree: tired of excitement of any kind. She wants Dulverton[1] and peace, just sitting in the sun, perhaps reading. Is it because we've had too much or because we're more mature? Both. I feel as though I wanted just to sit in the sun, outdoors, and let waves of green oak leaves and waves of small insect sounds, small rustlings and stirrings, pour into me, fill up all the wrinkles and cracks, make a smooth blank cool surface over everything. Then let impressions and thoughts come back clearly on that satin surface. But I do not want now to read or think or work; I just want to be filled up to the brim with quiet.

It was lovely sitting with Elisabeth. She was calm and happy. We felt in the same tone, and understood.

Long walk and talk with Mother. It seems as though she would have to bear and bear and bear sadness—and alone.

Englewood, Tuesday, May 31, 1932

In to Dr. Hawks.

Terrible, terrible apathy of mind, spirit, and body. "There's nothing in this world can give me joy." Must work out of it.

Elisabeth dressed up in a dark blue raincoat, plaid blanket under arm, cane over other arm, holding her waterproof roll. "English girl out for a walk!"

C. and I talk about house at Hopewell and our wanting "to start all over again."

[1] Dulverton in Somerset, England, where she was going to spend the summer.

I realize I will never get away from this. Now I realize either the crime numbly or my personal intimate loss numbly, never both at the same time.

I must start to work at something. I cannot write, even letters, or read, and my laziness makes me hate myself.

Englewood, Wednesday, June 1, 1932

Grand bustle for Elisabeth's leaving. E. at her desk up to last moment writing checks. Her high voice on long distance, "Oh, it was *so lovely* of you . . . I am *so* sorry," etc. Mary running shyly but impatient every three minutes to me at my desk. "Was my steamer letter ready? Her bag was all packed."

Her hat atilt, her fur over her arm, swinging her hand very thin and small in mine as she squeezed good-by.

Peter and I rather uncomfortable and confused outside of the bustle.

"Have you got your passport?"

A laugh—they're off.

Mary rushed to clean up both rooms and run the vacuum cleaner over the rugs. How I hate that still, closed-eyes look of a room when the person has left. It should not be cleaned up so quickly, as though it could forget the person, as though it could turn, from a living companion, into just "room," "master's bedroom," so quickly.

C. home late from Trenton.

TO E. R. M.   [*Englewood, June 1st*]
                                                  Steamer letter
Darling,

You have given me so much this winter and I don't express very much, but I feel close to you in thought and mood and everything, and it is great joy to have. I hope you let the sun and the pattern of beech leaves against the sky pour into you and make a cool green blankness over everything. I will do it here and think of you. Then we will sparkle again in the fall.

Don't worry about Mother, she will be so busy in the next two weeks with going to Grandma's and getting ready to go[1] that it will not be hard, and then Con and Dwight and Aunt Annie in an "all-on-a-spree" mood will put new life in her.

Do you remember James Stephens' "Goat Paths":

> "The crooked paths go every way
> Upon the hill—they wind about
> Through the heather in and out
> Of the quiet sunniness.
> And there the goats, day after day,
> Stray in sunny quietness,
> Cropping here and cropping there,
> As they pause and turn and pass,
> Now a bit of heather spray,
> Now a mouthful of the grass.
>
> . . . .
>
> If you approach they run away,
> They leap and stare, away they bound,
> With a sudden angry sound,
> To the sunny quietude;
> Crouching down where nothing stirs
> In the silence of the furze,
> Crouching down again to brood
> In the sunny solitude.
>
> . . . .

[1] E. C. M. was going on her first European trip after her husband's death, and would visit E. R. M.

In that airy quietness
I would think as long as they;
Through the quiet sunniness
I would stray away to brood
By a hidden, beaten way
In the sunny solitude,

I would think until I found
Something I can never find,
Something lying on the ground,
In the bottom of my mind."

DIARY   *Englewood, Thursday, June 2, 1932*
Laura and George [Stevens] out for evening. We sat outside on
the terrace and looked at the black shapes of trees and the lights
of the house shining out on the grass, and talked about where to
live—economically, safely, happily. City and stress, country and
lack of stimulus. I don't know—I can't talk theoretically. I am
just heavy and tired and want simple things and people: health
and children and a tree to sit under and Charles.

I do not want to be stimulated, or to think or to read or to
wonder.

Mother sits up and talks to George about books and people—
keen as a knife. My edges are so dull.

Englewood, Friday, June 3, 1932
Tried to write, pulling one heavy foot after another, on trip.[1]

Uncle Tom[2] and Mr. Birch[3] out for supper in the garden.
Daddy lives in their voices and their stories. I can hear the rich

[1] 1931 flight to the Orient.

[2] Thomas Cochran, Morgan partner and friend of D. W. M.

[3] Stephen Birch, president, later chairman, of the Kennecott Copper and
other mining companies; friend of the Morrows.

quality of his voice and feel his expansive warmth surrounding us all as they talk.

C. and I in swimming.

Mrs. Poole[1] to talk about piano lessons. C.: "Why don't you play something that's easier to carry around, like a mouth organ!"

Falaise, Saturday, June 4, 1932

C. playing tennis—hair ruffled, light and curly, eyes crinkled, intent, color high on his cheekbones, a lovely golden young look. I looked up suddenly at him and realized, "He has not looked that way for a long time," then, thinking back, "He looked that way on the boat after we were married."

Poor sleep—

TO E. L. L. L.   *New York, Monday* [*June 6th*]

Dear M.,

I started a letter to you out at Falaise and then couldn't finish it. We are at the Breckinridges' apartment, waiting to go out to Englewood. It was such a beautiful weekend, though very hot. Charles went fishing and played tennis, completely absorbed in what he was doing, but happily absorbed. I think he really relaxed.

I feel as though we would live more quietly from now on. Spectacular trips do not bring us much happiness because they lead to more publicity.

The doctor reports everything going very well with me and says it will be much easier this time. He has suggested—and though I hadn't thought of it, it appeals to me in many ways—having the baby in an apartment in New York instead of the hospital, to avoid publicity. The expense would be about the same and it would be much quieter, no new people, no curious people, quiet goings in and out. Charles could be there *all* the

---

[1] Constance B. Poole, for many years Director of Music at The Little School

time, or as much as he wanted. The baby could be right there with me in the next room. Plenty of room for C. to stay every night, for you if you should be here, for Mother if she should be here.

It appeals to me very much. We have no apartment but my father's big apartment is rented to someone who does not use it any of the summer and he would let us use it for August. What do you think about it? No matter how small and private, there is sure to be more publicity and quite a little talk and excitement even in the best hospital, and *I don't want it.*

No, I have written no poems about Charles Jr. or since I was married. I have been too happy and too active.

I found a very old one the other day that had your thought in it and that appeals to me very much, though it is old-fashioned in sound.

> "It is not growing like a tree
>   In bulk, doth make men better be;
> Or standing long an oak, three hundred year,
> To fall a log at last, dry, bald, and sere:
>   A lily of a day
>   Is fairer far in May,
> Although it fall and die that night;
> It was the plant and flower of light.
> In small proportions we just beauties see;
> And in short measures, life may perfect be."
>
> [BEN JONSON]

I like the line "It was the plant and flower of light."

DIARY   *Englewood, Monday, June 6, 1932*
Came back to find Skean and Bogey[1] lost, gone since Saturday night, probably stolen. After our desperate efforts to avoid it by

---

[1] E. R. M.'s Scotch terrier.

building a pen and keeping them in the house until it was finished. It was finished the evening they went off.

Banks[1] hated to break it to me, said they had "strayed," was "sure they'd be returned all right."

I feel hurt and terribly tired, terribly tired of perpetually trying to "think of other things." Terribly tired of having my bad dreams turn out to be true. It is such a little thing, but completely in tune with my insecurity and lack of faith in *anything*. I am tired of fighting.

Englewood, Tuesday, June 7, 1932

C. came in and handed me [a note]: "Mrs. Lindbergh, the dogs are here."

Then Skean wriggled in, showing his teeth in a smile, rolling on his back on the floor.

Englewood, Wednesday, June 8, 1932

Music lesson. I am so completely at the beginning, not able to read, keep time, or understand harmony intellectually, I wonder what I can get. My fingers are like old ladies going up and down stairs.

Mr. Bliss[2]—so very dear and sweet and understanding. [About music] "Something that gets better and better as you grow older—does not decrease as so many things do."

Englewood, Thursday, June 9, 1932

Miss Hawley[3] here—miniature.

Tried to plan day by hours, lost two hours! Music absorbing. Happy doing it. Is it just fiddling? Have I done nothing in last three years, or ever? Never given anything? Must you give *pub-*

[1] Septimus Banks, the Morrow butler.

[2] Cornelius Bliss. See note p. 111.

[3] Margaret Hawley, artist painting a miniature of little Charles from a photograph.

licly to give at all? Is giving measured in quantity too? Talk about writing but I don't write—I cannot write. I sit and think with the pad in front of me or, forcing myself, write flat things without heart.

I think, analyzing it, that women take and conquer sorrow differently from men. They take it willingly, with open arms they blend and merge it into every part of their lives; it is diffused and spread into every fiber, and they build from that and with that. While men take the concentrated bitter dose at one draught and then try to forget—start to work at something objective and entirely separate. So C. says, "Write about Baker Lake—that has no connection."

But that is just it—it has no connection; my heart is not in it. I can only work from the one strong emotion in me: my love for that boy, and the things that grow from it—wanting a home, wanting children, things to give and do for them, for Charles and my home. I will get beyond this almost animal feeling and want more, but not yet. The music is the nearest exit because that leads towards home. I wanted to give it to Charlie to sing and play and set his head swaying in time and his wide smile spreading. And if C. were dead would I want to write because he wanted me to? If I could live at all, I would. How dreadful that I can't free that emotion *now;* but perhaps it would be an unbearable weight.

I wake each morning (even when I do not dream) with the vague feeling that I have been close to the baby all night. I go to bed thinking of him—so vividly I almost see him—and then continue unconsciously in sleep. It is good, for by day he is getting further and further away—even the clothes, now I have looked at them three or four times, have lost his presence.

TO E. L. L. L.   *Englewood, June 10th*
Today is a nice day because I can say today (with good probability), "Only two months more to wait." It would be nice if it came a little early but C. says I must not expect that. When I say,

"What shall we name it, if it's a boy?" Charles just smiles and says, "Anne"!

I don't think he's planning any trip now at all, except one to Washington around the end of June, I think.

I am trying to play the piano again. Do you think that's silly? I wish I could have played little songs for Charles Jr. to dance and smile to—he did when I sang. And so I thought I'd learn just enough to do that for children. I love everything you say about him. It is good to hear. I have not yet played your music box. He used to turn it himself, you know, and swing and dance to it. I know it will bring such a vivid picture to my mind.

Don't think I am morbid about it, because I'm really not. Only it is such a warm joy to remember everything about him and keep him whole and happy in my mind.

About the house and our plans, we are completely at sea. I don't know that C. and I (he speaks of it a great deal) will ever feel secure in that beautiful place again. It is a long discussion and I want to talk to you about it. But he says he would never be able to go away to work—leave me and children there without armed protection—and yet we want our children to grow up independent, as C. himself is.

Englewood, June 10th

Darling Elisabeth,

It is always this way: you go and then the days slip by all alike and before I know it weeks have gone and I have missed you and never told you so. It has been terrifically hectic here, though. I'm glad you're not here.

Someone every day for lunch, supper, tea, and Mother rushing back and forth to town "in time to see" Ada Comstock[1] or Zaidee or Tom or Neil or Pauline, etc., etc., etc. In the middle of this Mr. Birch asked us [to his country home] for the afternoon

[1] Dean of Smith College; President of Radcliffe College, Cambridge, Mass. (1923-43).

and dinner and pressed it very hard; he is a dear, but you know he would, wholeheartedly. So Mother and C. and I went out one night, ate an enormous dinner: soup, plover eggs, soft-shell crabs, mushrooms on toast, suckling pig with an apple in its mouth, vegetables, pheasant (a stuffed pheasant, feathers etc., sitting on the platter looking at the sliced pheasant), ham, salad, ice cream, cake, etc.

Mr. Birch just wanted to do everything for us. He took us out and had us each catch a fish in his pool. Only I caught my fly on the willows above my head and Mother, minute, darling, wrapped in her big tweed coat, waving this enormous rod futilely and mildly over the pond, caught only weeds and sticks. Seeing Mother leaning over the pond with that *enormous* rod, I suddenly saw her as Daddy would.

[Later]
Darling, we seem to be living in death and horror. Violet[1] has just been found in the pantry—at first they thought in a faint, then dead, and now we know death by suicide. She had just been told that the police wanted to question her again, as her story has never been the same. Oh, what a terrible train of misery and sorrow this crime has pulled behind it. Will the consequences never never cease? It seems as though they go on multiplying, like waves from the splash of a rock. Mother and Jo were with her when she died, trying to bring her out of the supposed faint. Mother is shaken, but she will leave so *blessedly* soon. Charles has hold of things.

I am so glad she is going to such peace and beauty.

DIARY   *Saturday, June 11, 1932*
Smeared all over the papers' front pages again [because of Violet Sharpe's suicide]. And the memory of my boy wiped out in this

[1] Violet Sharpe, English maid in the Morrow household.

avalanching crime. Nothing found out yet in spite of conclusions jumped at.

Mr. Rublee out for lunch. "We have too many things, let's make life simpler."—"I think the things we possess should be as transitory as the rest of life. Don't build a stone house, live in a tent or a portable shack. Then when life changes, breaks up, you can take your tent with you."

Out to Port Washington, Falaise. Honeysuckle, the sea very calm, small ripples, smooth patches that reflect the gold of the sky. And the Guggenheims very calm and cool and generous and, thank God, conversation about broad world problems, merging of industries, prices fixed by Government, Labor to share in ownership, five-day week.

I feel as though *their* world were secure, as though dreadful things could never happen in it, because they have faith in it. As though ours were toppling, anything could happen, because we have lost faith in it. As though once you had lost your faith you were vulnerable and nothing you did could stop evil and sorrow and misery from pouring in. "The loss of faith surpasses the loss of an estate"—Emily Dickinson.

Falaise, Sunday, June 12, 1932

Terrible argument about managing publicity and our lives, C. arguing to live somewhere else for more peace.

Harry [Guggenheim]: "As long as you do anything constructive all your life, you will have to meet it, you can't get away from it. The only thing to do is to change your whole attitude. Conquer it *inside* of you, get so you don't mind. You've got to stop fighting it, stop trying to get away from it."

C. A. L.: "It isn't what they *say*—it's their physical presence in your life, not being able to step outside your door without having a flashlight explode in your face."

A. M. L.: "Suppose you *do* give in to it, stop fighting, stop guarding your private lives, throw open your doors to them, let them do anything they want, take anything—*then what?* Will we have peace then?"

Harry: "No—not unless you're willing to live in vegetating oblivion. And you never will be."

But we are too sore and hurt to argue on this subject. We quiver when we're touched.

TO E. L. L. L.   *Falaise, Monday morning* [*June 13th*]
When I wrote you Friday morning it was before we knew anything had happened. Just after that they told me that Violet, the waitress, had fainted after being told she must see the police again. Then they found she was dead and had taken cyanide chloride.

Everyone in the house had tried and tried to help her, telling her it would be all right if she would just give the right story. But she was evidently terrified. It looks as though she were the highly nervous-hysterical-unbalanced type. Really had nothing to hide but had worked herself up into such a state that she could not stand the police questioning; although she never had anything very bad from that standpoint. She was never questioned late at night, never touched (none of them were). Violet was continually watched by a doctor.

The whole thing seems, though, so terribly cruel and sad. How little we understand people.

DIARY   *Englewood, Monday, June 13, 1932*
Feel so weak spiritually—no strength in me. My mind and spirit unanchored and tossed about, insecure and terrified so easily, as if anything could topple me over. Dreadful feeling, on brink of lack of control. Great strength in Charles.

Terrible criticism of police, in papers: "Bullied innocent girl to death." Blaze of criticism in papers in England. Girl appears innocent. It is very sickening. What a crude, imperfect world—we understand nothing.

I feel as though people who take their own lives are not as completely, irrevocably gone as the others who die. Can they escape so swiftly and so comparatively easily? The fact that they come up to Death with open eyes, walk open-eyed across the thread that separates Life from Death, must give them a knowledge of the passage across. A knowledge that lets them come and go easily. Perhaps she would rather not linger around this life, but I feel that she is, in spite of herself, not very far away.

Englewood, Tuesday, June 14, 1932

One of those hectic *before-Mother-leaves* days. People coming up to say good-by: "I *just* want to see her a *moment.*" Mother sorting out books, dictating letters, trying on dresses. Jo at the telephone with pencil and pad; Aunt Edith waiting to speak to Mother. Mother saying every fifteen minutes: "I must go down and arrange those tiles for the table! Anne! Jo! Edith! Come on now, I'm going down," then someone would interrupt. "Miss Cutter has arrived" . . . "Mrs. Kerr" . . . "Miss Sullivan." A lot of people waiting around and a few people running.

Cars in and out of town. "Henry is going to call up before he comes out, to see if there is anything more." Dwight very leisurely: "No, Mother, I don't think I want those Baedekers."

Aunt Hattie[1] and Uncle Jay up before supper. The chiropodist. Con blows in, wispy curls straggling out underneath her cap, coat open, hands full of books and bags and a glowing face. "Well, I got here!"

The final loading up of bags, coats, baskets, and presents in the front hall. Mother: "I'm going to stop on the way at the Duncans'—*just for a second.*" They pile in. Dwight has forgotten a book and goes upstairs, slinging on a coat casually. Con, pretty and pert, puts up her round cheek to be kissed—so smooth and round and whole—all youth. Mother squeezes Charles' hand— swift little steps over the threshold. The cars pull out. The house

---

[1] Wife of General Jay J. Morrow, brother of D. W. M.

is very still. We sit down and read. All life has left the house, and with it . . . the baby again.

Mother darling—

You said last night, just like a little girl: "You're not going to miss me at all!" And I shall miss you terribly. I don't suppose we any of us face what you are to us—I know I don't. I am afraid to realize it, as though, if I did, it would be taken away from me, as though one's only security lay in unconsciousness. A pagan feeling: "If I let 'them' know how much she means, 'they' will be envious."

I can only think of that first week in Hopewell, of you as an ultimate fortress I had, an ultimate source of strength. First: "Well, Mother will be here . . . when Mother gets here . . ." Then, morning after morning when there did not seem to be any reason to get up, "Mother is downstairs already," and then those days you went to New York, so terribly long, but "It will be all right tonight, when Mother gets back." And you would always bring back a flurry and breath of life, even in those deathlike days.

I don't know where your ultimate source of strength is, and I feel that I have taken and taken and taken and not given anything back. Perhaps I can't give anything now. It is as though all of us close to this had lost our faith and once it was smashed we were vulnerable—anything could happen. As though your faith, a beautiful shimmering armor of glass, protected you infallibly as long as it was whole. But it's so fragile—once it's gone to pieces you have nothing.

But Dwight and Con have theirs. Can't you see Con sheathed in smooth and gleaming amethyst and gold, and Dwight in sparkling sapphire? And their faith will make you whole. I do feel as though we needed Daddy terribly now. I don't think his was ever smashed. It was so wonderful that I can feel it now. I think we all do. We are all so close together, Mother, and always always will be—life or death. That is wonderful, and I do honestly believe it.

This is such a sad letter, and goes too far in. But there is so little time to say things. I am always putting away things that are too real to say, and then they never get said. We are always bargaining with our feelings so that we can live from day to day. And you must know—and knew last night—that I love you terribly and humbly and that I'm going to miss you, but you said, "You're not going to miss me at all!" So really you're to blame for this letter!

And when you get back we'll go up to North Haven and make ourselves new sheaths out of the blue of the Camden Hills and the bleakness of the stones and the sharp edges of pine trees!

And if I *should happen* to have *twin girls* early before you get back, do you think it would be unfair to Elisabeth to call them Anne and Elisabeth? Don't worry, I won't name them till you get back. (And I wouldn't if she'd rather not have us both have Elisabeths. She should have whatever she wants.) But Elisabeth means more to me than any other name because of both of you. And two sisters named Elisabeth and Anne would be so lovely. . . . Never mind, I wouldn't if it made her even a little sad or wistful. Anyway, I won't have twins, and I'll be good and wait for you to come back and then have—perhaps twin boys!

DIARY   *Friday, June 17, 1932*

At night the different things in my mind lose their identity but not their emotional content. They are just as poignant and just as real even though they become, in dreams, different-colored ribbons twisting among themselves. Then in the morning, waking up, I untangle them: "What is this thing I've been fighting all night—this strand here? Oh, yes, the baby is gone. . . . And this little one knotted? Amey is coming out on my—his birthday" etc.

Friday

Sue [Vaillant] out for lunch—stimulating, quick and keen, and just as understanding. Reassuring: "How can you *give* any more than to give children and give through them, making finer, fitter individuals of them? Aren't you making the world better that way?"

"You are essentially *'being'* and he is essentially *'doing.'* I don't see why you don't perfectly counterbalance each other. Why doesn't your 'being' make the perfect medium for his 'doing'? How can you give more than through him? Then, if as an interesting individual for your own happiness you want something else too, all right—but your greatest *giving* is in the other."

Englewood–Long Island, Saturday, June 18, 1932

Out to the Harry Davisons'.[1]

They playing bowls on the lawn, I sit and watch the figures in the distance. The sudden unexpected flash of pleasure in watching C.'s characteristic walk—easy, poised, rhythmical, and yet loose—among strangers. My feeling all the time: "I must remember this—I must remember that—I must make this an eternal moment, before it's taken away from me."

I like her [Anne Davison's] clear objectivity, and the self-contained rigidity like a beautiful animal, and the shape of her head.

And they are "just terribly nice." Mrs. Davison[2]—I feel I expand and glow in her presence. It is the whole warm rich world of my father and mother.

---

[1] Family friend, banker, and J. P. Morgan partner, who had been a Naval aviator in World War I.

[2] Mrs. Henry P. Davison, Sr.

Long Island–Englewood, Sunday, June 19, 1932

Frances'[1] two little girls in very short skirts and hair ribbons playing on the lawn, with a ladybug. Little Harry's[2] red head almost touching their pale gold: "Aren't there any *men* lady-bugs?"

I long for a lawn and children and peace, forgetting they do not always come together.

Back to Englewood. The house very big and dark.

Skean followed me upstairs to the baby's room as he did so many times before. I wonder if he misses him.

Englewood, Monday, June 20, 1932

Abysmal morning—

I have *taken*, all my life, from family, friends, and the social organization and have not given anything back. And I must not wait for perfect conditions before I try to give back. I've had a good enough chance and have only procrastinated.

You can best give probably by carrying out what you specialized in at college, or if you don't want to do that, do something else—but make up your mind and do *something*, something constructive.

My theory:

1st, I *must* live *consciously*. Then I can act and give from that.

2nd, that my fundamental job is creating clearer, stronger, better children—giving through them and through C. what I have learned from living, as clearly conscious as much of the time as I can be.

Right now, everything springs from the physical and, I think, always with women.

Supper on the terrace and bowling on the lawn and happy not thinking about "constructive gifts."

[1] Mrs. Ward Cheney, Harry Davison's sister.

[2] Harry Davison's son.

Tuesday, June 21, 1932

Heavy and hard to breathe. The child pushes up into my lungs.

Reading the *Fountain*.[1] This is it. This is what I want—*here.*
This man knows!

"The stilling of the soul within the activities of the mind and
body so that it might be still as the axis of a revolving wheel is
still."

Englewood, Wednesday, June 22, 1932

Little Charles' birthday—and mine.

Amey and Chester for supper in the garden.

Chester playing the Chopin preludes.

Could see the baby's face for a moment in my mind, for the
first time.

Dreamed thick dreams of the new baby. "Well, it *laughs* like
Charlie." The laugh was so clear and distinct—bubbling, spontaneous, like little C. playing upstairs at night at hide-and-go-
seek.

Aunt Alice's[2] film [of the baby] disappointing: not the boy I
knew, except in flashes, shaking his head and talking, saying one
word over and over.

Englewood, Friday, June 24, 1932

Got quite elated planning about the new wing, the new baby, etc.
Starting over again in a new place, even a new part of the same
house, is invigorating.

Night—so long to live forgetting that baby—with the picture
getting dimmer and dimmer. The ghost of a little boy whom I
can't even see in my waking mind. Then, as though something in

---

[1] Novel by Charles L. Morgan.

[2] Alice Morrow, D. W. M.'s sister.

me denied this, I dreamed heavily about him. Under the crust of consciousness lay another consciousness that held the image of him securely. Only I could not bring it back with me when I woke early in the morning and cursed the birds and could not get to sleep again.

TO E. L. L. L. *Englewood, June 25th*

The larkspur was so very beautiful and tall, and that lovely blue still is like a garden on the table by the piano. They said it came from Detroit (before I got your letter) so I knew it must be from you and I was touched to have you do that, though I knew we would all be thinking about one thing that day.

So little happens here that there does not seem to be anything to write. Charles and I go in swimming, he works in town and reads a great deal. I practice slowly on the piano.

Last weekend, at young Harry Davison's, it was very nice. C. did a litle flying (the first in a long time) with the men and I just walked around and watched the children, one little boy and two little girls.

You know C. is wonderful with children, not self-conscious the way I am. And they *always* love him. He squatted down on the grass with a large handkerchief and a dime and made the dime disappear. They were right at his knees and adoring him. He does not fuss over them at all and is perfectly direct and natural— I think that's it. I do long to see him with his own.

Tomorrow we go to Hopewell. The Curtis trial is at Flemington, nearby. It may be two or three days. They think that Curtis's defense is going to try to prove that Curtis was "brutally treated"—bullied by the police—and that's why they want Betty and Whateley to testify. The defense thinks that Betty and Whateley will say *they* had cruel treatment too. I don't see *what* the defense can prove and what good it would do for Curtis anyway. I *do* hope it's over quickly and then we can live quietly.

DIARY   *Englewood, Saturday, June 25, 1932*
I dread going to Hopewell. To live there in no hope, where I
lived so long *just* on that.

Hopewell, Sunday, June 26, 1932
C., Betty, and I to Hopewell; hot, bumpy ride. The house gleams
white and fresh after the Whateleys' work. It is cool and peaceful,
a home again—no sign of the case except that Whateley had
dusted and set up on the radio the old faded tintype that some
crank woman sent us in the mail and we had put up for a joke. It
did not look funny.

Then the burnt marks on the stairs of the baby's fingerprints
where the men had tried to bring them out chemically.

The baby's room was still and peaceful, the big French windows wide open, just the same secure intimate room it was in
that other world. I left the door open.

This place does not suggest crime now, but I realize here intensely what I am realizing at Englewood more and more: that
the new baby will not make any difference to me in this feeling I
have for Charlie. I thought vaguely that it would be better after
the baby came, but it won't be at all. It won't change things. I'll
miss him just as much. The feeling for the new baby will grow
up separately, a lovely, different thing, alongside of this feeling.
I'll live with that always, always all my life, only it will be
perhaps easier to live with because more and more separate from
my daily life. I don't want it to be otherwise.

Hopewell, Monday, June 27, 1932
To see Mrs. Hibben[1] in the morning, nice and clarifying. ("I
hope you like my daughter. She is very lovely but she is very
shy.") She is so impulsive and honest and sweet. Thick heavy

---

[1] Wife of the President of Princeton University, who quoted D. W. M.'s
remark about A. M. L.

day, sky heavy and brown, tropical green, lush growth, rain sheets.

Wrote letters.

Wrote in afternoon two hours or more on Point Barrow.[1] Not so difficult though I have no impetus of pleasure as you have when you say "This is *good*." I do not see it whole with a single clear idea in it. There is no design—it is just narrative. I like better to work around and around and around one single idea—a polished stone in its setting. But then I do neither.

At night out for a drive to Princeton, chased by boys who recognized us. C. hot and nervous; I, bitter and angry. Driving over that road: "They went this way with the body of my boy, looking for a place to hide it. Why not there? Too near houses? That river? Too easily found." Through quiet Hopewell past all safe homes, past orphans' home, up that lonely hill—"Here."

I do not get past that moment. I am always trying to realize it more vividly, thinking that realities are easier to accept—can be accepted, met, and passed. (I can only get past it by bolting it, by falling back into universal platitudes: "It was a long time ago," and "He didn't know it happened," and "We all die.")

That night when we discovered it and I said, "It *isn't possible*," and C. said bitterly, "It seems to be," I said to myself: "Now you will face a reality. You've lived in a smooth world of unrealities so far, but you've come up against it now." And yet I never, never meet it. If I had seen the baby's mutilated body, would I have met it? I don't think so. For I begin to think that the reality of a thing you try to realize is in you and not in the thing itself.

Hopewell, Thursday, June 30, 1932

Letters.

Musical theory.

Writing—Point Barrow—not good.

Stifling heat. Skean pants under my chair.

[1] Chapter in *North to the Orient.*

I don't believe I can ever live in this house in freedom and sanity. That window, that side of the house, the approaches—I shall always be trying to know just what happened in terror and curiosity and misery.

Hopewell, Saturday, July 2, 1932

Jury's verdict on Curtis: guilty.

Four months since I saw the baby—longer than that trip abroad. I feel, as then, desperately, that I never had a baby—he is so gone.

I used to think that having sorrow would make one feel more secure—as though you could say, "Now I have borne suffering, I am strong, I will not be afraid again. Now the blow has fallen—I need not fear it again." But it does not effect me that way. I feel all foundations shaking under me. I feel next to Death. A year ago I had Daddy and the baby. Next year who will be gone, who will be here, will I still be here? I don't know and I dread it—I have no weapon against it.

And death so near me—I feel as though I walked hand in hand with it.

TO E. L. L. L. *Hopewell, July 2nd*

At last the trial is over.[1] Everyone is relieved. C. has been there every day, leaving here at 9 and not getting back until 7. And it has been very hot. Still, he has had such a training in that kind of reserve and mental preparedness that they say he was very cool and unruffled by the questioning, handling it all without any difficulty.

One of the things this week here has proved is how lovely this place is. C. goes about with such satisfaction, saying, "This really is a wonderful house, certainly beautifully planned, and what

[1] The trial of John Hughes Curtis; see note p. 247.

good material. It still looks absolutely new, in spite of the wear and tear it's had."

Then we go on planning about it, about plowing and sowing the fields in front of the house, and I think about furnishing and various small improvements, and we really don't see how we could leave it. It seems like a different place—the place it was before anything happened. It was so perfect and lovely, I wonder if we can ever make it so again. I do not like to think of winter here, but I suppose we can't look ahead that far yet.

Hopewell, Tuesday, July 5th

Mother darling,

I thought of you on your wedding day. It is strange but I have thought so much, so very much, about Daddy lately as though a superficial shell had dropped off and I could feel the reality again. As though, in a way, the pendulum swing of numbness to unhappiness had somehow stopped and a constant value had remained and I am not afraid of its going. It has been lovely to see President and Mrs. Hibben down here (during Curtis trial), for they have spoken so much of him.

And I have thought of this time last year, We were almost ready to go[1] and yet very happy. I can remember what fun C. and I had sitting on Daddy's bed each morning with the rolls of maps. And Daddy letting C. talk, with a half-amused and half-incredulous expression on his face—kind of a "Whee! What'll he be up to next!" expression—and he'd poke me as though to say so. "You think you'll go right around *there*, do you!" A grin and a poke at me.

We have had to stay here longer than we thought, because of the long-drawn-out trial. Tomorrow we go back.

Charles said the other day (we went by the place on the hill where they found the baby), "That doesn't count at all, Anne.

[1] On the flight to the Orient.

I'm not sure that any of that really counts. We think only in finite values, in terms of 'beginning' and 'end.' " Then he talked about that philosophical question, "Which is longer, the past or the future?" Col. Henry says the past, because the future keeps feeding into it. "But," says C., "I see that question in this picture: a man is standing watching an enormous flywheel, a wheel so big that he can only see a very small part of one side, and it looks to him as though it were *all* going away from him."

Then he said, "Man has always feared the unknown, and yet when he has understood it, it has been good, *not* evil." He talked and talked, and I felt great strength and comfort, so I've written this long letter. I wonder if I've got any of it across to you. He keeps saying, "The more I study science, the more convinced I feel . . ." etc. And most people use science as a road to a completely negative philosophy.

Dear Mother, I wish you could see the rambler rose with six pink roses on it, and the lilies that looked dead, sprouting out of the clay; also my big blue bowl full of Madonna lilies and larkspur (from Englewood) in the dining room. And orange tiger lilies balancing the Ming horse in the living-room alcove-place. This is another house now—one in which there was tragedy years and years ago.

TO E. L. L. L.   *Hopewell, Tuesday* [*July 6th*]
Dear M.—
We have been "planning" things for the house and grounds, the chief thing being in C.'s mind: How can we make it *safe* to live here? Guard it all the time with an armed guard or have several well-trained police dogs? He got quite thrilled about the idea and Sunday we went over to Princeton and saw some of the latter. The best one, a beautiful big "wolf" who does not make friends easily but is devoted to one person, appealed to C. very much. C. tried to make friends with him, to whistle, to touch him. At the last this great animal bared his teeth and growled. "That's fine!" said C. "I want a dog who won't make friends with strangers."

The trainer[1] said it would take fourteen days to get the dog to feel that C. was his master; then C. could do anything with him. But for the first few days we'd have to lock him up and not approach him without the trainer there—not try to touch him or go near him as he might spring at us. When one of these goes for you you're pretty well mauled up. (I was getting more and more nervous.) He went on to tell of how he had the dog in a car once and stopped to ask the way of a policeman and the policeman leaned on the open window sill and the dog tore a great hole in his uniform! None of this seemed to discourage C. He said it would be wonderful. The dog would be kept in a pen right outside the house here, and sleep out there at night and walk with us anywhere in these woods and no one would get near us without our knowing.

Well, the trainer brought him in something that looked like a police wagon with the dog bolted up inside. Then we wired up one door of the garage with heavy wire, put a bowl of water and a box of straw in it before the trainer left, so we wouldn't have to go in again. He was coming in the morning to feed it. Skean and Wahgoosh pranced and barked around the wagon. The police dog thundered back and we shut them up in the house. Then the trainer took him off on a leash and C. and I went with them for a walk. Apparently the dog won't attack anyone if his master tells him to keep quiet. But I felt like keeping out of his way.

Then the trainer left "Pal," the dog, locked up in the garage. C. and I sat and watched him and let Skean and Wahgoosh out. They pranced up to the wire and barked. The dog bared his teeth and gave one bellow. Wahgoosh fell over about three times and Skean held up a lame paw and yip-yip-yipped back to us. The dog was very restless, knocked over his water pail and then yelped for water. C. began to talk to him, giving orders through the wire, got him to lie down, put his fingers through the wire and scratched his back. Pal wagged his tail.

[1] Joseph Weber, breeder and trainer of German shepherd dogs.

Then C. decided he was going in the lion's den. I was worried. But he took a stick with him and opened the door slowly ordering the dog to lie down, which he did very easily. Then C. got his water bowl and filled it. He kept the dog under control all the time. Then he decided to take him out on a leash (with a choke collar), which we did, C. trying all the time to get more and more control of him. The dog gradually obeyed every signal (the trainer had taught them to C.), and by the evening he followed C. every step, and we all felt safer.

We had quite a time with Wahgoosh, who showed no fear at all after the first introduction and is wild to play with him. The big dog never hurts him though he could knock him over with his paw, and they are by now very fond of each other, playing for hours. Skean still yips and hides under sofas.

The next morning the trainer was surprised and delighted to see how C. had won the dog to him. C. feels sure now that he is our friend and protector for good. He means to leave him down here "when" we live here, but right now C. wants him around every moment so he can feel sure of him. So when we go to Englewood C. is going to take him.

Did you know C. was a lion tamer? I'm afraid I've made this all sound terrifying. I was frightened at first but he is so docile, now he knows this is his home, and is so beautifully trained that you only have to speak to make him stop anything.

I don't think I'd leave him alone with a child. But C. says yes; if he got to know our child it would be the best protection—too *much* so, really. If there were strangers' children there and they slapped our child the dog might hurt them. So you'd have to guard against that.

This is a long letter but it has been so absorbing, and it makes C. feel safe about this house. Of course I think that even if it just got *known* that we *have* a "police dog," *that* is half the battle. People won't come around. It isn't necessary to keep the dog wild and fierce as long as he has that reputation. And he certainly isn't fierce now, except last night, C., to test him, said to him when the trooper came up, *"What's that,* Pal!" And the dog bristled up and roared to get out. Then a word from C. and he calmed down.

DIARY   *Hopewell-Englewood, Wednesday, July 6, 1932*
I take charge of "Pal" and feel like Una and the lion—great creature padding up and downstairs with me, his big soft heavy paws like socks of sand, padding behind me.

Supper out on the terrace, Charles disciplining one or the other of the dogs all through the meal, like a mother constantly correcting her children, and you think in exasperation, "When *will* she stop talking to them?" Skean and Bogey, tied together, nearly pull the table down. Peter keeps up a constant growl under my chair; Pal roams around like a panther.

Englewood, Thursday, July 7, 1932
Ridiculous struggles with the sun-bath tent. Pal into the pool.

The dog fight: Peter, panicky, bites my cheek; Pal leaps on him and grabbing him by the hind quarters shakes him.

All terribly excited.

Englewood, Saturday, July 9, 1932
Great tearing wind in the oak trees—completely washes your mind and spirit of any desire for activity, pours into you and fills up that need.

Fireworks behind the trees—the cool dark—light from the house spreading at our feet—Pal stretched out in peace.

The devotion of this dog following me everywhere is quite thrilling, like having a new beau.

Monday, July 11, 1932
Elizabeth Bacon [Bisgood][1] out for lunch and afternoon. Hurt and courageous [after tragic experience with her baby].

[1] A college friend of A. M. L., now Mrs. F. K. Rodewald.

To have been through something makes it easy to talk. One earns the right to understand—and give sympathy. We talk and talk and understand.

Pal leaping on us in the dark.

Tuesday, July 12, 1932

Chester and Amey for swim and supper on porch.

Amey in her red, shiny hat—cool and quiet. Talk about death: "I don't think any of us intellectually fear death, intellectually doubt that the course of nature is good and right, but the instinctive physical panic . . ."

I feel so terribly far away from the baby, in one of those numb periods the pendulum has swung into. I do not try to pull him back, I only feel the inevitable farawayness and do not try to fight it. Heavy, thick, unfeeling—I still feel dumbly and mutely sad. And yet it is not that poignant and comforting *missing him* that is, in its way, possession.

Amey says it will come back. She is comforting and I, who dread, in a way, this new baby, feeling it will stand between me and Charlie, feel comforted at her saying that the new thing will be a contrast to bring him back, that he will get closer. And then, at night, I dream, as though to justify her saying this, that I am looking at the new baby and, for the first time, I see next to it—Charlie's face.

Friday, July 15, 1932

Amey brought a "cobweb" [blanket] for the new baby, because I had used the other one so for Charlie. Sermon on Politeness: "Someone once sent Chester and me some wild ducks. I don't like wild duck, but I wrote back how delicious they were, how my brother seldom ate meat but loved these, etc., etc., and we've got them every year since. We keep giving them away; they come steadily!"

Saturday, July 16, 1932

Really followed schedule: Harmony, sun bath, swim, lunch, practicing, dogs, nap, sight reading. Felt a little gain in the reading.

I feel obsessed now when I say good-by to people—that I will not see them again. Something in me that says perpetually: "Seize this while you have it, remember that gesture, it is the last time." Something in me that wants to make everything significant because, perhaps, I did not make significant enough the few hours I had with Charlie, spending them recklessly, looking ahead to endless years of him.

But you are always fooled—it is not what you expect that waits for you.

C. very patient with my heaviness and apathy.

Pal wakes me in the morning, with his nose on the bed.

Englewood, Sunday night, July 16th

Darling Elisabeth,

We are sitting on the "sun porch" in complete darkness except for a little halo around C. on the sofa reading, and one around me at the desk; all the dogs at our feet limp and quiet, and the radio playing "Unfinished Symphony." It is lovely, peaceful, and cool.

Almost as England sounded in your letters—your wonderful letters—the two that were written during the visit of Vernon.[1] I read them over and over and really dreamed of buggy riding and the moor and little lambs. They were so cool and refreshing.

Then the next day Vernon called up and came out and we had the most lovely satisfying day, talking and walking and swimming, in spite of my bulk and age (I feel so old). But I was surprised at how much older he was too, in understanding and living; I didn't expect that. He met me on my own grounds. Isn't

[1] Vernon Munroe, Jr., friend of Dwight Morrow, Jr.

it a marvelous, cool, refreshing, stimulating relationship! I think of Mrs. Neilson: "There is one nice thing about being married: you can tell someone how much you think of him."

In the meantime I practice constantly (can read "Hushaby, Baby" slowly, you know) and keep the police dog from tearing through the screen door after the Butlers, Jim McIlvaine,[1] etc., who come to use the court and the pool. He makes the most terrifying bellowing when he sees them skirt the corner of the house, and I hold his collar but, just on general principles, pat him and say "Good dog. Good dog!"

I could almost hug Aubrey Morgan[2] for getting to you before the Violet news, but don't worry, I won't mention it, even if I should ever meet him. But it is one of those things—perfectly done at exactly the right moment. Such a rare and perfect thing, so beautifully timed for your need that it stands out in your life as a golden moment. And you feel about it out of all proportion to the thing itself.

You have been away too long now, I'd like to see you again. But your letters and knowing you are there are wonderful.

DIARY   *Sunday, July 17, 1932*
C. and I alone all day, he studying bacteriology; I, music—really enough—too much!

Cannot walk without cramps, but swimming is glorious—I am young and slim again.

I am in a kind of stupor now about the baby. I do not go up to his room or look at his things or write in his record or go over the pictures. I feel in a kind of hopeless numbness. He is gone. I can't get him back that way or any other way. He is just gone. There is nothing to do. How futile to try to hang on to him by these scraps. How futile to hope that a miniature would have

[1] Cousin of A. M. L.

[2] Aubrey Niel Morgan, of Cardiff, Wales.

some of him—and even so, what comfort would it be in the face of that complete loss. The picture gets dimmer and I, hopeless, do not fight the inevitable.

Perhaps the numbness is partly physical protection. Perhaps Emily Dickinson's

> "After great pain a formal feeling comes—
> The nerves sit ceremonious like tombs;
> The stiff heart questions—was it He that bore?
> And yesterday—or centuries before?
>
> . . . .
>
> This is the hour of lead
> Remembered if outlived
> As freezing persons recollect
> The snow—
> First chill, then stupor, then
> The letting go."

Monday, July 18, 1932

Work all morning at Harmony and afternoon too, feel too much time spent for what I get out of it. No time left for the things I want most: sight reading, sight singing, timing.

Wednesday, July 20, 1932

Miss Hawley— Nothing to criticize in the miniature and yet it leaves me cold. I realize the futility of this hanging on to shreds of a person, thinking that will bring the person back.

Thursday, July 21, 1932

Mrs. Lindbergh comes.

Friday, July 22, 1932

Frightful walk with Peter, Pal, and the two black dogs, pulling Peter, chasing Pal ahead of me, shouting, stamping—very hot and angry. Every time I shouted my stomach contracted. Then I was trying to talk to Mrs. Lindbergh and my mind felt distracted and crowded, as though full of the mussy sound of stiff paper being crunched up.

The world we talked about was so cruel and shifting, no one and nothing in the world to pin one's faith to. I felt weary and discouraged yet conscious of my own faith pushing up stubbornly again like a weed that has been plucked out over and over —and always bobs back.

Mrs. Lindbergh shows me blue prints of C. as a little boy and I realize with a rush of emotion: "This I will never have, never see pictures of my son, my son Charles, growing up, with his first gun, learning to swim, etc." As though no other son could possibly be really "my son."

Mrs. Lindbergh's dream: "And you and Charles were leading him by the hand and I said: 'Can this be really little Charles?' and you said it was"—a flash into the depths.

Saturday, July 23, 1932

To Hopewell—a long hot ride with Pal slobbering and panting and restlessly turning round and round trying to find a comfortable seat.

Hopewell, Sunday, July 24, 1932

Feeling of terrible insecurity and cowardice in facing this ordeal of having a baby. This time (I wasn't before) I am afraid of death, afraid of going anywhere without C., afraid because death now seems so near. I feel as though there were no escape from that inevitable and dreadful moment when we must be separated. And it does not seem, as before, a hazy, unreal, distant moment banishable from this world of youth.

Tuesday, July 26, 1932

I do not know why we all live counting on the laws of Chance, when it is always the exception that affects our lives.

Saturday, July 30, 1932

Still absolutely numb about baby: "This is the hour of lead."

I am waiting for the pendulum to swing back again from numbness to realization, and I dread the blow of it, yet this freezing is worse, for I grope for realization and cannot put my hand on it—only a dull ache.

Sunday, July 31, 1932

A year since I said good-by to Daddy, patting his back on the *Mouette* in North Haven.

Wednesday, August 3, 1932

M. R., thin and starved for life, envying me. "But *you* are happy," she said. I thought of Daddy and of the baby, of Elisabeth and Charles and my life, and I said: "Yes, I am happy." I knew she was right.

Mother [back from Europe] calling for me, running down the hall in her little black dress and white collar. So eager, almost trembling with relief, it seemed, to be home and things still safe.

Thursday, August 4, 1932

Mother and I walk in the garden and talk of Elisabeth and of Daddy and of Charles Jr., and English people understanding suspense because of the war.

Of C.'s belief (at least his courageous and open view) of immortality and the picture of the wheel. "You married a wonderful man—a wonderful man." Mother breaks down my numbness.

Emerson on his deathbed saying, "That beautiful boy." Heartbreaking. I hope it is true.

Friday, August 5, 1932

Every once in a while I realize the miracle that boy was, the miracle we lost, not just a child, but the miracle of a child, a first child—the miracle of immortality, of life, of love. No other child can mean the same.

Sunday, August 7, 1932

Mother and I plan for the new wing. She has Tom moving bureaus, pulling out the drawer tenderly, "and all lined with cedar!" Bird pictures out of the attic, chintz from the sewing room, a little heart-shaped mirror—"No, the other one"—and the room begins to look charming, with the charm of Mother's rooms, like a woman whipping a dress into shape—snipping here, pinching here, a ribbon there. And you hardly see her doing it.

Mother looking over her diaries at night, looking back—all that is precious behind her. I can't say anything and can hardly bear to leave her to go to C., who whistles.

TO E. R. M. *Englewood, August 8th*

Darling,

The crickets are a thick curtain of sound around the house tonight. Nothing else penetrates. But it really isn't very hot. And I rather like it.

It is so lovely to have Mother back, and the burst of life that always attends it, is fun after our quiet summer. And unpacking of presents. Did you see the cradle?[1] It is just what a cradle should be (like Chaucer's "horsly horse"), but quite narrow and long (evidently intended for that long lanky girl I am about to have!). But so darling that it doesn't matter.

Mother is all prepared for a girl, with the most enchanting pink dresses ("Annekin pink"—really it does remind me of Twilight Park, that fresh cool pink, wild-rose pink I think it is). I had no preference before but with those pink dresses ready to spoil I shall want a girl.

[1] An old cradle Mrs. Morrow had bought in England for the new baby.

Tomorrow we have the larger Aunts[1] here *en force*. They all expect daily events. I feel rather mad, waiting around. Do you remember that panicky feeling in *Romeo and Juliet*, in the tomb where Juliet hasn't quite died yet and people are banging on the doors? And you feel like saying, "Hurry up, hurry up! You ought to be stretched out in peace." That's the way I feel.

C. really wants to go to North Haven and thinks we can stay "at least two weeks" (I plan a whole month) and take the baby and nurse. Will we really be there together? Is it possible? I do not believe it. I haven't been there in peace (for more than one or two *too precious* days) since before I was married. I have great faith in what it will be and do for me, as though I could recapture that security, the feeling of endless time and endless youth and endless happiness (not that one was always happy, but one felt it was there in reserve). But I suppose that is just youth and can't be recaptured. Not that one is old when one is still in the twenties, but I feel so definitely on the other side of the fence from Con.

C. has trained Thor [Pal renamed] to lead Bogey and Skean on the leash: he yanks them around like an arrogant nursemaid. Perhaps he could be as useful as "Nana" in *Peter Pan*. C. thinks he might help in The Little School.

DIARY   *Tuesday, August 9, 1932*

I thought today, looking forward to the pain of this labor, that I would and have suffered more pain than he did that night—at least I hope that is true. And that helps me. I'm glad I can feel what he felt and much more. I'm glad he felt no more.

The Morrow aunts as opposed to the smaller Cutter aunts.

Friday, August 12, 1932

They start work on the bathroom in the new wing.[1]

Mother and I putting the baby's toys away in the attic. I remembered what hard work he had pulling the blocks out of the cart—they fitted in so neatly—and how he wanted me to do it: "Out!" or "Eee!" Washing a bottle in the bathroom (with a backache) made me think of washing dishes after his lunch. He should be there behind me in his chair with hands and face and tray all cooky, chewing slowly and wetly on the cooky and mashing it on the tray and then reaching up toward the tin box for another, watching me abstractly and with arrogance.

Saturday, August 13, 1932

So tired and hot and hurt at having to wait so long for this baby, so sick of the discomfort and pains that mean nothing, and going to bed each night thinking, "Perhaps tonight," and waking up, "Perhaps today," and looking ahead and thinking, "This is the last music lesson" or "the last doctor's appointment" or "the last Sunday" and finding it isn't.

Sunday, August 14, 1932

Out in the sun with C. by swimming pool, C. making Thor dive for the ball, putting the ball on a string and tantalizing him. Skean jumping for the string, hoarse fierce little barks.

Told C. about new wing bath. We are up and down the stairs all morning and afternoon, C. measuring, planning, correcting to get more room: "I've got it now." A whistle from the top floor: "Could you come up here a moment?"

The dogs run away, C. after them; finds many reporters at gate—were eight yesterday. Terribly hot and discouraged at night. Is it all starting over again? Shall we move out into the

---

[1] The Lindberghs, in an attempt to obtain privacy and security, had decided to make their home temporarily at Next Day Hill, the Morrows' house in Englewood, N. J.

"sticks"? I cannot bear to think of it in terms of the baby—starting all over again. If it were not for the publicity that surrounds us we might still have him.

I see him sometimes when I am not trying now and the shock makes me gasp a little and then the picture goes. As he becomes more real the tragedy becomes more of a horror, especially at night.

Monday, August 15, 1932

Jerry Land[1] and C. talk of Means[2] and Curtis. I can hardly bear to go back in imagination, as I do when they talk of Curtis, to my hope, my real, surging hope of those last three weeks when I got C.'s telegrams from Norfolk. "Greatly encouraged—too many things check," etc.

Tuesday, August 16, 1932

Labor pains start about 12 Monday night. About 3:45 into town, slowing up for each pain. I felt so strange (in the grip of something inevitable and tremendous, an iron hand) passing through the everyday streets of New York, past milk wagons and trucks, newsstands and advertisements, and I going to the biggest thing in life except death, and the nearest thing to that. Arrive at apartment at 4:35. Miss Cummings, Dr. Hawks, Dr. Flagg arrive.[3]

First gas: just the same. First "This isn't working" and then a sudden loosening, your fingers lose their weight, shake it off; your body shakes it off as a snake its skin. Gradually you are just *thought* and you whirl through time and space rhythmically.

I had exactly the same mental concept I had before under gas. Someone questioning me (perhaps part of myself), but someone

[1] Rear Admiral Emory Scott Land, cousin of C. A. L.

[2] Gaston B. Means, who had posed as a negotiator with the kidnappers, as Curtis had done.

[3] Miss Marie Cummings, nurse; Dr. E. M. Hawks, obstetrician; Dr. P. J. Flagg, anesthetist.

was listening for my answers, as to what the *greatest thing* was, the riddle of the universe—what did everything boil down to in the end? And I would give one answer after another and always the answer was wrong, and I heard *The Thing listening,* laughing at me and showing me that all my answers proved my egoism, my smallness, but especially my egoism. It all came back to self, and I was ashamed. "Everything is Charles," "Everything is Mother," "Everything is rhythm," "Everything is space," "Everything is motion," "Everything is the same."

I wanted to find the answer so I could merge into this most important thing, and I kept saying to myself: "I must be humble, I must get away from self, I am not humble enough—next time I will find it." For with each answer I dropped from one whirling cycle (one universe, one cycle of existence) into another, each time nearer the truth but not quite there.

Then my body coming to, a singing fire of pain and bliss: "I am having a baby, my first baby. No" (my eyes fastened on the picture on the wall covered with newspaper—I clung to that as a drowning man to a rock), "no, I am in the apartment, my second baby, and is it all over?" (It seemed so long.) "That was quite easy." Then I realized with a leap, "This is my second baby, my first baby was killed and this is just the first pain" (with gas) and I woke up into the heavy helplessness of my body in uncontrollable tears.

I always knew whether C. was in the room or not, a second or two before I woke and found my eyes drawn inevitably to his. I *had* to turn to him: it was the one compelling thing in me, like Thor leaping pell-mell over things to get to me—a blind instinct. Sometimes my hand in his was the first thing to come back to life—my hand in his; while I was still blind and deaf and dumb, I could feel his forefinger stroking my wrist. Like the first tip of rock rising above the receding flood of unconsciousness.

The time under gas seemed so long—aeons. I lived through one cycle after another, one universe after another, and I would wake and say, "How long was that?" and they answered, "A minute and a half." It was unbelievable. And I would come to and they would be talking about such trivial things of this world when I had lived in such vast worlds. And I looked down on them amazed (as Narwitz in *The Fountain* [Charles Morgan's novel] or *Lazarus* in Browning) and then corrected myself, "Remember —you must be humble, humble."

Sometimes the answer to the question was "deception": "*Everything* is false, a cheat, a cheap trick with no meaning." And I would rebel and say, "It *can't* be—I *won't* believe it."

The pain was just as terrible, so terrible that you are not yourself any more—you are pain—everything in the world is pain. Sometimes more particular than that: you are impaled by it, unable to escape. Racing with pain, trying to escape into the gas while the tongues of pain lick at your heels, like the tide overtaking you.

But the labor was so much shorter this time (only four hours in the apartment) that I was not tired out and much more conscious in between pains and much more rebellious: no restraint of courage or endurance. And I was conscious, even when unable to talk or move and when the people around me thought I was unconscious. And I was amused at them: "How funny—they think I can't hear them and I can." Perhaps it will be like that when I die.

I was conscious of the different stages, of something between my legs, of being carried into the other room, of Dr. Hawks' gentle "Not much longer now," of Mother's drawn patient face. (I felt a profound pity and almost contempt for men: "How can a man ever understand a woman who has been through this?") I was conscious enough to be afraid (and to care) that everything was not going all right, that they'd found something wrong with the baby.

Finally waking up very sore but with the weight free from my abdomen, and that same unmistakable shrill bleat—uncertain hesitating bleat, across all other sounds, as though it were the only sound—of the baby. Mother's voice quiet, dear, and full of humor: "A little boy, Anne." I could not answer but went under again—I knew she would repeat it. "A little boy." I wanted to know over and over again if the baby was *all right,* perfectly all right, then thought how lovely it would have been for Charlie—a little brother. Miss Cummings telling me I must not think of that, I must start all over again fresh and forget that—*"Forget it!"* I could not help crying.

They brought me the baby. "He's not very beautiful, but . . ." "Oh dear—he has a nose just like Grandma Morrow." Emily called them for breakfast. It was only 9 A.M.! I *could* not believe it.

Then later all day (with a wheeling head and the recurring afterpains) I was blissfully happy, relieved, saying and thinking over and over, "The baby is all right, all right, he is here, he's all right," until C. said, "He has a wart on his left toe," and began teasing me. But I could not get over it. Out of last fall, out of this winter, a perfect baby. It was a miracle.

And I felt years removed from the night before and the months before that night. I felt I had given birth to more than a baby: to new life in myself, in C., in Mother. C., a teasing boy again; Mother, gently, softly gay as she used to be with Charlie. And I felt as if a great burden had fallen off me. I could not imagine the baby would do this for me, but I felt life given back to me—a door to life opened. I *wanted* to live, I felt power to live. I was not afraid of death or life: a spell had been broken, the spell over us that made me dread everything and feel that nothing would go right after this. The spell was broken by this real, tangible, perfect baby, coming into an imperfect world and coming out of the teeth of sorrow—a miracle. My faith had been reborn.

TO E. L. L. L.   *Englewood, August 16th*
Dear M.,

I must write you tonight just a scribble because I am so happy and relieved. *The baby here*—a fine big (7 lb. 14 oz.!) boy, strong and well and *absolutely perfect physically.* I cannot tell you what a relief it is, and what a miracle it seems.

Oh, to have that baby here, and so strong and fine and fit—*nothing* wrong! If I stress that, it is because I have felt since this winter so unsure of *everything* and so afraid that something might go wrong. But it was all right. C., I think, is very happy though he was certain it would be a girl. It is wonderful to have a son—a Lindbergh. He seems in grand spirits because he is teasing me.

What does it look like? Just as ugly as most babies. Really it is, with a nose (I hope it will change) like mine. Big eyes, wide space between the eyes, and—this thrills me—the Lindbergh dimple in the chin. The coloring looks fair, though the hair is that funny dark no-color of newborn babies. He cries lustily, has big feet and hands. His features are all bigger than Charles Jr. and the body bigger. But such a well, perfect baby—I am terribly happy. I hope you are. C. won't discuss names, and says if it can't be *Anne* it will have to be *Andy!*

DIARY   *Wednesday, August 17th*
C.: "You'll wear the baby out, looking at it."
Mother says it has a mouth like Daddy's.

C. talks with Mother about making a Children's Home out of the Hopewell house. "The only way its history can be used constructively." C. gives out plea to press for privacy for baby.

           Thursday, August 18th—rainy day
What name? Birth certificate filed without name. Slight reaction to elation; talk with Miss Cummings about case. I find that I have accepted, swallowed whole, one picture of it, and the

slightest shift in that, the moving of a trifle, a different light, again makes it unbearable.

The weather puts me back into last winter's mood and I realize, "It is still there, it will always be with me."

Mother told me that Emily, the morning the new baby was born, put her arms around Mother and said from her heart: "If only he were here to see his little brother!" I love her for it and cried at such heartbreaking sweetness and understanding—cried and cried.

Mother says she can see him reaching up to look in the crib. I must remember that the other night, in that freeing of the spirit from the body, I felt near death and it was not terrible. And C. talking of death last night, "None of the natural things of nature are terrible—they are good," and "The more I go into science the more I feel that one cannot say that everything ends with the death of the body. . . . I think it's very egotistical to say everything ends when the collection of atoms that was you scatters." "But I don't want to be separated from *you.*" "Maybe you won't be."

August 19th

Mother to Englewood. Dr. Martin to see baby. Says he looks like a three-weeks-old baby. He has Morrow blue eyes and long hard arms and legs, like C., and C.'s fair skin and (I think) a curl to his hair.

I love to watch my little rabbit, stretching his mouth, wriggling, and his nostrils quivering with a yawn. And as I look at his inarticulate efforts (and we watch and say something trivial) I think: Perhaps you are perfectly conscious but unable to say so, as I was (half under gas) and waking up to this world. You are still half in the other world and look down on our mundane talk with contempt and bewilderment.

Saturday, August 20th

Breasts sore, and a temperature, and rather depressed. I realize I am thinking too much about that night. I must definitely accept the theory we have. I must learn by heart what we believe until we know better and put the other possibilities out of my mind. If I try to face other possibilities I shall go mad. As to the rest, I feel I must turn my mind and emotions to some compensation—I do not know what—for him, for children perhaps. Perhaps for my own, perhaps for others—I haven't it clear yet. I like C.'s idea of the house at Hopewell being used for children.

The new baby brings him back to me in so many ways: a pucker of the mouth. A droop of the eyelids made me remember the way I used to make Charlie go to sleep when I was holding him in the car on the way to Princeton, by closing my eyes. Then he would close his, open them a little to see if mine were closed, a game.

Mother in her soft gray flowered chiffon, her hair just the right silver gray (pewter gray), makes one think what a lovely color gray is—cobwebs and mist and gulls' breasts. Mother reads Elinor Wylie to me.

Sunday, August 21st

Breasts better. The city quiet and cool. C. teasing Marie [Cummings]. Mother and I miss Elisabeth and Con terribly, wanting to tell them the news. I can hear Elisabeth bending over him and interpreting the funny little wriggles of his mouth and nose. Mother and I both called him "Charlie"—it slipped out so naturally. Although he is very different, he arouses the same emotion of gaiety and tenderness. I love the way he opens his mouth wide like a baby robin the minute Marie tucks the cloth under his chin, before the bottle.

It seems to me that what Narwitz meant in *The Fountain* when he said Death was the answer is that death is the crown to all our attempts throughout life, our perpetual endless struggle to lose ourselves in something bigger than ourselves, to lose ourselves in pleasure or excitement or love or work or art or creation; and as the greatest joy in life comes when we succeed in this in a small way, why should it be terrible when we completely succeed? Only this rests on the assumption that we are not snuffed out at death but absorbed into a greater flame.

Monday, August 22, 1932

I *hate* eating in bed. The tray is not level and there is no room for your knees and you spread your toast on the bias and eat it, crumbs falling down your neck and into the bed, always creeping ahead of your hand down into the hollow where you're sitting. Then the butter knife slides off the plate onto the clean tray cloth and you reach for it and it tumbles onto the sheet. The worst is drinking on the bias. The water climbs up the side of your face instead of going in your mouth. And your food is so *very* far away from you, down over that mountain of chest, over your tummy and knees and the expanse of rumpled sheet and smooth tray cloth. To carry it all that way on a fork from plate to mouth is an ordeal.

The baby starts to gain.

It is as though, having another child, I now see the tragedy in the flesh. It is much more real. "He was as real as this on my arm. . . . His eyes closed that way. . . . *That* happened to a child like this one."

It is strange that looking back on anything in your life, no matter how terrible, it seems bearable to you, and anything different seems unbearable (even less terrible things). You look on other people's tragedies or other possible tragedies to yourself and say, *"That* I could not bear."

Almost you would not have it otherwise (your tragedy). In your acceptance of it, I mean, almost you would not have it undone, because by wishing it undone you admit *it might not have been*. And that is the door to the torture chamber.

Tuesday, August 23, 1932

Aunt Alice sees the baby, brings him a lucky Turkish bead, turquoise blue.

The soft softness of his hair, brown and velvet, a rabbit's nose. I stroke it.

Wednesday, August 24, 1932

His first bath.

Emily sticks her red face in the door to say confidingly, "I thought all de time it was goin to be a boy."

Pris's husband killed. I think if it were I I should feel the terrible paradox that "He is the only person who could help me through this ordeal, he is the only person who could give me faith to meet it. His wisdom, his strength, is the only thing that could comfort me. He is the only person who could give me faith in his immortality."

I wonder if she feels that terrible shock at the speed with which telegrams, flowers, and letters of condolence come in; the shock of everyone's accepting the fact of his death so quickly and so easily, without a murmur of protest, without one rebellious "It *cannot* be," when you cannot accept the realization yourself, when it is almost treason to.

C. looking at me over the footboard as I hold the baby at night over my shoulder, his look for an instant, and I think, "No—now I am satisfied, I will not plague you any more to ask you how you feel . . . I am satisfied."

Thursday, August 25, 1932

Baby up to his birth weight.

Friday, August 26, 1932

C. to Baltimore. I must get over this mother-hen complex, afraid whenever he goes away that he may be hurt or killed.

C. home at 9. Ida had left a huge pot of spare ribs of beef, vegetables, hot dogs, stew, etc., on the stove. "He'll come out and fix it himself—he likes it that way." (They are so proud of knowing his taste and of its being the same as theirs.) And Emily: "Oh yeah—he'll come out and put the whole pot on the table."

Saturday, August 27, 1932

Glorious letter from Elisabeth. English country life with a bloom over it all, like a child's golden world at the beginning of summer. Is she in love?

C. rolling the baby up in a blanket, jelly-roll-fashion, to illustrate a good cover for airplane travel.

Mother reading Morgan's *Portrait in a Mirror*. Her voice (and the fact that the story is held only in the spoken word and I do not see it before my eyes in print) glazing the story with a dream quality, I float in and around it—a delicious feeling.

Feeling young and irresponsible one moment as I hadn't for nine months. Strange how that self-protective instinct unconsciously rises in you with a child. In spite of your own desires, something more fundamental rises in you while you are carrying a child and says, *Take care.* Feeling very happy, and very sad at the same time: C. and the baby and feeling well again—and little Charlie and the long year behind us. I felt I could not carry both the great burden of joy and of sorrow. Life too heavy to hold.

Sunday, August 28, 1932

Baby gains—first gain over birth weight: 7 lb. 15 oz.

I woke with a weight on my chest, an old, old weight, but I could not recognize it. Then I remembered my dream: Mother and I putting away some little shoes of Charlie's. I said, "I don't believe I've really faced it that he's dead, Mother. I keep thinking ahead in terms of him, as I did when I was away on the trip."

C. sat me up in chair.

The baby up-chucking milk and my unreasonable terror. "He must *not* be sick, I must not lose this child," and then like a returning wave the thought rushing back, "I must not let this terror spoil my child's life."

And I looked back to my realizing last winter (before we knew) in a dark moment, "He will not come back. This will eat into our whole life." But it must not.

Monday, August 29, 1932

Tom gives a George Ist mug to "Baby Lindbergh." I can see Daddy admiring it: "This is a lovely mug."

Elsie and Whateley, glowing with happiness and sunburn, up to see baby, bring silver napkin ring. "Such a *big* baby!" "The very *image* . . ."

Tuesday, August 30, 1932
Out to Englewood

Wake early—too excited to sleep—like children's birthday mornings.

C. carries me out to the tree by the pen. The dogs bark wildly, Skean *tearing* toward me, leaping on me, his teeth showing in a smile. Then Thor, leaping on me, licking my shoes when C. carried me up into Grandma's room, the baby in the cradle covered by the old pink-embroidered cover. Skean and Bogey rush at the cradle, jump up on the sides, Skean especially wagging his tail, looking at the baby. When Marie picked up the baby to give him the bottle Skean leaped up and licked his toes. He seemed very happy—really—to see him. Thor not very interested, but licked his head.

To bed for afternoon with a neck wooden with excitement. Thor and Skean and Bogey at the foot of my bed.

Elisabeth and Con home, Elisabeth's eyes shining out of her tan and Con glowing and enchanting-looking. A new Greta hair wave, a snappy black dress, a black and white Paris hat. We had so much to say, we couldn't. But at night when I sat upstairs in bed at the window and could look down on candles and their heads at the table on the terrace and hear their voices in the dark—Elisabeth high, swift, laughing, Con quick, sharp, pointed, Mother low, even, assured, with a snap of emphasis somewhere; C. low, without emphasis, a burst of shouting after it—then I felt a glow of realization. They sounded very charming, too—like a family in a novel.

Wednesday, August 31, 1932

Talk with Elisabeth: her winter, how to keep Dulverton calm here—"a tempo within the tempo."

Why are we all so nervous here?

1 So near New York—too accessible to telephones, people, plans, going in and out, etc.

2 Mother's energy—without a good outlet.

3 All naturally nervous.

4 Too many people waiting on us—too big a house.

5 Footsteps—no carpets.

Friday, September 2, 1932
Very hot

Elisabeth talks with me about Aubrey shyly, humbly—sweetly. And I am so afraid of stepping on something tender. Con drives off gaily to Connecticut, Elisabeth's hat on her jaunty curls.

I dream of Daddy—vividly, very vividly. He is sitting in a chair and he asks me for a kiss, half wistfully, half humorously. I go to him (how it hurt me to think of this when I woke) slowly, reluctantly, and absent-mindedly as I did as a child so often. Then a change, as though I realized, "But *think* of being able to kiss Daddy—I won't always be able to." And I went towards him lovingly and looked at his eyes and thought how beautiful they were—how they were *His Eyes,* brimming over with blue and twinkle (that brimming-over quality I had forgotten)—and I loved him and kissed him.

TO E. L. L. L.   [*September 3rd*]

I laughed at that lovely white rabbit for *the* rabbit. There is a slight resemblance—I think the nose, if you see what I mean!

We moved out here [from New York] Tuesday and have had a *terribly* hot spell. Has it been like that in Detroit? The baby has had prickly heat but otherwise is not at all upset by the weather and has gained steadily; now weighs 8 lb. 5½ oz. He sleeps outside on the porch with the dogs on guard. The only trouble is they bark so fiercely at anyone who comes around (even a gardener cutting grass) that they wake him. But I like them there. (There is always someone listening for their bark who goes to see what it is.)

The baby looks better since he's been in the air a little. I am taking things quite slowly, not to have any setbacks, but hope to be normally active in a week or so. We hope to go to Maine for two weeks as soon as the doctor lets us. Perhaps when the baby is four weeks old (a week from Monday or Tuesday). I want to take care of the baby myself with Elsie to help me up there. (There's a doctor on the island.)

His hair *is* curly. I think he may have side dimples (sounds like side whiskers!). The doctor calls him "Ajax" because of his big brawny arms and fists ready for a fight. I long to have you see him but will not press it. Whenever you can, we want you.

DIARY   [*Englewood*], *Saturday, September 3, 1932*

Harmless half-wit calls up at Marie's window late at night. C. calls the police. We laugh about it, but it puts me completely back in last winter's mood—a half-mad world where nothing is safe, nothing is sure, anything can happen.

M. [Marie]: "Do you think it's all right to leave the baby in there?"

A. (bluffing): "Oh yes—we'll leave the doors open!"

C. (not bluffing): "It might not be a bad idea to have the baby sleep with someone for a while."

A.: "And in the daytime—on the porch?"

C.: "I've been thinking about it, and I think someone better watch him."

We give in. Will this haunt us forever?

Sunday, September 4, 1932

Yellow leaves falling slowly, gently, from the tulip trees.

Mr. Marshall [the night watchman] wakes us up at five to ask about Bogey.[1] I lie awake and think about Hopewell nights, and that first night. Will I live through that night in horror and imagination *every* night in my life? Is there no way I can get around it except by pushing it back and not facing it, pushing it back and thinking about "plans" or "shopping" or "the new wing" —something trivial and worrying?

Began to realize Proust's conception of *time*. Time is *not* a string on which events are strung in sequence like so many beads you can count off and forget. I will never get past that night, because it is in *me*. I shall be near it or far away from it according to mood. Mood controlled by sensation and association. Nearer at night than morning, nearer in winter than in summer, nearer when the wind is howling or when I hear a child breathing peacefully asleep.

Monday, September 5, 1932

I wake and feel relieved. It is gone—that weight of horror. It is not there in the morning. I feel fresh and strong and able to conquer it.

Outside by the pool with Charles.

I find I am thinking of this baby as though he *were* the other baby starting again. And sometimes think half madly, "How lovely it will be when he is big again. . . . How lovely when he knows me again." Then I fight it and say, "No, this is another child. I must not try to see Charlie in him."

But why fight it? C. says, "You can't tell—we know so little."

[1] The dog was temporarily lost.

Tuesday, September 6, 1932

Getting jittery planning to get up to Maine, thinking about all the things I ought to do and not feeling strong enough to do them all. And it is so hard to rest.

Bad night. That dreadful feeling when the ache in your chest pushes and pushes; you can't get away from it. Trapped. And I wanted to reach out and find Thor or Skean to lick my hand, to do something mute and loving (C.'s sympathy too sweet and hard to bear because I know what he is feeling). I remember Mother saying that when she went up to North Haven after Daddy died and the baby came to her it eased a pain in her chest *physically*, like a poultice.

Thursday, September 8, 1932

In to Dr. Hawks. Shopping at Macy's. Crowds of people—too bright, too active, pushing people, all in a dreadful hurry; I feel pushed and jostled and left behind. I run into myself in the mirror, a pale, worried-looking girl: "Not as young as she once was." Not really a girl, that's it—you think of yourself as one, but you're growing old. Shoddy shoes, stockings the wrong color, matronly hat, suit that doesn't fit, and a body that feels slung together. Can't keep my tummy in, my chest out. Don't feel absolute control over my legs.

The mob in the hat department. "There she is!" Madhouse. I must get out.

Relief at home. In your own surroundings, even in an old shawl, you feel somehow regal. "I'd better stay here where I belong."

Tuesday, September 13, 1932

Baby's weight 9 lb. 4 oz.

Flight up to Maine in the Bird.[1] Left Long Island Country Club at 1:15; arrive North Haven 6:15.

[1] Bird biplane, in which C. A. L. had taught A. M. L. to fly.

I flew from Portland up. It was so beautiful again, the coast, islands, peninsulas, bays, and rivers all flowing southeast as though swept in a great wind out to sea. It was lovely to be flying myself. This last lap of the trip is always intimate and thrilling, like galloping home on your pet horse.

There's *Monhegan!* Yes, *Monhegan* way ahead, that dark blue strip, just one more bay and then another point and then high up for the jump to North Haven! We are very high. There is Mount Desert, a cone above the mist, and Isle au Haut, and Monhegan behind now. Behind, all the islands running away, pulling in one direction like little boats in a harbor with the tide, all amethyst, running away over the edge of the round world.

But the hair is whipping in my eyes, I have to turn and face the wind. There are the Camden Hills, those ripples in the earth, and the breakwater like a straight flagpole laid flat on the harbor. And the two islands of North Haven spreading towards me, reaching out points and bays towards me. The long arm of Crabtree Point approaching—now our point.

It is still there, it is all there—these islands sweeping out to sea, these islands floating on the top of the world, spilling over the edge of the world. They are all here, beautiful and still, spread flat before me, as they were the year before—and many years before—as they would be always. Daddy had died since last year, and the baby (I'm glad he lived in this beauty for a while). But these would be here, always. And I was happy as though I had recovered *them* for a moment, as though I had recovered everything ever lost, as though I had everything—everything worth having. And I tried to know why, to keep something from this moment of ecstasy, some secret to comfort me when I came down to the human world again.

What was it, what was the key I had? Was it the divinity of seeing familiar things in a new and clearer light? The island had always been like that, but I had never seen it from that angle. Was it seeing things in their right proportion—or more in their right proportion? Seeing how the island fitted into the bay, how our point into the island, or seeing so much at once that had been separated and confused before, seeing it all as one, Mount Desert, Rockland, North Haven, Monhegan.

I looked down on the little house and figures—at Mother and Elisabeth, two tiny figures clinging together on the lawn. They looked so frail. I felt a terrible pity for them and for all of us struggling in this great plan we can't grasp or understand, trying to see when we haven't the power, or the height. If I could only have this height always—but we were coming down now, the pine trees were near and familiar, everyday and human; I was coming down into the world again—the human world. The wind was cold on my face and I had been crying.

Wednesday

Elisabeth tells me about Aubrey.[1] It is just what I wanted and I can't realize it.

The shock is that strange new firm loyalty thrusting itself up between you.

I try to realize it.

Thursday

Dwight and Con arrived.

Hilarious, talk loudly, shout and laugh across the table, glory in our family jokes. Elisabeth making delicious delicate fun of Dwight, pricking the bubble at just the right moment. Dwight reads his diary. I like to get that look into him. Old-clothes party: Elisabeth in blue and white smocked dress, Con in my organdy ball dress (battleship-dance, Panama), Mother in gray-blue cloth suit, with Biarritz sweater, low-waisted, short-skirted, dear old dress. I, in pink Shantung "under-the-apple-blossoms" dress.

[1] Elisabeth Morrow had become engaged to Aubrey Niel Morgan.

Friday

North Haven weather: mist, rain, third day perfect. North Haven feeling, after lunch: eaten too much, too little exercise, too much inside, too self-conscious with guests; feel like fifteen.

Elisabeth tells Mother.

Mother's whole life swings again.

Mother's straw bag (with red flowers) always in her hand, holding letters, pencil, paper, scissors, and tape measure.

Saturday, September 17, 1932

Elisabeth tells Con, Dwight, C. about Aubrey, talks about her plans.

Con and I feel very queer here. Why? A terrible effort to get back to North Haven and to live the same life. And we *can't* do it. Partly because the very essence of our old life was its being-taken-for-granted. We want really to get back into our old selves, and we can't. It's like trying to get back into your old clothes; they don't fit.

And we are all strong individualists, bent on our own lives, our loyalties; instead of facing in to one center we are all facing out—Elisabeth to Aubrey and marriage and a new life, I to C. and the baby, Dwight to independence, work, and girls. Con is still quite a spectator, so she is not so egotistical. All except Mother—Mother is still facing the same ideal, the same loyalty. She is in the center and we are all around, all looking outwards.

Our old associations have worn thin and we haven't made new ones.

C. says at night outside, going to the point: "I don't know any place I like as much as this now." New associations!

Sunday, September 18, 1932

Can hardly bear to think of the little, real body that was Charlie going to nothing. Why is it harder to think of his going to nothing than to think of his coming from nothing? One direction is just as dark as the other.

Monday, September 19, 1932

Last night C. talked about the fun of landing in a little field, flipping in like old days, side-slip, stalling, wobbling (to see better). Can't do it any more on the big fields, it's horseplay if you do. In the old days you *had* to—flying was an art.

C. leaves 9 A.M. New York.

Writing. Sat in sun all afternoon with Elisabeth and Con and Mother—little front yard, with the shadow of the chimney creeping towards us and Bogey and Peter nosing in and out between the heliotrope and the hedge.

Tuesday, September 20, 1932

Go in after breakfast to see Elisabeth.

Lunch in sun in court. Elisabeth and I wear bandannas and get baked. Elisabeth: "Oh, I think we're going to have fun!"—"We?"—"Yes, you and I—I think we're going to understand each other's lives."

Wednesday, September 21, 1932

Elisabeth and Mother walk to the point with the dogs, Peter and Bogey. I watch them from the window—slowly through the garden, Elisabeth with her stick, her black and white polka-dot bandanna, her old purple tweed coat over her black dot suit, Mother in white, carrying her little straw bag with red flowers. I said, I must remember this, I must keep this picture. Then, childishly, I want to be in *their* minds too, so we can all have it together (like Alice's panic when she found she was in the Red King's dream). I knocked on the window and they looked up and smiled. Now I have that too.

Feel tortured with "I must appreciate this—I may never have it again." Why is life speeded up so? Why are things so terribly, unbearably precious that you can't enjoy them but can only wait breathless in dread of their going?

Saturday, September 24, 1932

Golf in morning: a lovely glistening day, the birch trees shimmer, the pine trees prick the sky, the golf balls click, all the yellow daisies bounce up over the grass; life is good and rich and still, the sun is warm through our sweaters.

C. and I play tennis. "But I haven't done any work." "Neither have I, but what are we up here for, anyway?"

The northern lights piercing the dark, up and down, like firelight in a bedroom at night.

Sunday, September 25, 1932

The wind howls at night. I think of last winter. I will never accept it—*cannot* accept it or get used to it or get past it. It is not like a death—not like Daddy—which I knew would happen sometime. It is not a "normal" sorrow. Back of it is always "It need not have happened," and that is a torture. I suppose I can only swallow it whole. It will not be absorbed but always be there, and always hurting, like something in your eyes. Nature does not absorb it but gradually provides a protective covering which numbs the sharp pain, but you are always conscious of it.

Monday, September 26, 1932

A lovely, soft, sunny day. Picnic to the White Islands. C. takes the wheel. Lighthouse, bright white sides. C. and I climb up "our island" (Big Garden Island[1]) and find a path up over gray rocks, through prickly juniper, over that springy moss, crushing shells and sea urchins under our feet, to an old well and stone walls; see the bare green knob of "Little Hurricane Island" and, beyond, the blue line of Matinicus. Lobster pots and sea gulls. Running along steep rocks with rubber-soled shoes.

What is there about North Haven so satisfying, comforting: the permanence of its beauty, the permanence of those moun-

---

[1] Given by her parents to A. M. L. as a wedding present; later given to the Nature Conservancy as a wildlife reserve.

tains, an attempt to mingle them with our lives, to try to make our lives stand still, to persuade ourselves that our lives are always going on the same (though we know better)? So we say and plan, "Some summer we must do this . . ." "Next summer . . ."

Tuesday, September 27, 1932

I felt last night bitterly and passionately that I had lived too much in the last few years, had lived too intensely, been too sad and too happy. That I had felt too much. That life was too precious—much too precious. I want to be delivered from that feeling. Make life humdrum, ordinary. I want routine and dull rounds—I want monotony like Chrysis' fable: "for our hearts are not strong enough to love every moment."[1]

It isn't for the moment you are struck that you need courage but for the long uphill climb back to sanity and faith and security.

TO E. L. L. L.   *Englewood [early October]*

So much seems to have happened since we came down Thursday (three days of fog delayed us up in North Haven). In the first place the baby was such a wonderful surprise. He looks so big, his face has rounded out, his cheeks are full and pink and his eyes *very* big and round. His arms and legs (long and lanky) have filled out. Also his nose does not look as big! He weighs 10 lbs. 6½ oz. It is really thrilling for me to take care of him. Miss Cummings has gone for a week. We hope, though, she will stay for the two or three weeks we are on the trip west.

C. has seen Dr. Carrel again and seems interested and happy in looking forward to work this winter, both in aviation and in that other line. I don't know definitely plans for the winter, but C. doesn't like the thought of Hopewell. He doesn't think it safe without a guard and I think the winter there would be quite

[1] In Thornton Wilder, *The Woman of Andros.*

hard. It seemed like a different place in the summer, and everything that happened in the winter unbelievable.

TO E. L. L. L. [*Englewood, October 15th*]
Dear M.,
We think we've got a name! At least it is one that we're both
pleased with for a good many reasons. We wanted quite a plain,
simple name that would not mark him too much, that would not
be too much of a burden. One that would mean himself and
no one else, that would sound well with Lindbergh and also with
Morrow, as we wanted to put Morrow as a middle name.

C. says, "It's logical to have a child carry the name of both
parents," and I like having something of my father in the name.
We had strong leanings toward *John* but it is a very common
name and people would guess it was taken from So-and-So on
my side of the family or on C.'s. Carl sounded better than anything but it was so near *Charles*—and we called little Charles that
for a few months. I felt I wanted a name with no associations.
Looking through the dictionary we became quite weary.

Finally we found in a Scandinavian history book the name *Jon*
and we both liked it, and Jon Morrow Lindbergh sounds quite
right to me. *Jon* (among the English) is a nickname for Jonathan
and so is not very strange, and it sounds like John, so in school
it won't mark him too much. And, as C. says triumphantly, "It is
phonetic spelling!"

He smiles now at me and moves his mouth in a gurgling
imitation of talking, when I talk to him!

TO E. L. L. L. *Englewood, Sunday, November 6, 1932*
Dear M.,
Great excitement here with Elisabeth's engagement. I think
she is very happy. She was *made* to be married and have a
happy home, and I am so glad about it. No career would ever
satisfy her.

Jon is very sweet. He notices his own hand now and stares at it for long minutes. Also (don't laugh!) we put some pictures up on the wall the other day and he stares and stares at them.

Last night at ten I picked him up to give him his bottle. He just looked up with an *enormous* smile on his face—from ear to ear—so appealing and amused (like C. when he's played a joke) that I had to laugh at him. I have a feeling it will always be like that.

TO E. L. L. L.   *Englewood, December 15, 1932*
It has been a long time again but the party for Con involved quite a lot. I moved the baby out. He is such a joy, is very well, has rosy cheeks, seems taller every day, and is so gay. A week ago when I was bathing him he laughed out loud—for the first time. Today he turned over from his tummy to his back (pushing himself over with his hand). His big eyes take everything in. He holds his head up very well. Smiles when he's sung to or talked to—is, in fact, four months old tomorrow!

C. says he has written you about our idea.[1] Like all the good ideas with vision, it was of course his idea. We wanted to talk to you about it. It seems to me a very good solution. It satisfies something in me—"to make it up to the boy," to make it up to children, anyway, to make good out of evil, if that is possible. I think this would do it. If it is practical—that we don't know yet. But normal use of that place does not seem possible for us or for anyone else (I should dislike any other family using it carelessly, rudely). All this means a great deal of thinking, and we will not do it quickly, and then to start new somewhere else, on our own—that is way ahead. In the meantime C. is working hard and seems happier, more active than in a long time. He says, "We are getting things well in hand," and he's pleased.

[1] The Lindberghs were considering giving, and later gave to the State of New Jersey, their home and property in the Sourland Mountains, near Hopewell, to be used for children (see p. 303).

Wedding guests mentioned in the following diary entry:
Lois Healey, roommate of E. R. M. at school; "Aunt" Maud and
"Uncle" Dutch Hulst, old Englewood friends of E. C. M.; Aunt Annie
Cutter and Aunt Edith Yates, sisters of E. C. M.; David Yates, son of
Edith Yates; Louisa Munroe, daughter of Mr. and Mrs. Vernon
Munroe, old friends of the Morrows; Mr. J. P. Morgan; Amey and
Chester Aldrich; Mrs. George Olds, widow of President Olds of Am-
herst; the Nortons, old family friends; Ruth (McIlvaine) Voorhees and
Katherine (McIlvaine) Leighton, cousins; Lucia Norton Valentine
(Mrs. Alan Valentine); Jean Monnet; Constance Chilton and her
mother, Mrs. Chilton; Mrs. Loomis, friend of E. C. M.; Mrs. Thomas
Lamont; Mr. and Mrs. Russell Leffingwell; Mr. George Rublee; Mrs.
Henry P. Davison, Sr.; Uncle Jay Morrow, brother of D. W. M.; Mr.
Carl Elmore, minister of the Presbyterian Church in Englewood;
Guthrie Speers of Union Theological Seminary; President and Mrs.
Allan Neilson of Smith College; Corliss and Margaret Lamont; David
Munroe; Mrs. Cornelius Bliss.

DIARY Elisabeth's wedding day, Wednesday, December 28, 1932
Breakfast upstairs in Elisabeth's bedroom. I try to be efficient,
writing down presents in wedding book with Lois. Aunt Maud
brings up two new-laid eggs for luck. Aunt Annie and Edith and
David. "Hello, Banks? I'm calling from Miss Elisabeth's room.
Have you got a corkscrew down there?" "Yes Ma'am. You want
some glasses too?"

The big room cleared out, ferns in its window, two potted
trees. Dwight, running down.

The musicians arrive. Louisa in purple. No hangers for coats.
"Could we have a few chairs?"

Con and Louisa and I practice walking in to "Here comes the
bride." (Can you hear the baby crying?)

Mr. Morgan arrives. "I shouldn't have come, but I should have
been so hurt if I hadn't been invited."—"Your house in England,
Mr. Morgan . . . a bench like Jane Austen's . . ."—"But it *was*
Jane Austen's bench. . . ." Amey and Chester, Mrs. Olds, the

Nortons, the Relatives—suddenly everybody. "And how is Elisabeth?"—"Well, she has been fighting a cold. . . . Oh yes, we do think he is splendid."—"Oh, she will be *so* glad you're here."—"Well, I'm glad you like it—it came from Macy's. Oh, hello, Katherine. Oh, Lucia . . ."—"Yes, but *your* present, Ruth . . . What is that you're saying? 'Where is my man?' Oh, he won't come, says he's a member of the no-function club."

Trying to introduce, to smile at everyone, can't talk. Introduce Lucia to Margaret Lamont—old friends. Too many people on this side of the room; go across—M. Monnet, Mrs. Chilton. Mrs. Davison ("Lovely Waterford glass."—"Oh, did it come? Like sending coals to Newcastle!") The music; we line up—for hours. "Say, Anne, how'll I know Aubrey?"—"Oh, Uncle Jay, you don't know him. Well, he'll be dressed up!"

No one talking to Pat and husband; go down. Aunt Annie has a bad cold. Uncle Dutch sitting down. Mrs. Loomis—Mrs. B. kisses me—didn't remember in time to avoid. All lined up for a long time; look across—Mrs. Lamont, the Leffingwells, Lucia, Mr. Rublee, M. Monnet. The music, *Pastorales* by Rousseau. Then—a hush. Aubrey and Uncle Jay stride in, in a hurry, men's feet in unison like horses' hoofs, Uncle Jay trying not to cry. Then the march: Con, in blue velvet, blue velvet leaves over her curls, looking down demure, serious, trembling. Pink spray of orchids, lilac, mimosa, African daisies. Con—little, demure, and swaying, swaying skirt and little blue shoes. I look at her even while Elisabeth comes around the corner.

Then Elisabeth on Dwight's arm, Elisabeth radiant and triumphant. And in that flood of emotion which seized me as I looked at her, I felt—so strongly that it was like a visual impression—I felt Daddy. I felt him there with as much reality as I ever did when he was alive. It was not association, not a conscious thought—not that all his friends were there or that dear serious Dwight in his sweet dignity reminded me of him, or that Elisabeth did. (Later I could see that also.) It was just that flood of emotion, the catch of the breath, the blood pounding, and sharp as a knife—*Daddy*. Then the breath giving way, the blood pounding back, my eyes swimming a little, I began to think, fastening my eyes on her beauty. This was Elisabeth.

I felt as though I had not seen her for a long, long time, almost as though the whole thing were in my memory and I an old lady and this an Elisabeth raised from the dead. This was Elisabeth. This was the old Elisabeth as I thought of her—her straightness and her clarity and her radiance. This was the sharp blue flame of Elisabeth. I remember as a child watching the flame of a candle suddenly soar to a height two or three times its normal size, a strong smooth spear of flame soaring, and I would watch with bated breath. And this was Elisabeth. Here and now, this beauty, this radiance—this is the essence of Elisabeth; not as with most brides one says, "Doesn't she make a lovely *bride!*" I wanted to say, "Doesn't she make a lovely Elisabeth!" This was the *real* Elisabeth—not that person we had watched at the table, fussing over food, refusing eggs. This was the real Elisabeth. The veil, the train, the band of orange blossoms in her hair, the color in her cheeks, her slim body in a sheath of satin.

I thought, looking at her, that I was going to cry, then they stopped in front of Mr. Elmore and Guthrie Speers, and Mr. Elmore began to speak and my eyes dried quickly.

I looked at the back of her head and the curve, like a calla lily, of her body, and I saw her bend her head to hide a laugh, saw the wrinkles of the smile in her cheeks. She was so sure—her voice, her carriage, the turn of her head. Guthrie talking to Elisabeth's blue eyes. Dwight stepping back with dignity, a little confused by the sea of train on the floor that he must cross, then gently he tiptoed around it.

Then Elisabeth turning to Mother. The pause and her "Turn me around, somebody!" I did. Then a surge of people. "Wasn't she lovely!" Lovely—lovely—lovely—lovely.

The receiving line—on the sofa with President and Mrs.

Neilson, Corliss with a fountain pen, Dave and the wedding book. Mrs. Bliss: "A very blond Italian beauty, don't you think? What picture is it?" I thought of the one in the old hall in Englewood. The flowers, the people with flowing, windy skirts clinging to their legs. "What is it, Mother?" [I remember asking as a child]. "She was going to be married, but Death took her."

Elisabeth in a brown suit, rose petals, and her hand up waving, running through the crowded hall.

INDEX

Aircraft: autogiro, 73; Bird biplane, 9, 11, 162n., 313 and n.;
Falcon, 56, 57, 120, 128;
Fledgling, 126 and n.; Fokker,
79, 159n.; Ford, 56–57; gliders,
9, 10, 124–27, 128; Lockheed
Sirius, 76n., 120, 121, 128,
161n., 202n.; Lockheed Vega,
76; Moth, 72; Pan Am S–38,
103n.; *Spirit of St. Louis,* 124n.
See also Aviation
Aklavik, Canada, 164, 169–73
Alaska, 161n., 173–80
Albuquerque, New Mexico, 55,
76, 77, 78
Aldrich, Amey, 41 and n., 109,
113, 139, 223, 262, 277, 280,
290, 322
Aldrich, Chester, 41n., 109, 111,
262, 280, 290, 322
All Quiet on the Western Front
(Remarque), 58 and n., 60–61
Anabasis (Xenophon), 37 and n.
Anna Karenina (Tolstoi), 112–13
Antilles, 75n., 79n., 87–88
Argentina, La, 113 and n., 114
Aspects of the Novel (Forster),
80
Austen, Jane, 161
Aviation: air races, 71, 73, 74;

breaking of transcontinental
speed record, 9, 10, 131–34 and
n.; commercial crashes, 74 and
n., 75, 122 and n., 123, 159
and n.; first passenger lines, 7.
See also Aircraft; individual
airlines

Bailey, Miss, 175
Baker Lake, Canada, 167–69
Banks, Septimus, 269 and n., 322
Barranquilla, Colombia, 97–99
Beck, Eman, 20 and n., 21, 26
Beck, Susanna, 20 and n., 21, 99
and n., 100–1; letters to, 99,
243. *See also* Vaillant, Mrs.
George C.
Belize, British Honduras, 102,
103
Berkshire Hotel, N.Y.C., 47, 74,
75, 109, 110
Big Garden Island, Maine, 318
and n.
Birch, Stephen, 266 and n., 271–
72
Bisgood, Elizabeth Bacon, 289
and n., 290
Bixby, Harold M., 7, 52n.
Bixby, Mrs. Harold M., 7, 52
and n., 53

Index

Bliss, Cornelius, 111n., 269
Bliss, Mrs. Cornelius, 111 and n.,
112, 322, 325
Block Island, Rhode Island, 6,
42
Bogey (E. R. M.'s terrier), 268
and n., 269, 289, 297, 309, 312
and n., 317
Book of Tea, The (Kakuzo), 194
Borcic, Dr., 197
Borno, Louis, 85 and n.
Bowlus, Hawley, 124 and n., 125–
27, 128
Boyd, Robert, 16 and n. *See also*
Lindbergh, Charles A.
Brandt, Laura. *See* Stevens, Mrs.
George
Brandt family, 107 and n.
Breckinridge, Col. Henry, 142
and n., 162, 228, 229, 230, 231,
232–33, 237, 247, 252, 260, 267,
286
Breckinridge, Mrs. Henry, 142
and n., 232–33, 252, 260, 267
British Honduras, 96
Brown, Dr. and Mrs., 199
Brown, Mr. and Mrs., 122
Brown, Dr. William Adams, 41
and n.
Browning, Robert, 301
Brownsville, Texas, 20 and n.
Buroton Bay, Japan, 188
Buzzards Bay, Massachusetts, 247

Camagüey, Cuba, 82
Canada, 161n., 164–73
Candle, Alaska, 178

Capone, Al, 245 and n.
Caracas, Venezuela, 95
Caribbean islands, 80–90
Carmel, California, 130
Carnegie Institution, 96 and n.
Carrel, Dr. Alexis, 158n., 244n.,
319
Caulkins, Dan, 117 and n.
Caulkins, Mrs. Dan (Anna Fay
Prosser), 117 and n., 136
Central America, 7, 75n., 79n.,
96–97, 102–4
Century, 34
Chagrin Falls, Ohio, 71
Chekhov, Anton, 111, 112
Cheney, Mrs. Ward (Frances),
279 and n.
Chiang Kai-shek, 196
Chiang Kai-shek, Mme., 196
Chichén Itzá, Mexico, 103
Chilton, Mrs., 322, 323
Chilton, Constance, 110n., 205n.,
322
China, 10, 161n., 192, 194–202;
floods in, 194n., 195, 197 and
n., 198–99
China Flood Relief, 224
Churchill, Canada, 167
Churubusco convent, Mexico, 32–
33
Cleveland, Ohio, 69–70, 71, 205
Clovis, New Mexico, 54 and n.
Cochran, Thomas, 266 and n.
Columbus, Ohio, 49 and n., 54n.
Comstock, Ada, 271 and n.
Condon, Dr. John F., 241 and n.

Conrad, Joseph, 81
Coolidge, Calvin, 18, 129 and n.,
  130n.
Coolidge, Mrs. Calvin, 129
Coppermine, Canada, 169
Crime and Punishment
  (Dostoevsky), 80
Cristobal, Panama, 96–97
Cuba, 80–84
Cuernavaca, Mexico, 5, 18 and n.,
  54, 83, 107
Cummings, Marie, 140 and n.,
  145, 299 and n., 302, 303, 305,
  309, 311, 319
Curtis, John Hughes, 247 and n.,
  249, 251, 253, 254, 281, 284 and
  n., 299 and n.
Cutter, Annie Spencer (aunt), 32
  and n., 41, 69–70, 159, 160,
  265, 322, 323
Cutter, Mrs. Charles Long
  (grandmother), 15 and n., 32
  and n., 41, 69–70, 156, 158, 160,
  252, 265

Daffin (Morrows' terrier), 29
  and n., 46, 50, 121, 135, 136,
  153–54
Davison, Harry, 278 and n.,
  279n., 281
Davison, Mrs. Harry (Anne), 278
Davison, Mrs. Henry P., Sr., 278
  and n., 322, 323
Detroit, Michigan, 67, 70–71, 117
D'Harnoncourt, René, 111 and n.
Dickinson, Emily, 273, 293

Dulverton, England, 263 and n.,
  310

Earhart, Amelia, 56 and n., 62,
  121, 257 and n.
Eastland, Thomas, 7, 59 and n.,
  60, 63–64
Eastland, Mrs. Thomas, 7, 59, 60
Eastman, George, 65
Edison, Charles, 65
Edison Company Committee, 65
  and n.
Edison family, 65, 66, 67
Edo Pontoon Company, 163
Egoist, The (Meredith), 80
Elizabeth and Essex (Strachey),
  16
Elmore, Carl, 322, 324
Emerson, Ralph Waldo, 295
Emily (servant), 110, 111, 302,
  304, 307, 308
Englewood, New Jersey, 67 and
  n., 68. *See also* Next Day Hill
Eskimos, 166–81 *passim*
*Everyday Child and Its Everyday
  Problems, The* (Thom), 141

Fairbanks, Douglas, 121–22
Falaise (Guggenheims' home), 62
  and n., 141, 144, 257 and n.,
  258, 267, 273
Flagg, Dr. P. J., 299 and n.
Flores, Guatemala, 103
Ford, Henry, 65
Foster, Dr. Nellis, 107 and n.,
  108, 110, 139

Fountain, The (Morgan), 280 and n., 301, 305

"Garden of Proserpine, The" (Swinburne), 260 and n.
Gatty, Harold, 132 and n.
George (gardener), 153–54
Gilbert, Seymour Parker, 60 and n.
Gilbert, Mrs. Seymour P., 60 and n., 61
"Goat Paths" (Stephens), 265–66
Goddard, Robert, 144n.
Gold Medal of the Congress, 143 and n.
Gómez, Juan Vicente, 96 and n.
Gow, Betty, 155 and n., 159, 161, 163, 164, 224, 226–27, 231, 232, 233, 249, 253, 260, 262, 281, 282
Graeme, Mrs. Cecil (Jo), 156 and n., 272, 275
Gray, Greta, 242
Greist, Dr. and Mrs., 174–77
Greist, David, 175, 176
Grenfell, Edward Charles, 60 and n.
Guggenheim, Daniel, 144 and n.
Guggenheim, Diane, 258 and n.
Guggenheim, Mrs. Harry (Carol), 142
Guggenheim family, Harry, 7, 62n., 67, 142, 258, 273–74

Haiti, 84–86
Hamilton, Edith, 213–14
Harvey Houses, 7, 54, 55
Havana, Cuba, 80–81, 83

Hawks, Dr. E. M., 263, 299 and n., 301, 313
Hawley, Margaret, 269 and n., 293
Healey, Lois, 322
Hermes, H.M.S., 12, 199–202 and n.
Herrick, Myron T., 28 and n., 33 and n., 34, 35 and n., 144
Herrick, Parmely, 35 and n., 72
Herrick, Mrs. Parmely, 72
Herschel Island, Canada, 173
Hibben, John G., 285
Hibben, Mrs. John G., 282 and n., 285
Hinghwa, China, 198
Hoover, Herbert, 66, 67, 68, 69, 106, 143n., 245
Hoover, Mrs. Herbert, 66, 67, 68
Hoover, Herbert, Jr., 68
Hopewell, New Jersey, 229; Lindberghs' home in, 144 and n., 156 and n., 157, 205, 206, 211, 227, 238, 246, 259, 263, 271, 282, 284–85, 286, 303, 305, 319–20, 321 and n.
Hopkins, Mr., 175
Hopper, Edward, 167, 223
Hotel Chase, St. Louis, 50
Hotel Lincoln, Indianapolis, 48
Hotel Muehlebach, Kansas City, 51
Hudson's Bay Company, 165, 167
Hulst, "Uncle" Dutch, 41 and n., 322, 323
Hulst, "Aunt" Maud, 41 and n., 322

Index

Humanity Uprooted (Hindus), 182 and n.

Ida (servant), 307, 308
Indians, 165–66, 167, 170
Innocent Voyage, The (Hughes), 69
Isabel (servant), 133, 154
Ixtacihuatl (volcano), 83 and n.

Jackson, Mr. and Mrs. Grant, 179–80
Japan, 10, 161n., 186–94
Jeffers, Robinson, 130 and n.
Jonson, Ben, 268

Kamchatka Peninsula, U.S.S.R., 161n., 180–85
Kansas City, Missouri, 51
Karaginski Island, U.S.S.R., 180
Ketoi Island, Japan, 186
Kidder, Dr. Alfred V., 64 and n., 65, 101, 103n.
Kidder, Mrs. Alfred V., 64–65
Kidnapping of Charles, Jr., 211, 226–51; evidence in, 213, 227, 244, 251, 255; false leads in, 213, 228, 229–30, 238, 241, 242, 243, 244, 245–48, 249; negotiations in, 211, 228, 230, 233, 234, 240, 241; police and, 212, 228, 229, 231, 233, 239, 245, 246–47, 258, 272, 274; press and, 211, 226, 228, 229, 230, 231, 232, 233, 234, 235, 238, 239, 240, 241, 245, 247, 249, 272, 274; ransom for, 211, 213, 227, 228, 240, 243; reconstruction of, 253, 254–55, 258; underworld help in solving, 231–32, 245 and n. *See also* Lindbergh, Charles A.; Lindbergh, Mrs. Charles (Anne Morrow); Lindbergh, Charles, Jr.
King John (Shakespeare), 215
King Lear (Shakespeare), 118
Kingman, Arizona, 58
Knight, Harry H., Jr., 7, 52 and n., 53
Knight, Mrs. Harry H., Jr., 7, 53–54
Kunashiri Island, Japan, 189–90
Kyushu Island, Japan, 193

Lamont, Corliss, 322, 325
Lamont, Mrs. Corliss (Margaret), 322, 323
Lamont, Thomas W., 60 and n., 136
Lamont, Mrs. Thomas W., 322
Land, Charles H., Jr., 70 and n., 71, 146, 155, 193
Land, Rear Admiral Emory Scott, 299 and n.
Land, Robert, 145
Leffingwell, Mr. and Mrs. Russell, 322, 323
Leighton, Katherine, 322, 323
Lenin, Nikolai, 184
Leonardo da Vinci, 34
Lindbergh, Charles A. (C. A. L.): in air races, 71, 73, 74 and n., 75; in airplane accidents, 18–19

Lindbergh, Charles A. (*Cont.*)
and n., 20, 21, 200–2; in Alaska,
173–80; and Anne, 3–4, 8, 9,
16, 18, 22, 29, 36–38, 62, 66,
67, 140; archaeological exploration flights of, 75n., 96 and n.,
101, 103 and n.; broke transcontinental speed record, 9,
131–34 and n.; in Canada,
164–73; in Caribbean, 80–90; in
Central America, 96–97, 102–
4; and Charles, Jr., 138, 147,
162, 204–5, 207, 224–25, 226,
260; and Charles, Jr., death of,
249–61 *passim*, 283, 285; and
Charles, Jr., kidnapping of,
226–48; in China, 194–202; and
Chinese floods, 197 and n., 198–
99; courage of, 249, 251, 274;
and Curtis trial, 284; on death,
304; disguises of, 42, 107, 108,
113, 114; on Edison Committee,
65n.; engagement and marriage
of, 3–4, 5, 6, 15, 16 and n., 17
and n., 18, 23, 40 and n., 41, 44,
252; fears for safety of family,
271, 286, 311–12, 319; flight
over great-circle route of, 10,
76 and n., 161n., 163 and n.,
164–202, 285; and gliding, 9,
121, 124–27 and n., 128; grief
of, 231, 254, 260, 270; and Herrick, 28 and n., 33, 35 and n.;
honeymoon of, 6–7, 40n., 41–
45, 47–48; and Hopewell home,
156, 157, 158, 238, 246, 263,
271, 284–85, 303, 305, 319–20;

321 and n.; in Japan, 186–94;
and Jon, 303; and lack of
privacy, 5–7, 44–45, 105–6, 108,
113–14, 118, 154, 283, 311;
letters to, 17, 25–33, 35–37;
Paris flight of, 52n., 124n., 235;
and pets, 135, 154, 156–57, 286–
89, 297, 298; as a pilot, 123,
128–29, 143, 162 and n., 165–
202 *passim*, 317; and press, 5,
6, 7, 45, 56, 59, 81, 82, 122, 127,
137, 138, 242, 273–74, 303; in
Princeton house, 144–47; received medal, 143 and n.; and
reconstruction of kidnapping,
253, 255, 258–59, 261; research
of, at Rockefeller Institute, 158
and n., 244 and n., 245, 252,
258, 259, 261, 292, 319; and
search for a home, 105 and n.,
107, 109–10, 137, 142n., 143,
144, 145; surveyed and
organized routes for Pan Am,
7, 10, 20, and n., 75 and n., 79
and n., 80–104; surveyed and
organized routes for TAT, 46
and n., 48–62, 75, 76–78, 122–
23, 127, 159 and n.; in U.S.S.R.,
180–85. *See also* Kidnapping of
Charles, Jr.
Lindbergh, Mrs. Charles A.
(Anne Morrow; A. M. L.):
and air races, 71, 73, 74, 75; in
airplane accidents, 18–19 and
n., 20, 21, 200–2; and archaeological flights, 75n., 96 and n.,
101, 103 and n.; on being alone,

Lindbergh, Mrs. Charles A.
  (*Cont.*)
151–52; and Charles, 3–4, 8, 16,
18, 22, 29, 36–38, 62, 66, 100,
140, 141, 142, 200, 213, 249–50,
252, 266, 267, 274, 278, 281,
286, 291, 294, 295, 300, 304,
307, 313; and Charles, Jr., 138
and n., 140–47 *passim*, 152,
155–64 *passim*, 168, 182, 186,
193, 196, 204–7, 224–25, 226,
251–52, 268, 271, 280, 282, 291,
295–96, 298, 302, 304, 305; and
Charles, Jr., death of, 211,
248–61 *passim*, 270, 277, 283,
284, 285, 297, 306, 308, 314,
316, 318; and Charles, Jr.,
kidnapping of, 211–17, 226–48,
272, 276, 304, 305, 309, 312;
and Charles, Jr., memories of,
216, 251, 254–63 *passim*, 270,
271, 290, 292–93; and Charles,
Jr., record of, 234, 239, 261;
on communication, 6, 10; and
Constance, 15–16, 17, 29, 32–33,
37, 39, 41, 58, 63, 66, 76, 107–8,
121, 152; on crashes, 74–75, 78,
122–23, 159–60; and death,
203, 213–15, 254, 275, 284, 294,
304, 305–6, 307; diary of, 211,
213, 247–84 *passim*, 289–319
passim, 322–25; disguises of,
108, 113; dreams of, 164, 196,
247, 252–53, 262–63, 270, 277,
280–81, 290, 308, 310; and
Dwight, 63; and Elisabeth, 4,
29, 40, 41, 47, 63, 66, 112, 124,

130, 139–40, 161, 260, 263,
264–65, 315, 320, 322–25;
engagement and marriage of,
3–4, 5, 6, 15, 16 and n., 17 and
n., 18, 23, 40 and n., 41, 44, 252;
and faith, 254, 257, 269, 273,
274, 276, 294, 302; on fame, 8,
39; and her family, 9, 10, 41,
57, 62–63, 67n., 74, 75, 118,
213, 223 and n.; and father,
11–12, 25–26, 29, 41, 63, 65–66,
99, 124, 130, 203–4, 225, 237,
238, 266–67, 272, 276, 284, 285,
295, 309, 310, 314, 318, 320,
323–24; on flight over great-
circle route, 10, 76 and n.,
161n., 163 and n., 164–202, 285;
and gliding, 9, 10, 124–27;
grief and sorrow of, 12, 213,
214–15, 237, 247, 250–61
passim, 264, 270, 272, 284, 294,
295, 318, 319; honeymoon of,
6–7, 40n., 41–45, 47–48; and
hope, 211, 212, 213, 244, 299;
and Hopewell home, 156, 157,
158, 205, 206, 227, 238, 246,
259, 263, 271, 282, 284–85, 286,
305, 319–20, 321 and n.; and
horror, 213, 216, 248, 256, 299;
and Jon, 304–13 *passim*, 319–
21; and Jon, birth of, 299–303;
on lack of privacy, 4–7, 8, 9,
36, 44–45, 59, 105–6, 108, 113–
14, 118, 131, 153, 155, 283, 311,
313; on love, 3; mail of, 26, 28,
29, 155, 230, 234, 235, 239; on
men and women, 52, 53, 301;

Index

Lindbergh, Mrs. Charles A.
(*Cont.*)
and mother, 10, 16, 39–40, 45–
46, 57, 63, 66, 67, 72, 79, 106–7,
114, 120, 124, 236, 248, 276–77,
296; and motherhood, 8, 10,
141, 156; and mother-in-law,
10, 21, 70–71, 138, 144–46; as
a navigator, 4, 47, 132, 133–34;
piano, learning, 254, 267, 269,
271, 281, 291, 292, 293; as a
pilot, 4, 11, 162 and n., 163n.;
and poetry, 118–19, 194, 203–4,
217–18, 223–24, 260, 265–66,
268, 293; and press, 5, 6, 7, 31,
32, 45, 56, 59, 70, 79, 80, 81,
95, 117, 122, 127–28, 137, 138,
143, 155, 229, 231, 232, 234,
235, 240, 242, 245, 258, 261,
267, 268, 272, 273–74, 298–99;
in Princeton house, 144–47; on
progress, 89–90; as a radio operator, 4, 10, 11, 163n., 169,
173, 174, 178, 179, 180, 186,
187; reading of, 16, 27, 58, 69,
80, 111, 112–13, 141, 161, 182,
194, 254, 264, 280; and rebirth,
214–16; and reconstruction of
kidnapping, 253, 254–56, 258;
and remorse, 215, 216, 250–51,
254; and search for a home,
105 and n., 107, 109–10, 137,
142n., 143, 144, 145; self-confidence of, 3, 4, 9, 67, 200; self-
discipline of, 212, 237; on
suffering, 213–14, 215–16; on
tragedy, 213, 216; and trans-

continental speed record, 9, 10,
131–34 and n.; on travel, 7, 8,
267; at White House, 68–69,
143; and writing, 6, 10, 12, 17,
23, 28, 35–37, 164, 211, 223 and
n., 224, 254, 264, 266 and n.,
270, 283. *See also* Kidnapping
of Charles, Jr.
Lindbergh, Charles, Jr., 138 and
n., 140–47, *passim,* 152, 155–64
passim, 168, 182, 186, 193, 196,
204–7, 224–25, 226, 251–52,
260, 262, 269n., 271, 280, 298,
305; death of, 211, 248–61
passim, 270, 277, 283, 284, 285,
297, 306, 308, 314, 316, 318;
kidnapping of, 211, 226–48. *See
also* Kidnapping of Charles, Jr.
Lindbergh, Evangeline Lodge
Land (E. L. L. L.), 10, 67, 70–
71, 147, 158, 211–12, 248, 251,
252, 293, 294; letters to, 21, 122,
137–38, 142–45, 152, 154–56,
159, 162, 192, 204, 206, 224–
35, 238–43, 244–46, 249, 250,
258, 261, 267, 270, 274, 281,
284, 286, 303, 311, 319–21
Lindbergh, Jon Morrow, 302–13
passim, 319–21
Lippmann, Walter, 239
Little School, The, 110 and n.,
139, 140, 205 and n., 206, 267n.,
297
London Conference on Naval
Disarmament, 124 and n.
London Daily News, 134
Long Island, 109–10

Long Island Aviation Country Club, 11, 162, 313
Loomis, Mrs., 322, 323
Los Angeles, California, 56, 59
Los Angeles Times, 124

MacLean, Admiral Colin, 199
MacNab, Colonel Alexander, 25 and n.
Maddux, Jack, 7, 56n., 63–64, 65, 119, 120, 122, 131
Maddux, Mrs. Jack (Helen), 7, 56 and n., 63, 64, 65, 119, 120, 121, 122, 131
Maddux, Junior, 121
Madison Square Garden, N.Y.C., 235
"Magnificent Universe, The" (Frost), 34
Mamba's Daughters (Heyward), 16
Mansfield, Katherine, 28, 111, 146–47, 214
Marshall, Mr., 312
Martin, Dr., 304
Mary (servant), 264
Masefield, John, 203–4, 224
Mayan cities, 96n., 101, 104
McDonald, Mr., 21
McIlvaine, Jim, 292 and n.
Means, Gaston B., 299 and n.
Mérida, Yucatán, 102
Merriam, Dr. John Campbell, 62 and n.
Mexico, 5, 31, 39, 102–4; rebellion in, 21 and n., 26, 31

Mexico City, 20 and n., 26; U. S. Embassy in, 5, 16n.
Miami, Florida, 81
Milton, John, 103
Milton, Massachusetts, 107
Milton Academy, 39n.
Mitchell, Dr. David, 206 and n.
Monnet, Jean, 60 and n., 322, 323
Montessori Mother, The, 141
Moose Factory, Canada, 165–66
Morgan, Mr. and Mrs., 174, 175, 178
Morgan, Aubrey Niel, 292 and n., 310, 315 and n., 316, 323
Morgan, J. P., 322
Morgan, Mr. and Mrs. Stokeley W., 37 and n.
Morgan & Co., J. P., 60 and n.
Morley, Sylvanus G., 101 and n.
Morris, Earl Halstead, 101 and n.
Morrow, Alice (aunt), 280 and n., 307
Morrow, Constance Cutter (C. C. M.; sister), 15n., 42, 50, 94, 112, 119, 124, 127, 129, 135, 138, 153, 261, 262, 265, 275, 276, 297, 305, 309–10, 315, 316, 317, 321, 322, 323; Anne and, 17 and n., 29, 32–33, 37, 41, 63, 66, 76, 107–8, 121, 225; letters to, 15–16, 18–20, 22–23, 34, 39, 48, 54, 56–58, 62, 84, 91, 102, 120, 132, 134–35, 141, 146, 151, 153, 161, 202, 205
Morrow, Dwight Whitney (D. W. M.; father), 16, 18n.,

Morrow, Dwight Whitney
  (*Cont.*)
  23, 56, 60n., 68, 71, 75, 106, 124
  and n., 129 and n., 138, 162,
  245, 251, 266–67, 272, 276, 285,
  303, 309, 310, 320, 323–24;
  Anne and, 25–26, 29, 41, 63,
  65–66, 124, 130; death of,
  11–12, 202n., 203, 204, 223n.,
  225, 237, 238, 248 and n., 284,
  295, 314, 318; Charles Lindbergh and, 22 and n., 99, 285;
  political campaign of, 134 and
  n., 135, 136
Morrow, Mrs. Dwight W.
  (Elizabeth Cutter; E. C. M.;
  mother), 10, 23, 32, 58, 62, 68,
  80 and n., 111, 124 and n., 129,
  134–35, 140, 153, 162, 204, 205,
  225, 257, 258, 260, 261, 262,
  265 and n., 266, 268, 271–72,
  275, 295, 296, 298, 301, 302,
  303, 304, 305, 308, 310, 315,
  316, 317, 324, 325; Anne and,
  16, 57, 63, 66, 67, 72, 106–7,
  114, 120; and death of Charles,
  Jr., 248 and n., 252; and death
  of husband, 202n., 203, 204,
  251, 263, 313; and kidnapping
  of Charles, Jr., 211, 230 and n.,
  234, 236, 245, 276; letters to,
  39–45, 50, 55, 60, 71–79, 94,
  104–9, 113, 117, 121, 124–31,
  133, 158, 159–60, 162–86,
  193–97, 223, 276, 285
Morrow, Dwight Whitney, Jr.
  (D. W. M., Jr.; brother), 31,
  127, 129, 138, 160, 261, 265,
  275, 276, 315, 316, 322, 323,
  324; Anne and, 63; letter to, 47
Morrow, Elisabeth Reeve
  (E. R. M.; sister), 6, 18, 22, 28,
  46, 57, 94, 106, 119, 124 and n.,
  127, 133, 135n., 136, 138, 153,
  154, 156, 158, 203, 204, 225,
  252, 257, 258, 260, 261, 264,
  265n., 277, 295, 305, 308, 309–
  10, 315, 317; Anne and, 4, 29,
  40, 41, 47, 63, 66, 112, 130,
  139–40, 161, 263; engagement
  and wedding of, 315 and n.,
  316, 320, 322–25; illness of,
  135, 139 and n., 140 and n., 160,
  161, 260, 261, 262 and n.; letters
  to, 51, 68–69, 87, 110, 139, 199,
  236, 264, 271, 291, 296; Little
  School of, 110 and n., 139, 140,
  205n., 206
Morrow, General Jay J. (uncle),
  96 and n., 97, 262, 275, 322,
  323
Morrow, Mrs. Jay J. (Hattie),
  275 and n.
Mouette (cabin motorboat), 6,
  40n., 41–45, 47–48, 295
Munroe, David, 322
Munroe, Louisa, 322
Munroe, Vernon, Jr., 28 and n.,
  29, 41, 291 and n., 292
Murry, J. M., 147
Muse, Mrs., 106

Nanking, China, 195–97 and n.
Nassau, Bahamas, 89, 91, 160
Neilson, William Allan, 92, 113
  and n., 322, 325

Neilson, Mrs. William Allan, 113
and n., 256, 292, 322, 325
Nemuro, Japan, 190–92
Neville, Mrs. Edwin, 193 and n.,
194
New York City, 49n., 109, 110
New York Herald Tribune, 239
New York Times, The, 32, 101,
239
Newark, New Jersey, 67
Next Day Hill, Englewood, 5, 6,
40n., 108, 110, 111–12, 255,
259n., 298n.
No Love (Garnett), 80
Nome, Alaska, 179–80
North Haven, Maine, 23 and n.,
27, 66, 71, 73, 74, 75, 78, 79n.,
140n., 163, 164, 223, 277, 297,
313–19
North to the Orient (A. M. L.),
11, 164, 223n., 283n.
Northland (ship), 178
Norton family, 322, 323
Nuttall, Zelia, 30 and n., 31

"Of His Dear Son, Gervase"
(Beaumont), 118–19
Olds, Mrs. George, 322
Orient, 10, 76 and n., 161n., 163
and n., 164–202, 285
Othello (Shakespeare), 27–28
Ottawa, Canada, 164
Ovey, Esmond, 18 and n., 111

Painted Pig, The (E. C. M.),
80 and n.
Pan American Airways, 7, 20n.,
75n., 79 and n.

Panama, 96–97
Paramaribo, Dutch Guiana, 75n.,
90–94
Pebble Beach, California, 130
Pecos Valley, New Mexico, 64
Peking, China, 196, 197
Pennsylvania Railroad, 49n.
Perry, Lewis, 65
Peter (E. R. M.'s terrier), 135
and n., 136, 153, 154, 264, 289,
293, 317
Peterkin Papers, The (Hale), 24
and n.
Petropavlovsk, U.S.S.R., 182–85
Pickford, Mary, 56, 71, 121–22
Point Barrow, Alaska, 172,
173–78
Poole, Constance B., 267 and n.
Popocatepetl (volcano), 83 and n.
Port-au-Prince, Haiti, 84–86
Portes Gil, Emilio, 15n.
Portrait in a Mirror (Morgan),
308
Prelude, Chorale, and Fugue
(Franck), 151
President Cleveland, S.S., 180
Princeton, New Jersey, 142 and
n., 144, 145
Proust, Marcel, 312
Puebla, Mexico, 23–24

Quintana Roo, Mexico, 103 and n.

Revillon Frères Limited, 167
Rivera, Diego, 95
Robertson, Major William B., 7,
53 and n., 77

Index

Robertson, Mrs. William B., 7, 77
Rockefeller Institute for Medical Research, 158 and n., 197, 244 and n., 245, 259, 261, 262
Rockne, Knute, 159n.
Rogers, Will, 56 and n., 62, 124, 130
Romeo and Juliet (Shakespeare), 297
Roosevelt Field, Long Island, 48
Rossetti, Christina G., 118
Rublee, George, 134 and n., 136, 273, 322, 323
Ryan Airlines, Inc., 124n.

Safety Harbor, Alaska, 179
Saint-Exupéry, Antoine de, 215
Saint Kitts, Leeward Islands, 88–89
Saint Louis, Missouri, 51, 52, 76, 77, 118, 133
Saint Thomas, Virgin Islands, 84, 87, 88
Salas, Tito, 95
Samuel, Harold, 120
San Juan, Puerto Rico, 86–87
Santa Anita, Mexico, 30–31
Santa Fe Railroad, 54 and n.
Santayana, George, 36–37
Santiago, Cuba, 83–84
Santo Domingo, Dominican Republic, 86
Schwarzkopf, Colonel H. Norman, 229 and n., 245, 246, 248

Selby, Miss, 63
Seward Peninsula, Alaska, 178–79
Shana, Japan, 188–89
Shanghai, China, 164, 200
Sharpe, Violet, 153, 272 and n., 274, 292
Sheffield, James R., 85 and n.
Shinshiru Maru (boat), 187, 192
Shishmaref Inlet, Alaska, 179
Siberia, 161n., 180–85
Skean (Lindberghs' terrier), 156, 157, 158, 253, 259, 268, 269, 279, 283, 287, 288, 289, 297, 298, 309, 313
Smith, Frances, 78 and n., 256 and n.
Smith College, Northampton, 26 and n., 39n., 104
Soledad Mountain, California, 124, 126
South America, 7, 75n., 79n., 90–96, 97–99
Speers, Guthrie, 322, 324
Spirit of St. Louis organization, 52n., 53n.
Stevens, George, 158 and n., 266
Stevens, Mrs. George (Laura Brandt), 107n., 158 and n., 266
Stratton, Samuel W., 65
Sullivan, Katherine, 164 and n.
Swift, Captain, 191

Teterboro Airport, New Jersey, 11

Thomas (servant), 134, 296, 309

Thompson, Ruth, 70

Thor (Lindberghs' police dog), 286–89, 290, 291, 292, 293, 294, 297, 298, 300, 309, 313

Time, 244

Tokyo, Japan, 164, 192, 193

"Toys, The" (Patmore), 104 and n.

Transcontinental Air Transport, 7, 46 and n., 49n., 54 and n., 55–59, 74 and n., 75–78, 120, 122 and n., 123, 131. *See also* Transcontinental and Western Airways

Transcontinental and Western Airways, 159 and n.

Trenton, New Jersey, 246–47, 250

Trindle, Mr., 175

Trinidad, 87, 90, 94–95

Trippe, Juan T., 79n., 88, 93, 97, 98, 106

Trippe, Mrs. Juan T. (Elizabeth), 79 and n., 80, 82, 88, 93, 95, 97, 98, 106

Tulum, Mexico, 104

Union of Soviet Socialist Republics, 180–85

Urquhart, Dr. and Mrs., 170–71

Vaillant, George C., 99n., 100–1

Vaillant, Mrs. George C., 278. *See also* Beck, Susanna

Valentine, Lucia Norton, 322, 323

Van der Post, Laurens, 216

Vancouver, Canada, 202n.

Venezuela, 95

Victoria, Canada, 202

Voorhees, Ruth, 322, 323

Wahgoosh (Lindberghs' terrier), 154 and n., 155, 156–57, 158, 205, 226, 229, 233, 259, 287, 288

Watson, John Broadus, 141 and n.

Waynoka, Oklahoma, 49n., 54 and n., 55

Weber, Joseph, 287 and n., 288

West, Mr. and Mrs., 165–66

Western Airways, 123. *See also* Transcontinental and Western Airways

Whateley, Oliver, 155 and n., 159, 193, 232, 233, 238, 281, 282, 309

Whateley, Mrs. Oliver (Elsie), 155 and n., 193, 227, 232, 233, 253, 282, 309, 311

Wichita, Kansas, 134n.

Williams (servant), 69

Wilson, Elsie Cobb, 110 and n., 111

Winchell, Walter, 225

Winslow, Arizona, 55, 56, 78

Woman of Andros, The (Wilder), 319 and n.

Woods Hole, Massachusetts, 44, 47

Wuhu, China, 198–99
Wylie, Elinor, 305

Yangtze river, 194 and n.,
   195, 200–2

Yates, David, 322
Yates, Mrs. Sheldon (Edith,
   aunt), 41 and n., 133, 275, 322
York Harbor, Maine, 45, 47
Yucatán, 75n., 102–4

Printed in the United States
60467LVS00005B/33